THE ANALYSIS OF IDEOLOGY

THE ANALYSIS OF IDEOLOGY

Raymond Boudon

Translated by Malcolm Slater

The University of Chicago Press

Originally published as *L'idéologie: ou l'origine des idées reçues*,
© 1986, Librairie Arthème Fayard.

The University of Chicago Press, Chicago 60637
Polity Press, Cambridge

© 1989 by Polity Press
All rights reserved. Published 1989
Printed in Great Britain

98 97 96 95 94 93 92 91 90 89   54321

Library of Congress Cataloging-in-Publication Data

Boudon, Raymond.
  [L'idéologie, ou, L'origine des idées reçues. English]
  The analysis of ideology / Raymond Boudon : translated
by Malcolm Slater.
      p.   cm.
  Translation of: L'idéologie, ou, L'origine des idées reçues.
  Bibliography: p.
  Includes index.
  ISBN 0–226–06730–0 (alk. paper)
  1. Ideology.   I. Title.
B823.3.B5913   1989   89–4930
140—dc20   CIP

This book is printed on acid-free paper.

Contents

For Stéphane

Preface

Malebranche said that, in explaining a phenomenon, we must never forget chance causes.

The chance cause of this book was a question which Raymond Aron asked me after a lecture I gave on 'Recent developments in sociological theory', in which I once again argued that individualist methods were enjoying a new lease of life among sociologists, and that the evidence showed that they were in fact helping us to understand social phenomena better.

Aron's question was the one which I had dreaded most – can collective beliefs also be explained by reference to the principles of methodological individualism?[1] I remember that I was bowled over by the question, even though I had expected it. In any event, I decided not to reply, since it was clear that the question could not be dealt with in a few sentences. I did not know at the time, however, that a whole book would be devoted to answering it.[2]

Raymond Boudon

Prologue

1

A question (among others) on ideology

According to Max Weber, the great German sociologist, the explanation of any social phenomenon has to start by reducing it to the individual behaviour patterns which gave rise to it, and moreover these behaviour patterns have to be regarded as 'rational'. His advice was that only if this kind of explanation fails can irrational elements be introduced into the description of the behaviour patterns of social actors. At first sight, however, it would seem unsafe to assert that these principles of method can also be applied to ideological phenomena. At any rate, instinctive feeling on social matters would find it hard to accept that this can be done, since it relies on a principle which runs counter to Weber: faced with a social phenomenon, it sometimes finds it difficult to resist the interpretation that irrational behaviour is behind this phenomenon. It may be that this irrationalist interpretation is rejected only after rather lengthy debate – this is when it can be rejected, and when it usually is. Many examples could be cited to prove this, but I will refer briefly to only one of them, taken almost at random.[1]

In the 1960s, the Indian government commissioned a study from a prestigious American university on how it could achieve its aim of birth-control. The first stage was a quite proper series of observations, and involved the distribution of contraceptive pills in certain Punjabi villages, while other villages were designated as a control group: obviously they wanted to make sure that any fall in the birth-rate in the villages where the pills were handed out was in fact because of this and not for some other reason. The experiment was a complete failure – birth-rates fell, but in the same proportion in the non-pill villages as in the ones where pills had been distributed. Clearly, this decline could not be attributed to the pill, and the simple conclusion was that handing out pills had no effect since there was the same decline in the birth-rate in both groups of villages. The researchers' immediate reaction was to interpret the result by reference to the fact that Indian peasants clung to age-old traditions, rejected innovation, mistrusted things from outside, and resisted the idea of changing natural processes artificially. In other words, the behaviour of Indians was interpreted as being determined by social forces outside the control of the individual. Once this diagnosis was made, the proposed cure, of course, was to persuade Indian peasants to take the pill. The danger was, however, that its beneficial effects would be emphasized too directly – people as irrational as Indian peasants would not be amenable to rational argument, so one had to go about it in a roundabout way, with a bit of guile. Anthropologists came up with the suggestion, which was put into effect, that the teams responsible should as far as possible be Indianized, since Indian women would be prepared to accept the pill more readily from fellow-Indians than from foreigners with fair skins.

This new 'communication strategy' was enormously effective, at least so it appeared. From the time of its implementation, the number of families who agreed to have a small supply of pills offered by Indians increased sharply and the proportion of people who said they were in favour of contraception rose to 90 per cent. In fact, the villagers were merely being polite to the research teams, on the grounds that the latter had come from such a long way off, and were so hard-working and anxious to be of service that it would be discourteous to refuse them. People therefore accepted pills and even went as far as saying they were in favour of contraception; the pills, however, were thrown away as soon as the teams had left. Why was this? The research teams had merely to listen to what the peasants said in order to find out, and in fact they did say why quite openly to those who had enough curiosity to ask them – the more children they had, the better off they were. This is course is true, in that in an economic situation such as the Punjab, a child is cheap to bring up, to look after, and to educate. Moreover, having children means that the productivity of land increases and there is no need to call on expensive paid-labour. If the child is employed outside the family, as is often the case, this adds to the family's income and helps to pay for the education of younger brothers and sisters.

It is not therefore because Indian peasants are subject to incorrigible superstitions that the research teams were unable to bring them round to their way of looking at things. Their behaviour regarding the birth-rate is perfectly understandable and, in this sense, rational when looked at from the point of view of the nature of the environment in which they live.

This example is a good illustration of the two propositions which I was putting forward: very often, the explanation of a social phenomenon amounts to showing that it is the result of behaviour patterns which are understandable and, in this sense, rational. Conversely, the *instinctive* explanation of the phenomenon is often based on an irrational view of the behaviour. In this respect, social scientists are as vulnerable as lay people.

It would be tempting to say that the research teams were responsible for the superstition. To depict Indian peasants as rational and Western researchers as full of prejudices, patronizing underdeveloped people who are offered the latest discoveries of Western technology, would go down well with certain sections of the public. However, just as we can refrain from advancing the hypothesis that Indian peasants rejected the pill because of superstition, we can similarly avoid the assumption that the research teams clung to this hypothesis for the same reason. Firstly, they came from countries where it *is* 'irrational' to have a large number of children. In France or in the United States, education lasts a long time and is expensive, even though theoretically free; and health care is also expensive. Moreover, adolescents and young people can not always expect to be kept by their parents, not only because this would be incompatible with their independence, but also because their job is likely to take them away from home. There is no need to pursue this analysis – because of differences between the two sets of circumstances, behaviour which is irrational in one context is rational in the other, and vice versa. In any event, it is not out of the question that the research teams approached their task saying, in effect, 'it is irrational, in a modern society, to have a large number of children', and that they readily accepted the obvious corollary of this proposition – that modernization and development imply that the number of births should be limited.

They were probably all the more ready to accept the truth of this corollary in that the Indian government, as well as those Indians with whom they came into contact, shared this view: after all, it was on the Indian government's initiative that they undertook the research. The government's aim was to lower the birth-rate. Why were the government and the Indian members of the research team in agreement on this political objective? The reason is obvious – the high birth-rate in India at that time was *as a matter of fact* a major cause of poverty and economic stagnation. As Malthus had shown long before, the increase in the number of mouths to feed accounted for (and exceeded) any increase in food produced. A high birth-rate was therefore *objectively* a bad thing, and it is easy to see why politicians as well as intellectuals tried to solve the problem.

Obviously, this involved a contradiction between individual rationality and collective rationality: the peasants had *good reasons* for adhering to the traditional model of the large family even if in doing so they contributed to economic stagnations and therefore to their own problems; but peasants readily perceived that abandoning the traditional model of the large family would create problems for themselves while helping only very slightly to reduce the general level of poverty.

The research teams could have immediately latched on to this kind of reasoning, but to do this they would have had to:

1 ignore their own circumstances which led them to see the relationship between small families and modernization as self-evident;
2 reject received ideas that peasants in general, and Indian peasants in particular, adhered to long-established traditions;
3 set aside their professional habits – that is, the theoretical guidelines normally used in their work. Sociologists and anthropologists find it natural to see human groups as conforming to traditions which vary from one context to another;
4 master the fairly subtle conceptual tools allowing them to differentiate clearly between cases in which individual rationality and collective rationality come into conflict and those in which both kinds of rationality converge. Many economists, as well as many mathematicians and philosophers, are familiar with these conceptual tools, but this is hardly true of anthropologists, sociologists, or demographers;[2]
5 avoid being influenced by the Indians with whom they worked – officials and research people who also tend to interpret the behaviour of peasants as 'irrational', thus reinforcing their own view of the situation;
6 have a wide knowledge of the characteristics of the social and economic environment of the peasants.

It is clear that these six conditions were unlikely to be fulfilled at the same time and without delay, and in fact this was the case. This is why a 'reality shock' was to be expected – in this case, the unfortunate failure of the experiment – before they could restart the operation on a different basis.

Overall, neither the behaviour of the peasants, nor the interpretation which the research team originally put on it, however wrong this was, stemmed from superstition and irrationality. It is true, however, that the first reaction of the researchers was to interpret the peasants' behaviour as irrational, and the first reaction of the observer at one remove, noting the failure of the researchers, is to picture them as full of superstitions.

We see therefore that Weber's advice, to which I referred at the beginning of the chapter, ought to be followed, even when analysing superstitions and ideologies, since *Homo ideologicus* is perhaps not as irrational as people think, as my example shows. This is the main hypothesis which I will endeavour to sustain in this book, though I must immediately point out that the meaning I will give to the notion of rationality will be a wide one.

In so far as I have a clear perception of my own aims I have to say that I think of this book as the latest in a series which began with *L'Inégalité des chances*,[3] in which I tried to show that in order to analyse the system of macroscopic data which social mobility represents, it was vital to take it for what it in fact *is* – the statistical imprint of the juxtaposition of a host of individual acts, which of course are not those of disembodied people or abstract calculators, but of individuals who are socially *situated*, in other words people who are part of a family and other social groups, and who have resources which are cultural as well as economic. Moreover, the choices which these individuals face are not abstract, but are choices the terms of which are fixed by specific institutions – for example, in the field of education; or by constraints – for example, the supply of and demand for skills in the context of career choices.

It goes without saying that these individuals cannot be looked at one by one; they have to be grouped into types, to which are ascribed patterns of behaviour which are of necessity idealized. In all these cases, however, we have to try, in accordance with Max Weber's advice, to reconstruct the individual behaviour pattern so as to make it meaningful and not interpret it, except in the last resort, as the effect of irrational forces. Once this microscopic stage of the analysis has been successfully completed, it remains to *aggregate* the individual patterns and show that, at the macroscopic level, there do in fact exist the general phenomena which we were trying to explain.

From writing *L'Inégalité des chances*, I was persuaded that individualist methodology, as it is called, was fundamental to sociological analysis: even for the analysis of phenomena at a very high level of complexity – for example, a national society – we must not forget that these phenomena cannot be anything other than the macroscopic imprint of microscopic behaviour, of individual behaviour.

Individualist methodology is not of course new – Karl Popper long ago stressed its importance for the social sciences.[4] When, however, he gave practical examples of it, he always took them from economics and gave the impression – or perhaps he believed it, which is more likely – that nobody except economists ever bothered with it. Weber's pleas for the individualist method have therefore gone unheeded in areas outside economics.[5]

In *Theories of Social Change*,[6] I turned from the study of social mobility to that of development and social change; development, like mobility, is an essentially macroscopic phenomenon – it can be examined only at the level of a whole society or group of societies. I was not trying to propound a new theory of development, but, using concrete examples, to assess the importance of individualist methodology in this area. My conclusion was that there was in fact a lot of research which could be done based on this method. Although the phenomena of development or stagnation, of social change or absence of it, are complex, and although they are on a macroscopic level, they can in fact be taken for what they *are* – the effect of individual acts, acts which are meaningful.

My book *The Unintended Consequences of Social Action* was another stage in the same series.[7] Here, I tried, by bringing together original research and interpretive analyses, to show the importance for sociology and political action of a classic notion – that the juxtaposition, or, as I would prefer, the *aggregation* of rational acts can give rise to effects which are unintended and sometimes undesirable.

In turning to ideology, my first intention was to continue this series of books. Just as social change seems at first sight to be a difficult area for individualist methodology to tackle, because of the macroscopic nature of the phenomena of change, so the theme of ideology also offers problems, but of a different kind – even if we can agree that the concept of ideology should be defined using the criterion of truth and falsehood, is it reasonable to regard adherence to false ideas as a *meaningful* act? It may after all be more plausible, as many theorists suggest, to regard it as the effect of passions, fanaticism, or distorted perception resulting either from self-interest, or inter-group conflicts, or tensions within an individual induced by living in society.

Obviously we cannot disregard those forces which are beyond the control of the subject; but I think (at least it is what I will try to show in this book) that even for ideology we can follow Weber's suggestion, and try to analyse adherence to received ideas like any other kind of behaviour, by regarding it as a meaningful act, while giving due attention to the irrational. Weber, of course, followed his own suggestion in his work on the sociology of religions.

The present book, however, was also inspired by other considerations. In *Theories of Social Change*, the problem of ideology had arisen, indirectly and almost unwittingly. Models in social sciences are inevitably always simplifications of reality. When a phenomenon involves a large number of actors and encompasses a large number of acts, economists or sociologists usually confine themselves to looking at, for example, two groups of actors (such as producers and consumers) and ascribe to them simplified patterns of behaviour. A model of this kind can of course represent reality only at several removes. The same is true of history, when, for example, a biographer often decides to depict the subject as having always had a final goal in life.[8] In the social and human sciences, any interpretation or explanation creates a gulf between itself and reality which can be enormous. The person interpreting or analysing, as well as the reader, is not always aware of this gulf, but in explaining why this is so, we need to steer clear of insubstantial hypotheses, and show that this lack of awareness, like other attitudes, can be meaningful.

I will devote a great deal of attention to this question, but for the moment I want to emphasize the direct relationship between what I am saying and the problem of ideology, since ideologies are often based on a realistic interpretation of interpretations or explanations which are themselves removed from reality. An extension of this line of thinking will help us to understand better why ideologies are often based on scientific reasoning and why they are to a great extent a normal product of what Kuhn called normal science.[9]

In *Theories of Social Change*, therefore, I unwittingly started to go down a road where I would encounter the problem of the origin of ideologies. It is true, however, that there were also more contingent considerations. Looking at intellectual developments in the last thirty years, one is struck by the dizzy succession of ideas that came and went. I am not convinced that the analogy of fashion is very helpful or correct to account for this, in that one merely has to think of an individual's personal experience to see that one does not subscribe to an idea in the same way as one enthuses over a piece of furniture, a painting, or an item of clothing. Belief is not a question of taste; and the feeling that something is true is not the same as the feeling that something is beautiful or attractive.

I touched on this problem in *The Unintended Consequences of Social Action*,[10] and suggested that when there was a quick succession of ideas, this was brought about by communication effects rather than mere imitation, as would be the case of fashions in clothes. I think that this class of effects is very important, in that they have a decisive part to play in the spread of ideologies. They are also part of the process whereby we can understand how false ideas can catch on so readily, without forcing us to assume that those who subscribe to them are in some way blind.

I was of course also aware of what I term the intrinsic interest of ideology, as evidenced by the amount of writing on the subject. Certainly, there are fundamental metaphysical reasons for this interest; after all, people find it difficult to accept that 'to err is human', despite the saying. The whole of classical philosophy reveals an effort to extirpate error and falsehood, to ascribe it to dark forces which have to be conquered. This attitude to falsehood has been extended to ideology, which for many people is a modern form of falsehood. This is why, from time to time, the 'end of ideologies' is announced; for example in the mid-1960s, and again today. In the Weimar era, some years before Hitler came to power, Mannheim said much the same thing – that movement of ideas and competition between intellectuals would allow a true idea to triumph over a false one. Where Tradition essentially involved a monopolization of the truth, Modernity, according to Mannheim, was characterized by competition between intellectuals, and therefore freer discussion and debate.[11] We must however do justice to Mannheim's memory by saying that he quickly abandoned this optimistic view, and revised his position well before Nazism was at its height.[12] The need to extirpate ideology is so strong that no reference to historical fact has been able to stop people prophesying the end of ideologies. There is no desire in this respect to move away from evolutionism, which reminds us that scientistic evolutionism also said at one time that religion was dead.

The final point is that the confusion in discussions on ideology is a kind of intellectual challenge and makes one want to bring a little order into the debate. I do not know whether I have been successful in this, but at least I have made the attempt.

In any event, I have tried to stick to one firm principle – not to embark on an ideological theory of ideology. Needless to say, this essentially self-destructive temptation is not always avoided by ideology theorists: moreover, the very nature of the theme means that it is usually present; and as soon as ideology is defined in a polemical manner (as the ideas of one's adversary), the temptation is certainly unavoidable. If we want ideology to be only – to parody a phrase which at one time was on everybody's lips in France – those ideas 'which have hurt us so much', one encounters an intractable problem: how to explain why ideas which were so obviously wrong miraculously came about and exerted such an influence.

Since I am aware of this pitfall, I have tried to avoid it and to confine myself strictly to the question of why people adhere so readily to false or dubious ideas, without at any time presuming that false beliefs are the responsibility of a particular Church, or true ones of some other Church.

In my mind, this does not in any way imply that all theories are of equal worth. I have not hesitated to show, as will be seen, that some theories which have held sway and helped to legitimate false ideas are wrong, not to say ludicrous. However, we have to recognize that some intellectual constructs may be readily subjected to the criterion of truth or falsehood, whereas with others it is more difficult to do this. I will come back to this point in the concluding chapter.

The fact that I have endeavoured to be axiologically neutral does not mean that I have no personal convictions. I have for a long time felt closer to liberalism than any other ideology, both for positive reasons which need no further comment since there exists a body of writing showing the importance and vitality of the tradition of liberal thinking on how to understand social phenomena as well as social behaviour,[13] and for negative reasons also, in that I have sometimes thought that those who consider they have a monopoly of finer feelings also tend to think they have *ipso facto* a monopoly of truth.

This book is not a *committed* book. I repeat that my sole intention is to make a modest contribution to sociological theory on ideologies by confining myself to one question – why do people adhere so readily to false or dubious ideas?

The reader may perhaps be surprised that, in the introduction to a book which is supposed to deal with ideology, I have not referred to any *isms*, and mention of Nazism, Fascism, Marxism, or Third Worldism has been purely incidental. This is because of certain strong feelings which I will go into in more detail at a later stage; for the moment, I will simply say how important it is, on a subject as difficult as this one, to put the questions into groups. It is impossible to discuss Nazism seriously without taking into account Hitler's rise to power, which is really a question for the historian. Hitler's view of the world cannot be studied without reference to his life, which is a question for the historian and the psychologist. Similarly, the analysis of fanaticism is the province of the psychologist. The task of the sociologist is to try to understand why ordinary social actors (*Homo sociologicus*) can adhere so readily to false or dubious ideas. If it were not for their consent, no ideology could start up, let alone establish itself. The question is limited, yet it is crucial for the understanding of ideological phenomena.

I have tried to show, firstly, that ideologies are a natural ingredient of social life; secondly, that ideologies start not *in spite of*, but *because of* human rationality. This is why I think the principles of Weberian methodology can be applied to this aspect of social life as well as to others. In other words, the received ideas which make up ideologies can be regarded, and probably deserve to be analysed, as *meaningful* ideas, provided one accepts that the irrational has a residual place in their creation and diffusion.

However, to reach this proof, we must realise that social actors are *situated* and that one's view of the world depends on one's vantage point. Moreover, what one sees from a vantage point depends on what one knows and what one does not know. Furthermore I have tried to show that ideologies are a natural and normal sub-product of the social sciences, not so much in that they are non-scientific, or that they fall outside the rules which usually regulate scientific endeavour, but in that they are in fact subject to them. Of course the social sciences sometimes fall outside these rules, and in doing this they help to strengthen ideologies; but they can also create and strengthen ideologies by following their normal course. This is not because, allegedly, they are incapable of being as rigorous as the natural sciences. This is another received idea which is false – the social sciences can be just as scientific as the natural sciences.

There are two reasons why the social sciences can give rise to ideology, even when sticking to their normal course: the first, which applies to the

natural sciences as well as the social sciences, is that they inevitably present images of reality which are far removed from reality; the second,
which applies only to the social sciences, is that they have what might be
termed a natural exotericism. In any event, I hope that I have in some
small way helped to answer the essential question of the sociological
theory of ideologies – why do people believe in dubious and false ideas?

The book is in three parts: since there is so much confusion about the
concept of ideology, it was crucial to attempt a *definition*. And the fact
that the concept has been written about so much means that I had to cover
the theoretical debates surrounding it and the kinds of *explanation* to
which it has given rise. On a subject such as this, a book which started
from scratch would inevitably have been of questionable worth; these
matters are dealt with in chapters 2, 3, and 4. The following four chapters
(5 to 8 inclusive) comprise part II and deal with the main problem raised in
the book restricted. Here what I call a theory of ideology is put forward,
and I have tried to show that social actors often have good reasons for
adhering to dubious or false ideas, and belief in ideologies should therefore not be ascribed to passion, fanaticism, or blindness. By way of
illustration, chapter 9 (constituting part III) applies this theory to two
modern-day ideologies – developmentalism and Third Worldism. The
discussions in part I are inevitably more abstract that those in parts II
and III. The reader who is in a hurry, and perhaps not particularly
interested in a survey of the classical theories of ideology, is invited to go
quickly through part I.

I have confined to chapter notes certain questions which are important
for any theory of ideologies, but which could not be dealt with fully in the
body of the text. For example, many theories of ideology introduce
implicity or explicit the concept of 'the unconscious'. This is hardly
surprising, since it is tempting to build *Homo Ideologicus* into an irrational being subject to barely controlled urges. However, the concept of
'the unconscious', like its variants (false consciousness, and so on) has to
be treated carefully. I have tried, in several chapter notes, to hint at where
the boundary between legitimate and illegitimate uses of this concept
should be drawn.

In conclusion, before launching into the discussion, I think it is vital to
underscore an important point which up to now I have dealt with only by
implication, and to which I will make copious reference later: namely,
that when I propound the hypothesis that collective belief in false ideas
can often be explained by postulating a *Homo Sociologicus* who is *rational*, I am taking the concept of rationality in a broad sense, not reducible
to the narrow meaning which it is sometimes ascribed to it.

The primary meaning of rationality in the social sciences can be called *utilitarian*. Here, rational actors are supposed to pursue objectives which accord with their most immediate interests, using the most appropriate means. This form of rationality is obviously very important in social life, and is illustrated by the first stage of the example cited in this introduction – Indian peasants reject the pill because, in the particular economic context, it is in their interest to have lots of children. This utilitarian concept of rationality is what English speakers have in mind when they talk of a *rational choice model*. However, it is obviously much too narrow to be of general application, as is evidenced by the many cases in which it is irrelevant in the explanation of behaviour (attitudes, beliefs, and so on) of actors, or in the analysis of *objectives* that they are supposed to be pursuing in behaving in this way or having these beliefs. To illustrate this, let us go back to our example: the diagnosis of the research team was that Indian peasants are victims of their superstitions. Obviously, they have tried to come up with a correct diagnosis and thereby make the campaign more effective. This aim, however, does nothing to explain the *content* of the diagnosis; in other words, the diagnosis cannot be explained by reference either to the utilitarian conception of rationality or to what might be called, following Weber, the teleological conception (*Zweckrationalität*) of rationality. This certainly does not mean that the diagnosis cannot be explained, since, as I have tried to show, the research team had *good reasons* to put it forward.

What I have said before has probably made it sufficiently clear that when I speak of rationality, I am using it in its broad sense. I will therefore apply Weber's approach (which was my starting point) in the following premises: explanation of the behaviour (attitudes, beliefs, and so on) of actors involves evincing the *good reasons* which have led them to adopt this behaviour (these attitudes, beliefs, and so on), while recognizing that these reasons may in some cases be utilitarian or teleological, or of any other kind.

A possible objection might be that in adopting so broad a definition, there is a danger that I am depriving the concept of rationality of all meaning. I do not think there is this danger, since one has only to think about it to see that the premises I have just put forward is very restrictive: it excludes the possibility of explaining the actors' behaviour by anything other than the *reasons* which they would give if they had time to reflect on the matter or the inclination to indulge in such introspection. It thereby excludes several explanatory processes and hypotheses commonly used in the social sciences and which assume implicitly or explicitly that actors can unwittingly be manipulated by forces outside their control.[14]

Part I

2

What is ideology?

The impression given by the literature on ideology and the explanation of the ideological phenomenon is very likely to be one of great confusion.[1] Definitions differ enormously between writers, and explanations of the phenomenon are based on a wide variety of principles. Overall, the impression is that the same word is used to describe a multitude of phenomena rather than a single one, that theories of ideology are at odds on something they define differently, and that the large corpus which they constitute seems therefore like a dialogue of the deaf.

In this chapter, I will look at the definition of ideology, and consider whether it is possible to discern categories within the range of definitions which have been propounded and whether it is reasonable to decide on a particular definition.

Let us look at some classic definitions by way of illustration, beginning with Marx's famous one in *The German Ideology:*

> The production of ideas, of conceptions, of consciousness, is above all directly interwoven into the material activity and the material interaction of people – and as such is the language of real life. Conceptions, thought, the intellectual interaction of people are still at this stage the direct emanation of their material behaviour. [. . .] The fact that in the whole of ideology, people and their relationships appear upside down as in a *camera obscura*, arises from their historical life-process, just as the inversion of objects on the retina does from their physical life-process.[2]

Ideologies for Marx, therefore, are the false ('upside down') ideas which the 'material interaction' of people inspires in them, as an inevitable process. The capitalist, for example, regards profit as the natural remuneration of capital, just as workers tend to regard getting a wage as normal.[3] Neither has a clear view of the truth which Marx thought he had made plain in *Capital*, namely that profit expresses the surplus value produced by the exploitation of the worker, and that wages correspond to labour, the value of which has been subtracted from this surplus value.

My intention is not to embark on a detailed discussion of the Marxian[4] theory of ideologies: at this stage I will not concern myself with all the discussions to which Marx's writing on ideology has given rise,[5] but will confine myself to the point that in most of the theoretical writing devoted to this question, Marx defines ideologies as *false ideas* which social actors possess because of their 'material interaction'.

The point has been made many times that the theory of ideology is a question on which the Marxist school seems the least united. It is not going too far, for example, to say that Lenin's definition is not really like Marx's. Lenin's view[6] was that ideologies are ideas systems, or theories, used by protagonists in the class struggle. Their truth or falsehood may of course vary, but the important thing is that they are, in varying degrees, *useful*. Moreover, their usefulness does not necessarily depend on their truth; and every class can have an ideology.

I will complement these two brief extracts from the Marxist school by quoting from Louis Althusser:

> It is sufficient to know very schematically that an ideology is a system (with its own logic and rigour) of representations (images, myths, ideas or concepts depending on the case) endowed with a historical existence and role within a given society. Without embarking on the problem of the relations between a science and its (ideological) past, we can say that ideology, as a system of representations, is distinguished from science in that in it the practico-social function is more important than the theoretical function (function as knowledge). [. . .] [I]n every society, we can posit [. . .] the existence of a basic economic activity, a political organisation and 'ideological forms' (religion, ethics, philosophy, etc.) *Ideology is therefore an organic part, as such, of every social totality.* [. . .] Human societies secrete ideology as the very element and atmosphere indispensable to their historical respiration and life.[7]

I have quoted Althusser at some length in order to give the reader something on which to judge his conception of ideologies – that basically, ideology amounts to the totality of ideas, concepts, and representations which do not come under the heading of science. They are neither true nor false; in any event, they do not correspond in the first instance to a need for knowledge. They are however indispensable, and act as a kind of respiration for social life. Althusser is dismissive of the idea that science can be inspired by non-scientific views.

A brief survey of the Marxist line of thought was necessary, of course, since the word 'ideology' developed particularly within this tradition. It is interesting to note that the classical sociologists of the end of the nine-teenth century, whether Max Weber, Pareto, or Durkheim, all appear studiously to avoid the word 'ideology'[8] probably because they regarded it as closely linked with the Marxist tradition, and they all had reservations about Marx's thought – of the three people mentioned, only Pareto gives any real attention to him. Their decision not to make use of the concept of ideology is perhaps also because within the Marxist line of thought itself, contradictory definitions of the concept are apparent, some being based on the criterion of truth and falsehood, and others not. Despite this, the concept of ideology has made headway since the heroic era of Durkheim, Weber, and Pareto. Nowadays it is considered to be a classic concept and indicates an area of social sciences of which nobody now doubts the existence or importance.

In looking at how some modern, non-Marxist, sociologists define ideo-logy, I will confine myself to a handful of examples, since my sole intention is to show the variety of definitions by authors whose common charac-teristic is that they have given a lot of thought to ideology, and not to try to cover all definitions comprehensively.

Raymond Aron wrote:

> Political ideologies always combine, more or less felicitously, factual propositions and value judgements. They express an outlook on the world and a will turned towards the future. They do not fall directly under the choice of true or false, nor do they belong to the same category as taste or colour. The ultimate philosophy and the hierarchy of preferences invite discussion rather than proof or refutation; analysis of present facts or anticipation of future facts changes as history unfolds and as we acquire knowledge of it. Experience progressively modifies doctrinal con-structions.[9]

This is of course one of the passages from *The Opium of the Intellec-tuals* which has given rise to the most thought and discussion. Aron is referring to the famous distinction in *Nicomachean Ethics* that some subjects derive from discussion – from dialectics, in the Aristotelian sense – and others from demonstration. To paraphrase Aristotle,[10] it would be just as absurd to apply to morality the kind of reasoning used in mathematics as it would to reason in mathematics in the same way as one argues in morality. On this Aristotelian distinction, Aron superimposes a later distinction, which Hume formulated in a clear-cut way – judgements of fact are demonstrable, value judgements are not. Ideologies, however, are made up of judgements of fact and value judgements, which is prob-ably why, though 'they do not fall directly under the choice of true or false', they come *indirectly* under this heading: value judgements cannot be proved true or false, but they are susceptible of being correct. Aron admits of course that judgements of fact can be proved true or false.[11]

As well as harking back to Aristotle and Hume, this quotation from Aron also makes a subtle reference to German historism; it may be that he was thinking particularly of Karl Mannheim in the penultimate sentence ('analysis of present facts or anticipation of future facts changes as history unfolds and as we acquire knowledge of it'), since Mannheim argued, as we will see later, that the perception of a historical fact is always itself historical, in that it depends on the historical position of the observer.

My next example is taken from the most striking part of the entry on Ideology in the *International Encyclopedia of the Social Sciences*; it is an important example, in that this work amounts to a kind of corpus of reference in the field of social sciences, and also because of the reputation of the author of this entry – Edward Shils.[12] Shils argues that ideology is another example of the positive and normative belief systems (here once more is the distinction between factual statements and value judgements) which flourish in any human society. Compared with *outlooks* (which the Germans call *Weltanschauungen*), ideologies are distinguished by the explicit nature of their formulation; but they are also more closed, inflexible, and resistant to innovation. They are promulgated and endorsed with a great deal of affectivity; those who subscribe to them are required to do so totally. They share with 'systems and movements of thought' (for example existentialism, pragmatism, or Hegelian idealism) the characteristic of being based on explicit or systematic intellectual constructs. Systems and movements of thought, however, are different in being more open to innovation and because they do not require total adherence from the believer. Shils also distinguishes ideologies from *programmes* (for example, the civil rights movements), where objectives are more circumscribed than is the case with ideologies.

To summarize, ideologies are distinct from other belief systems in the way they meet eight criteria. They are distinguished by: the explicit nature of their formulation, their wish to rally people to a particular positive or normative belief, their desire to be distinct from other belief systems past or present, their rejection of innovation, the intolerant nature of their precepts, the affective way they are promulgated, the adherence they demand, and finally, their association with institutions responsible for reinforcing and putting into effect the belief systems in question.

Later in his survey, Shils makes clear one important point – unlike Marx, he declines to define ideology using the criterion of truth or falsehood: 'no great ideology has ever regarded the disciplined pursuit of truth – by scientific procedures and in the mood characteristic of modern science – as part of its obligations.'[13] Marxism is nevertheless, according to Shils, 'the only great ideology which has had a substantial scientific content.'[14] For Shils, therefore, the nature of ideological activity, despite its systematic character, is far removed from scientific activity.

A major difficulty with Shils's position is obviously that it leads him to make an exception of Marxism, whereas his definition of ideology seems particularly appropriate to Marxism. Another problem is that it seems quite arbitrary to say that Marxism is the only ideology capable of having a substantial scientific content, since obviously liberalism is also based on a series of scientific works, from Adam Smith's *The Wealth of Nations* down to the writings of Friedrich Hayek. Robert Nisbet has clearly shown[15] that modern conservatism is also nurtured by sociology. Other modern ideologies such as developmentalism (I will look at this later),[16] which are probably less comprehensive but which have had considerable social and political influence, are readily seen to be based on a plentiful corpus of scientific theories.

Let us nevertheless bear in mind that, according to Shils, ideological activity is closer to that of the prophet or religious reformer than that of the scholar; for Marx, on the other hand, the ideologue is a scholar, even though a perverted one. It is interesting to note that Parsons, with whom Shils collaborated on several works, propounds a definition of ideology which is close to Marx's: 'The essential criterion of ideology is deviation from scientific objectivity . . . The problem of ideology arises when there is a contradiction between what one believes in and what can be established as scientifically correct.'[17]

I will conclude this survey, which I hope has adequately shown the confusion in debate on the definition of ideology, by quoting an extract from Clifford Geertz[18] which is often regarded as a milestone in the theory of ideologies. The best way to introduce Geertz's definition is to remind the reader of a telling example which he himself uses. When the US Senate debated the famous Taft–Hartley Act which was intended to reduce the influence of trade unions in the labour market, the latter called it a 'slave labor act'. Sociologists saw this reaction as a perfect example of the way ideologues tended unduly to simplify things. One of them, Francis Sutton,[19] achieved fame by suggesting that ideology was a distortion of reality which served to reduce the psychological tensions to which social actors are liable. He regarded the trade union reaction to the Taft–Hartley Act as a good illustration of this process of distortion:

> [I]deology tends to be simple and clear-cut, even where its simplicity and clarity do less than justice to the subject under discussion. The ideological picture uses sharp lines and contrasting blacks and whites. The ideologist exaggerates and caricatures in the fashion of the cartoonist. In contrast, a

scientific description of social phenomena is likely to be fuzzy and indistinct. In recent labor ideology the Taft–Hartley Act has been a 'slave labor act'. By no dispassionate examination does the Act merit this label. Any detached assessment of the Act would have to consider its many provisions individually. On any set of values, even those of trade unions themselves, such an assessment would yield a mixed verdict. But mixed verdicts are not the stuff of ideology. They are too complicated, too fuzzy. Ideology must categorize the Act as a whole with a symbol to rally workers, voters and legislators to action.[20]

Geertz reacted sharply to Sutton's analysis; he argued that Sutton had not understood the trade union response. Since he was imbued with the view that ideology is always a distortion of reality, or, to use Parson's phrase, a deviation from the truths established by scientific analysis, Sutton ignored the essential point, and failed to see that when trade unionists called Taft–Hartley a 'slave labour law', they were resorting to a classical rhetorical device. Their phrase was no more than a *metaphor*, and not a distorted perception of reality. It should be regarded rather as action – more precisely as *symbolic action* – intended to produce a mobilization effect, and Sutton admits this to a certain extent when he refers to the rallying function of ideology.

In other words, Geertz was arguing that ideology should not be seen as distorted perception or knowledge. Moreover, by insisting on defining ideology in relation to knowledge, one inevitably makes it into a polemical concept – what is knowledge for one person is ideology for another, and vice versa. Thus, for example, Marx regarded himself as a scholar, but saw Adam Smith as an ideologue, whereas liberals see Marx as an ideologue and Adam Smith as a scholar. If the concept of ideology is to retain a meaning in scientific discourse, Geertz argues that it has to be divested of the polemical character it assumes as soon as it is contrasted with knowledge. Not only is this possible, but his own analysis of the trade union reaction to the Taft–Hartley Act is a telling illustration of this particular way of looking at ideology. When the definition of ideology is based on the notion of symbolic action – that is, on that set of actions of which Aristotelian rhetoric is one example – the concept of ideology is divested of its polemical character. Geertz argues that it is then, and only then, that it can hope to describe an object relevant to scientific analysis. Proof of this relevance lies in the plentiful writing on the functions and the social uses of metaphor and other rhetorical devices.

To summarize, Geertz says that if the concept of ideology is to retain a meaning within scientific discourse, we must stop defining ideology in relation to science. In other words, we have to accept that, as Althusser would say, the 'knowledge function' of ideology is subordinate to its 'practico–social function'.

At this stage it would be useful to summarise (see table 1) the various definitions to which I have referred. I have classified these definitions by reference to two criteria – Marxist tradition/non-Marxist tradition; definition based/not based on the criterion of truth and falsehood. There is no correlation between the two; we see that in both traditions, ideology is defined either with or without reference to the criterion of truth and falsehood.

I was not quite sure where to put Aron in the table, in terms of the horizontal line, but certainly as far as the vertical column was concerned. I finally put him in the left-hand column for two reasons: firstly, because his definition indicates that ideologies are indirectly subject to the truth/falsehood alternative; and secondly, because it is clear from *The Opium of the Intellectuals* that the ideologies he attacks in this book are attacked because they are false, and that therefore he felt able to judge ideologies by the criterion of truth and falsehood.

I have put the consciousness-reflection theorists in the top left-hand box: all such theorists proceed on the assumption, firstly, that the way social actors represent things is a reflection of their position, and secondly, that the sociologist can rise above the mêlée, or, to use the Platonic image,

Table 1 Types of definition of ideology

Types of tradition	Based on the criterion of true and false	Not based on the criterion of true and false
Marxist tradition	MARX: ideology as false science	LENIN: ideology as a weapon in the class struggle
	THEORISTS OF CONSCIOUSNESS-REFLECTION	ALTHUSSER: ideology as the atmosphere indispensable to social respiration
Non-Marxist tradition	ARON: ideology as not deriving directly from the criterion of true and false, but deriving indirectly from it	GEERTZ: ideology as symbolic action
	PARSONS: ideology as a deviation from scientific objectivity	SHILS: ideology as a specific type of belief system

break free from the wall of the Cave and in this way make sense of the illusions held by social actors.

We see, therefore, that despite its confused nature, the debate about the definition of ideology revolves round one single question: should ideology be defined according to the criterion of truth and falsehood? All the authors I have quoted (and, I think, all the authors who could be quoted) come down on one side or the other, replying negatively or positively. Only Aron gives an answer which is neither wholly negative nor positive.

The *terms* of the debate are therefore clear, above and beyond the confusion; but which of the two answers to the question is better? Although a definition is not, of course, amenable to proof, and one can merely argue for it or against it, it is vital, on this point as on others, to beware of ready-made ideas. After all, a definition can certainly, in some cases, be proven to be untrue: for example, nobody would define a human being as a three-legged animal, unless, like the Sphinx, there was a play on words. Unfortunately, unlike the concept of 'human being', there is no class of objects with which 'ideology' is readily identifiable *before* an attempt is made to define it; so in this case one cannot resort to a comparison with reality (humans are two-legged and not three-legged) in order to accept or reject a particular definition of ideology.

It needs to be stressed that the debate on the word 'ideology' has helped to create confusion in the concept itself. For those people who thought up, accepted, used, and spread this term, it did in fact correspond to a reality which they regarded as new. This reality was no doubt a specific historical reality rather than one which corresponded to a class of objects; and it could not give rise to a definition by indicating something akin to it and the precise way it differed from it. On the other hand, it must be accepted that it is not very difficult to spot. In fact the word 'ideology' made its appearance, took on its present-day meaning, and became widespread when, at the end of the eighteenth century and in the nineteenth century, great efforts were made to use Reason and Science as a basis for a social order which until then had been built on Tradition.

My primary argument in favour of a Marx–Arons–Parsons kind of definition is therefore one that is both historical and logical. Originally, the word 'ideology' signified the reality of the increasing social role played by scientific reasoning in thought on political and social matters. If we keep this original definition, and take the concept of ideology as signifying the totality of theories which claim to teach us about political and social matters by basing oneself on a scientific approach (or at least an approach which appears to be scientific), then it follows that ideology does fall under the heading of the truth/falsehood alternative.

At this point, we need to look briefly at the history of the word 'ideology'. It was of course invented by Destutt de Tracy at the end of the eighteenth century, and signified for him the science of the origin of ideas, which he decided to found. Destutt de Tracy's intention was therefore that it should signify a discipline which took ideas as its subject matter, like mineralogy takes minerals and geology the earth. He thought that in content and direction, the discipline could take its inspiration directly from sensualist ideas, as epitomized in the well-known model of Condillac's statue. Condillac was convinced he could show that his statue was capable of the most abstract ideas if he attributed to it the most rudimentary of the senses – smell. Destutt de Tracy tried to take Condillac's ideas one stage further and analyse ideas as deriving from the senses. He called this *ideology* rather than *psychology* since the root of this word had too much of a religious connotation.

Originally, therefore, the word 'ideology' had a meaning which has nowadays almost entirely disappeared, apart from Marx's theory of ideologies, parts of which are close to Destutt de Tracy's scheme, in that he also tries to show that ideas derive from feelings stemming from the material conditions of existence. Except for this remote intellectual relationship between Condillac and Destutt de Tracy on the one hand and Marx on the other, the original meaning of the word 'ideology' has disappeared, no doubt as sensualism, and then materialism, dwindled.

It was Napoleon who, by chance, gave the word 'ideology' its modern meaning. When Destutt de Tracy and Volney tried to thwart Napoleon's imperial ambitions, he scornfully called them *ideologues*, meaning people who wanted to substitute abstract considerations for *real* politics, as it was later called. From that time on, ideology signified those abstract (and rather dubious) theories allegedly based on reason or science, which tried to map out the social order and guide political action. This is what Marx took it to mean, perhaps taking his cue from Hegel who used the word (in Napoleon's sense) only once, towards the end of his life.[21]

The reason why this meaning of the word gained currency is again because it corresponded to a reality – the idea, which had gained ground from Locke through Rousseau to Adam Smith, that it is possible, useful, and proper to look for the laws of the social world, just as Newton had looked for the laws of nature. Writing about Newton, Locke said: 'If others could give us so good and clear an account of other parts of Nature, as he has of this our Planetary World, and the most considerable Phenomena observable in it, [. . .] we might in time hope to be furnished with more true and certain knowledge in several Parts of this stupendous Machine, than hitherto we could have expected.'[22] This was later followed by Montesquieu's famous definitions: 'Laws, in the widest sense, are the necessary relationships which derive from the nature of things: and, in this sense, all beings have their laws: Divinity has its laws; the material world has its law; intelligences higher than humans have their laws; animals have their laws; human beings have their laws.'[23] Adam Smith's frequent reference to the 'natural order of things' is in the same vein. The history of the word 'ideology' shows therefore that it has signified an aspiration to think about, and set the foundations of, social order in a *scientific* way. At the same time, however, the pejorative aspect of the word, which survived from Napoleon to Marx, and from Marx to Aron and many other writers, showed how this aspiration could be illusory.

The traditional meaning of the word 'ideology' corresponds therefore to a *reality*, even though this reality can be neither as clearly identified nor as easily distinguished from other realities as human two-legged animals can be differentiated from other animals. This kind of concept is traditionally designated by the notion of *ideal type*. Thus, for example, the concepts of 'absolute monarchy' or 'capitalism' are ideal types – as with ideology in its traditional sense, they reveal specificities of history. Moreover, these ideal types usually appear first in the discourse of social actors themselves, and are only then absorbed into that of historians, sociologists, or economists. This is what happened in the case of ideology, as well as in the case of the two others mentioned.

My second argument in favour of what I will from now on refer to as the *classic* or *traditional* definition of ideology goes back to an objection (to which I have already alluded) to Shils's view. Shils says that Marxism is the only great ideology which has a substantial scientific content. It is important to stress again, however, that most nineteenth- and twentieth-century ideologies, major as well as minor ones, contain scientific reasoning. Marxism is an example, as Shils points out, and it is difficult, for instance, not to regard Marx's analysis of the crisis of feudalism in *The Poverty of Philosophy* as a very serious study in economic history. It is so unexceptionable that the main thrust of it was followed by Keynes;[24] and it is clear that *Capital* is an example of an approach which is scientific – which does not mean, of course, that all of its arguments are true.

The same can obviously be said about liberalism. Let us look at Locke's famous argument on property. If there were no property rights, an individual would have no real inclination to work if there was a danger of having the fruits of this labour taken away. This is a theorem which is amenable to the most rigorous proof, and the same can be said of Adam Smith's proof in *The Wealth of Nations* that colonies are harmful to colonial countries,[25] or Ricardo's 'law of comparative advantages' that international trade is a positive sum game benefiting both sides. Political liberalism, like economic liberalism, is also based on a corpus of classical theorems.

To avoid confusion, I must make it clear that I am not equating Marxism and liberalism (although this book is not about the content and relative validity of ideologies, I will make occasional reference to this aspect in chapter ten). I simply want to state that despite what Shils says, Marxism is not the only ideology which has a 'substantial scientific content'. Shils's view is all the more strange in that he is far from being a Marxist: it is probably because of his wish to convince himself and his readers that ideologies should be looked at in the way of religious doctrines rather than scientific doctrines, and this is why he treats Marxism as an exception which proves the rule. However, it is an exception which is difficult to accept in that, firstly, liberalism is clearly also based on scientific doctrines, and secondly, these doctrines are probably less fragile than those on which Marxism is base. Although it is difficult, for example, to refute Locke's argument on property rights, or Ricardo's 'law of comparative advantage', it is easy to refute the central element of Marx's thought – the theory of surplus value.[26]

I have also referred briefly to the fact that modern conservatism, which is a more *diffuse* ideology than the two I have just mentioned, has also found support, at least as regards some of its variants, in doctrines of a scientific nature, in this case doctrines derived from sociology.

In fact, by emphasizing the social and sociological importance of authority, charisma, social hierarchy, status, and solidarity, the classical sociologists – particularly Max Weber, Durkheim, and Pareto – helped to end the atomistic and egalitarian view of society which had been propounded by the political philosophy of the Enlightenment. By stressing the importance of *traditions*, they helped to give back a positive meaning to a concept seen as negative in the period before the French Revolution, though, as Nisbet clearly shows,[27] there are in the work of these classical sociologists themes which had been developed in a more prescriptive and normative way by conservative thinkers at the beginning of the nineteenth century, for example Bonald or Joseph de Maistre. It is not certain, however, that the classical sociologists were influenced by these thinkers, but it is certain that Weber, like Durkheim and Pareto, by analysing in a positive way phenomena such as those I have mentioned, helped to make them more important – tradition, authority, and hierarchy lost the negative drift of the Enlightenment period and regained their former positive tenor. These are of course values which are regarded as positive by conservative ideology.

Here, we must beware of an optical illusion with regard to history: sociology is often seen as a discipline dedicated to egalitarianism and 'social change'. In fact, egalitarian sociology, as well as the version which looks for social ferment since it is supposed to bring inevitable *progress*, is a recent development. Although they did sometimes appear in the past, it was particularly in the 1960s that they flourished, and they now seem to be in decline.

As I said, conservatism is a diffuse ideology and I do not claim that it is entirely based on classical sociology. In other respects, conservatism is based on Tradition, as will be seen in the example of Voegelin in Chapter seven. I am merely suggesting, following Nisbet, that some aspects of the conservative ideology have certainly been reinforced by the scientific analyses of classical sociology. Of course, social Darwinism, as its name signifies, was also based on theories which are of an undeniably scientific nature. It goes without saying that the precepts of social Darwinism cannot be regarded as deriving directly from Darwinism itself.[28]

What is true of the major ideologies is also true of the minor ones; these are just as worthy of attention, since they can have, and often have had, considerable political and social influence. I have already mentioned the case of developmentalism, based on a set of theories which regards foreign aid and the injection of capital as the necessary and sufficient conditions for economic development. These theories (whether they are true or false does not concern me at this particular juncture) are undoubtedly based on approaches which are scientific. They have also been challenged, and it was in fact their opponents who gave them the collective name of developmentalism: there was a critical intent in attaching an *ism* to them, and the idea was to create a pejorative effect. The arguments of their opponents, however, were often based on scientific arguments.

For the sake of balance, I will refer also to the example of Third Worldism,[29] which is not, as is often suggested, an ideology based merely on finer feelings. Here as in other cases, feelings are based on theories which, whether they are wholly or partly true or false, at least have the form of scientific theories. If it had not been for the large body of research and theories which come under the heading of 'dependency theory' (with which I will deal in chapter 9), Third Worldism would not be what it is today.

My two main arguments therefore in favour of the Marx–Aron–Parsons definition of ideology can be summarized as follows:

1 The word 'ideology' achieved salience in the nineteenth century because it described a new social *reality*, that is, the more and more widespread trend to explain the bases of social order and political action by analysis of a scientific kind. Simultaneously, the pejorative nature of the word showed the limitations of this and the risk of distortion to which it was open.

2 Most ideologies, whether major or minor, 'left-wing' or 'right-wing', are characterized by the fact that they are based on doctrines conforming to the scientific approach.

These two arguments lead to the definition of ideologies as doctrines based on scientific theories, but on theories which are false or dubious or have not been properly interpreted, and which are therefore given undeserved credibility. The basic sociological problem is therefore how these misinterpretations are possible, and why they are so widespread. This is the basic problem to which this book addresses itself, but before tackling it I will continue with my plea on behalf of the *traditional* definition of ideology – the Marx–Aron–Parsons kind, since not only does it correspond to a reality and raise an important question (why do false, dubious or weak theories so readily become widespread and authoritative?), but also, the *modern* definition (the Shils–Geertz–Althusser kind) has various faults, to the extent that it is not very clear what in fact it is signifying. Let us immediately dispose of one of Geertz's arguments which appears to be sound but in fact is not: that in its traditional meaning, the concept of ideology contains value judgements since it deals with beliefs of dubious justification; scientific concepts ought to be axiologically neutral, that is, not contain value judgements.

This argument is using in a totally wrong way the concept of axiological neutrality, which says that observers ought not to project their own preferences and values on to the object being analysed. They should not say that a white object is black simply because they *like* the colour black. However, the concept does not say that a falsehood or a truth should not be regarded as such; and axiological neutrality is not being broken by asserting that somebody who says that two plus two equals three is mistaken, or that somebody who is telling lies is a liar.

Clearly, some scientific objects cannot be defined by reference to value judgements of this kind. There can be no analysis of lies if no 'judgement' is passed on the liar. The phenomenon of magic, which has inspired much scientific work, is another example: not only does the research take account of the illusory nature of belief in magic, but it assumes that the observer can treat these beliefs as being in contradiction with scientific knowledge. In other words magic can be defined only on the basis of the notion of false belief. Why should something which seems not to be a problem in the case of magic be a problem when it comes to ideology?

A further point is that the *modern* definition of ideology does not, I think, match up to what one expects of a definition. Even if one rejects my previous argument that the word 'ideology' in its traditional meaning does in fact reveal a *historical reality*, the definition still has to allow a clear identification of the objects to which it refers, and to designate them using criteria which are not widely different. Thus, for example, one would not think very much of a definition which said that humans were (1) two-legged, (2) capable of double-dealing, (3) the inventors of negation, (4) clean-shaven, (5) creatures of passions, (6) reasonable. Yet it is a definition of this kind that the 'modern' conception of ideology seems to be propounding.

In fact, if ideology is defined by the concept of symbolic action, this would include all mathematical theorems, all insults ever addressed by one politician to another, children's stories, philosophical theories, even all political opinions. This is the kind of confusion to which a definition such as Althusser's leads, since the word 'ideology' subsumes moral, philosophical, religious etc. (*sic*) ideas, concepts, images, theories, and representations. Also, the definition is still wide even if one takes ideology to mean all symbolic acts connected with politics.

The final point is that it is arbitrary to assume, as Geertz suggests, that *symbolic action* is necessarily free from reference to the criterion of truth and falsehood. This can be shown by looking again at the metaphor he himself uses, which he regards as a paradigm of *symbolic actions*. If there is bright sunshine and I exclaim 'what foul weather!', it is clear what will be the reaction of those with me. My metaphor – symbolic action though it may be – will fall flat: it was *false*. It was false not in the logical sense of the word, but rather in the sense in which one says that a portrait is *false*. It is perhaps not an accident that the same word can be used in both cases. This is what happened to the trade union metaphor referred to by Geertz – it was *false* in the sense that the Taft–Hartley Act was not in fact *perceived* by the general public as a slave labour law. The metaphor therefore fell flat and had no visible mobilizing effect.

There is another argument for not considering symbolic acts in Geertz's sense as not falling within the criterion of truth and falsehood. Rhetorical devices often have value and effect only if they are based on ideologies (in the traditional sense of the term). This is clearly seen, for example, in the case of political debates: a member of the French National Assembly once declared, in oratorical flight, that 'the independence of the Kanak people is written in history.' The strength of conviction was less the result of his oratorical gestures than of the corpus of evolutionist theories which he was evoking in the minds of his listeners.

The objection may well be once again – what of value judgements? Does not every ideology contain them?; and are they not unprovable, as has been known since Hume?[30] Is it not true that ideologies, since they contain value judgements, fall outside the criterion of true and false at least to this degree? Aron stresses this point very well when he says that 'political ideologies always combine, more or less felicitously, factual propositions and value judgements', which is why 'they do not fall *directly* [Boudon's italics] under the choice of true or false.'

The question of value judgements is obviously a very complex one, and I cannot cover all of it here. I will therefore confine myself to emphasizing, without insisting on the point, that value judgements can be conditionally proved. In this sense, even physics contains value judgements. Thus, for example: 'People who do not like physical pain are *advised not* to leave their hand in door openings, where strong lever effects are in evidence.' The same applies to the human sciences – for example: 'Unless it is desired to make people disinclined to work, it is *necessary* to guarantee that they have control over the produce of their labour.'

Generally speaking, if we assume that B is unanimously thought desirable and A is, in an incontrovertible way, the necessary and sufficient condition of B, then putting them together, we will have proved the value judgement that A is good. Of course, there are value judgements which are not provable. It is probably a *good thing*, for example, not to cut off the hands of thieves; but it is impossible to prove this. Let us merely say that the question of the proof of value judgements is a complex one, but that it is not true that value judgements always fall outside the choice of true or false.

Similarly, it needs to be stressed that apart from particular judgements which in principle are always provable (if there is enough information available), factual judgements can be not provable. It is easy to decide whether a statement such as 'there exists a purple hen' is true (all that is needed is to produce one), but one cannot be sure whether it is false. It can easily be proved that 'all hens are not purple', but not that 'no hen has teeth.'

Finally, we are well aware that however sound a scientific theory is, it is always based on unproved statements. Without going further into this discussion, I will conclude that the contrast between value judgements which are unprovable and factual judgements which are always provable has to be approached with care.

On the assumption (and I have not tried to go further than this in what I have just said) that it is useful to define ideology, following the *traditionalists*, as beliefs based on scientific theories which are false, dubious, or in any case given more credibility than they warrant, then *ipso facto* one defines the concept of ideology on the basis of the concept of *scientific* reasoning. This does not mean that there are not other kinds of reasoning. One may ask whether the modernists are not throwing out the baby with the bath water when they suggest that ideology can be defined without reference to the criterion of truth and falsehood. Is it not more simple to recognize that there is a type of reasoning – scientific reasoning – which cannot be conceived independent of the criterion of truth and falsehood, but that there are others which do not depend so clearly and closely on this criterion?

Rhetorical reasoning is another classic form of reasoning, different of course from scientific reasoning. Geertz is perfectly correct on this point and, in making the distinction, he is simply restating an old Aristotelian distinction. We have nevertheless seen that in many circumstances, rhetorical reasoning can also be subject to the criterion of truth and falsehood, as when the metaphor falls flat, or when oratorical effect tacitly invokes a doctrinal corpus. However, rhetorical reasoning can also function autonomously as far as this criterion is concerned.

The same applies to *exegetical* reasoning, which calls on an authority which is either widely recognized or recognized by particular important groups, and establishes what the authority in question '*really* meant'. A classic example of exegetical reasoning is *The Praise of Folly* by Erasmus. Pretending to call on Folly (which means that he can challenge what is being said if he so desires), Erasmus in fact calls on the Bible for authority. The Bible *really meant* that it is preferable, in order to serve the glory of God, to lead an honest and effective life in this world rather than to prove one's piety by 'good works'. Erasmus's exegetical reasoning was of course destined to have considerable influence, in that it was an important stage in the development of Protestantism.

It is probably because of the existence of these different types of reasoning that Pareto, one of the more interesting theorists of ideology did not use the word, but preferred a neologism – 'derivation'. According to Pareto, derivations are all those intellectual constructs which people devise to show that their feelings are justified. However, depending on circumstances and the particular point in history, the reasoning on which the derivations are based can vary – exegetical when Tradition held sway, but usually scientific in modern times. Putting it like this is not of course how Pareto describes it, but it does give an idea of his thinking. The reason why he avoided the word 'ideology' was that he regarded it as too bound up in Marxist tradition, but also that he wanted a single word to describe the different kinds of reasoning which people used to cover their feelings. At the same time he was clear that, among these intellectual constructs to which he gives the generic name of derivations, it was important to differentiate those which are based on scientific reasoning.

Pareto had yet another reason, however, for finding his own word to describe the kind of construct which we call 'ideology': he saw clearly that, although intellectual constructs based on scientific reasoning are characteristic of modernity, other kinds of reasoning nevertheless survived. Just like Geertz, he recognized the importance of rhetorical reasoning, and did not underestimate that of exegetical reasoning in modern times (again I am paraphrasing Pareto). The latter still plays an important part among groups which look to traditional authorities, whatever these may be. People still ponder on what the Bible *really meant*; the same applies to the American founding fathers, the creator of the French Fifth Republic, or the father of Marxism. In a more general sense the whole of case law is an unending reply to the question of what the original legislation really meant. At a more mundane level, there are sociologists who spend an enormous amount of time pondering on what Weber or Durkheim really said rather than whether what they said is true or informative.

In other words, all three kinds of reasoning play an important part in modern society, which is probably the main reason why Pareto preferred to use 'derivations' rather than 'ideology'. If Pareto had to be included in the table on page 23, I would put him in the same box as Aron and Parsons, since although he does recognize that there are different kinds of reasoning and, like Geertz, he stresses the importance of rhetoric in those constructs that he calls derivations, he does not conclude that derivations cannot be judged against truth and falsehood. In fact, Pareto's *Treatise on General Sociology* suggests (here it is perhaps going too far) that all derivations, whatever kind of reasoning they use, bear the stamp of falsehood and blindness.

I will come back to Pareto's theory of derivations, which I believe to be important.[31] It goes too far in some respects, however – for example, it is not true, as I will try to show, that, except in special cases, ideologies can be regarded simply as rationalizations intended to justify and legitimate feelings. If this were so, it would hardly explain why the illusions of ideology are so perfect. Secondly, I think that, although we have to recognize the existence of several kinds of reasoning, the scientific kind is particularly significant in that it explains how the word 'ideology' came to have its most common present-day meaning. A final point is that Pareto certainly exaggerates the provable nature of factual judgements and the unprovable nature of value judgements, which leads him to conclude too readily that the latter can be based only on feelings.

At this point, however, I will return to the problem of the definition of ideology, having been diverted by Pareto into looking at the theory of ideology. I will proceed on the basis that the concept of ideology is a doctrine based on scientific reasoning and endowed with excessive or unjustified credibility. The main sociological question stemming from this definition concerns the reason why the credibility is excessive. By limiting my analysis to this question, I am looking at only one part of the field which Pareto covered in his theory of derivations, but it is a part which I believe to be essential.

3

Is *Homo Sociologicus* (always) irrational?

I argued in the previous chapter that one of the main reasons for the confusion in discussions on ideology is that writers use different definitions of the concept, which means that they are not all referring to the same thing. Some define ideology in relation to the criterion of truth and falsehood, while others do not. It is to be expected, of course, that explanation of the phenomenon of ideology will vary according to the definition used. One's view of the causes or the grounds for existence of ideology will depend on one's conception of what ideology *is*, which leads on to the question of whether there is a correlation between the way one defines ideology and the way one explains it.

A reply to this question, however, must be preceded by a survey of the kinds of explanation of ideology which can be, and which have been, suggested. As in the previous chapter, I will again not attempt to be exhaustive, since it would be futile to try to give a detailed survey of all the theories of ideology which have been propounded. I will therefore merely *classify*, by covering the main areas apparent throughout the range of theories.

In *Novum Organum*, Bacon develops his well-known theory of *idols*. As Mannheim rightly points out,[1] this foreshadows the theory of ideologies, or, to be more precise, a variant of the theory of ideologies. The idols in question are all those 'phantoms' or 'preconceptions' which stem either from human nature itself or from the psychic make-up of certain individuals, and which are the main cause of our mistakes: 'The idols and false notions which have already preoccupied the human understanding and are deeply rooted in it, not only so beset men's minds that they become difficult of access, but even when access is obtained will again meet, and trouble us in the instauration of the sciences.'[2]

These 'idols' therefore not only disrupt our access to truth, but they are also so rooted in people's minds that it is difficult to be aware of them. Not only do we wear distorting lenses, but we are not conscious that we are wearing them – the modern phrase would be 'the unconscious'. Also, it is of course difficult not to resort to the concept of the unconscious as soon as one is willing to interpret literally the metaphor of blindness. However, we must also bear in mind the last point in the quotation – it is not enough to be conscious of one's blindness, to realise the ghostly nature of idols; we must also will ourselves into a state of vigil – otherwise we may lapse back into a dream world.

In this splendid book, Bacon is putting forward for the first time what might be called the classical theory of falsehood, which can be regarded as irrationalist in that it attributes falsehood to forces outside the control of the subject. The latter can always master them, but only by means of efforts which might slacken. Descartes says much the same thing in a different way; and Spinoza's distinction between understanding and the will leads to a similar diagnosis – the move towards truth which defines understanding is continually threatened by interference from the will. Pascal sees the imagination as a 'mistress of error and falsehood', and in doing so is suggesting that the human mind can be occupied and dominated by outside forces. I think Mannheim was perfectly right when he stated in 1929 that Bacon's theory of idols foreshadows the modern theory of ideology, but in making this link, he took 'the modern theory of ideology' to be the one outlined by Marx and Engels.

It is a theory which is complex, incomplete, and scattered throughout many of his writings, so that it is doubtful whether it can be regarded as one single whole. In fact I believe that, for Marx at least, an examination of all his works on ideology (which are mainly short and full of allusions) reveals two very different theoretical orientations. I will return to this briefly at a later point,[3] since my aim in this chapter is to establish a classification of theories of ideology, rather than offer a complete analysis of a particular theory.

Putting aside for the moment, therefore, the question of the coherence and unity of Marx's theory of ideology, I think it important to emphasize that many works by Marx and Engels refer significantly to the principles of what I have called the classical (irrationalist) theory of falsehood. The originality of Marx and Engels lies (I was going to say lies *only*, but this would unjustly reduce their originality) in the fact that they attributed *social* causes to the 'idols' whereas Bacon and the classical philosophers said there were *natural* causes – that is, part of human nature as they conceived it.

In order to support my view that there is a direct link between the classical theory of falsehood and the 'Marxian' concept of ideology, I will quote a famous letter from Engels to Mehring dated 14 July 1893 (i.e. after Marx's death), and which has been quoted and commented upon many times, for two reasons – firstly because it appears to be the first attempt by, as it were, the Marx–Engels 'team' to put forward a proper definition of a phenomenon on which they had both written at some length; and secondly, because it was the first time that, as a 'team', they had made use of a concept which inspired so much later writing, that of 'false consciousness': 'Ideology is a process which the would-be thinker certainly accomplishes with consciousness, but with a false consciousness. The motive forces (*Triebkräfte*) which really move him remain unknown to him; otherwise it would certainly (*eben*) not be an ideological process.'[4]

It is not difficult to recast this quotation using Bacon's language: people whose reasoning is based on preconceptions or idols are certainly undertaking 'a process [. . .] with consciousness' – they are fully awake and able to come up with coherent arguments. However, their speculations about the real world have very little to do with reality, since this is perceived through distorting lenses (the 'idols' or 'preconceptions'). Since they think they are seeing reality as it is, we have to assume that they do not know either that they are wearing such lenses, nor *a fortiori* why they are wearing them. As Engels said: 'the motive forces which really move them remain unknown to them, *otherwise* [Boudon's italics] it would certainly not be an ideological process.' Ideology implies being blind to matters, and this implies the existence of an unconscious, which can by definition invade the consciousness of the subject without the latter realising it.

We come now to the question of what the 'motive forces' are which fill the unconscious with particular matter. Here, the paths of Bacon and (Marx–)Engels diverge – human nature as the classical philosophers see it means that social causes can be adduced: '[The ideologue] works with purely intellectual material which he deals with in an unconsidered way as produced by thought, and which he does not try to explore further by setting it against a more distant process, independent of thought. And that seems to him to be self-evident.'[5]

The ideologue therefore takes on board arguments without seeing that they contain concepts, images, and 'idols' which do not derive from the activity of thought itself, but which are inspired unwittingly by 'a more distant process', that is, by social relationships and economic relationships or, to use a less precise phrase which crops up frequently in Marx and Engels, by 'material life' or 'material activity'.

To show that Engels's famous letter to Mehring can be regarded as giving an insight into the thought not only of Engels but also of Marx (or more precisely into how Marx conceived ideology in much – but not all – of his writing), I will quote another famous passage, this time from *The German Ideology*, some of which I have already used in the last chapter:

The production of ideas, of conceptions, of consciousness, is at first directly interwoven with the material activity and the material interaction of people – and as such is the language of real life. Conceptions, thought, the intellectual interaction of people are still at this stage the direct emanation of their material behaviour. The same applies to intellectual production as in the language of the politics, laws, morality, religion, metaphysics, etc. of a particular nation. People produce their conceptions, their ideas, but they are conditioned to be real, active people by the development of their productive forces and the interaction which these create, including the most advanced forms of this interaction. [. . .] The fact that in the whole of ideology, people and their relationships appear upside down as in a *camera obscura*, arises from their historical life-process, just as the inversion of objects on the retina does from their physical life-process.

This quotation can be put with the one from Engels's letter: here again are the distorting lenses, and we are no more aware of them than we are of the image on our retina. The distortion is caused by the fact that people's ideas and conceptions are directly inspired by their 'material activity' and their 'material interaction'. Of course, they can no more be aware of the real cause than they can of the image on their retina, nor *a fortiori* of the fact that this image is upside down in relation to the image actually perceived. Moreover, although Marx does not do so, the analogy can easily be extended further – just as the biologist can study sight and observe the phenomenon of inversion, so the writer can point out the inversion which ideology imposes on reality.

The extracts from Marx and Engels can also, I repeat, be tied in with the quotation from Bacon: the only point of difference (though it is an important one) is on what I will call the location of the cause – human nature in Bacon, society in Marx–Engels (when Marx and Engels speak of 'material life' and 'material activity' they mean 'social life').[6]

One final point needs to be made, to clarify the interpretation of the *camera obscura* image, and the importance which it should be given. This is that Marx and Engels normally use the word 'ideology' in the singular (no doubt because of the influence of the Marxist school on this aspect of ideology, the use of the word in the plural is in fact a modern, not to say recent, development). This is important in that it confirms that Marx and Engels conceived of ideology as a *process* – a word they use frequently, as evidenced by my quotations from them – that is, as an easily identifiable mechanism with its own laws, like sight or digestion.

Marx's comparison of ideology with sight should be seen as being for him not a *metaphor*, but an *analogy*; whereas the two sides of a metaphor are linked by a chance or superficial relationship (for example, 'an iron fist'), an analogy involves an actual resemblance between the two sides of the pair (for example the Cartesian theory of 'animal–machines', or cybernetic analogies in modern political science).[7]

We see therefore that for Marx and Engels, ideology is a process which is *analogous* to sight. The question then arises as to the mechanisms by which 'material activity' can in fact produce the inverted images characteristic of ideology in the minds of 'real, active people'.

The principle behind these mechanisms is well-known: it is class interests. At this point, however, a surprise is in store for us. Although Marx overemphasizes class interests in the origin of ideologies, his analyses of the way in which these interests have influenced a particular ideology are not only often unexceptionable, but also they are not derived from the general theory and the analogy to which I have just referred. As Pierre Ansart wrote: 'when the industrial bourgeoisie theorized about the benefits of the parliamentary monarchy, it was endeavouring to promote a regime which would allow it to increase its power and defend the interests of trade and industry.'[8] When the feudal aristocracy extolled the king's greatness, it was because it thought that the monarchy was the keystone of a system which ensured its privileged position in society.

There is no problem in accepting this kind of analysis, once its fairly rudimentary nature is realised. The structure of the argument is: a particular institution (the Monarchy, the parliamentary system) serves my interests, and so I am likely to think it a good institution. There is nothing original or doubtful in this: the strategy of arguing that what is good for oneself is good for others is commonly used by political actors and social actors in general. The teacher says 'you are going to fall and *hurt yourself*' to the pupil leaning back on two legs of a chair, thus making the benefits of good behaviour into a 'theory'. It is not surprising, therefore, that the industrial bourgeoisie should have made the benefits of parliamentary monarchy into a theory. The analysis must be taken further, since political philosophy is not the preserve of one particular class, whether the industrial bourgeoisie or any other, but of intellectuals whose interests do not necessarily coincide with those of the class in question,[9] and who moreover may be inspired by considerations other than those of their interest. Apart from this caveat, it is difficult to find fault with these analyses. In fact, the only difficulty is that they fall completely outside the theory of ideology outlined by Marx and Engels, for example, in the extracts I quoted earlier. In this instance, ideology takes the form either of 'preferences' (as economists would say) which are easily explained by reference to the social position of the actors involved, or of 'theoretical constructs' which amount to symbolic action (in Geertz's sense) with a strategic purpose. The 'theorizing' we are looking at there (for example, theorizing about parliamentary monarchy by the industrial bourgeoisie) is different in degree rather than in kind from that symbolic action with a strategic purpose which is common in social and political life, such as 'You are going to fall and hurt yourself', 'Freeing industry is defending jobs', 'Increasing demand by raising wages will breathe new life into industry . . .'

It can be seen, as these three examples show, that 'symbolic action with a strategic purpose' can be in keeping with reality as well as the opposite. It is true that the pupil who leans back on two legs of a chair is in danger of falling and sustaining injury; it is also true, in the context of France in the mid-1980s, that 'freeing industry is defending jobs'; but it is doubtful that increasing wages will stimulate firms – in certain circumstances, it may well kill off some of them. Similarly, parliamentary institutions may serve the interests of the industrial bourgeoisie without necessarily being harmful to other interests.

These clarifications are necessary because Marx assumes, in the examples he adduces, that the aim of 'symbolic action' with a strategic purpose is always to camouflage untruths. This of course is not always so – I might try to persuade somebody to subscribe to a 'theory' which suits me perfectly, by suggesting that it will be extremely beneficial to the other person, without its being necessarily false. As Pareto said, there is a difference between the *truth* of a theory and its *usefulness;* and there is no reason in principle why the two criteria should necessarily either converge or diverge.

The reason why Marx's analysis always emphasizes the case where X tries to persuade Y of a theory which benefits X but is counter to Y's interests is that *the dogma of the class struggle is ever present in his mind*. This dogma can be summarized as follows:

1 the only real actors are classes;
2 they are by definition in conflict with each other;
3 hence what is good for class X is *always* bad for class Y and vice versa;
4 X and Y can sometimes be a coalition of classes; if so, just as in the case of (3), the relationship between the two coalitions is *always* a zero-sum game.

The confusion and difficulty of many of Marx's analyses of a particular ideology are caused by interference from this dogma. If one ignores it and concentrates on those analyses which Marx outlines at various points, some examples of which I have given, then one discovers what is nowadays called symbolic action with a strategic purpose. Up to this point, there is no difficulty. The problems start when one assumes:

1 that only X (the ruling class) is capable of such action;
2 that X is always trying to dupe Y (the underclass);
3 that Y is in fact taken in;
4 that X allows itself to be taken in by its own stratagem, and perceives as *true*, theories which are false, but nevertheless useful to it.

Marx of course adheres firmly to statements (1) and (2) in this list but usually hesitates over (3) and particularly over (4). Occasionally, he tries to put forward meaningful reasons (in Weber's sense) to explain why the ruling class lets itself be taken in so readily – I will come back to this point later. In addition, he frequently describes the ruling class as *conscious* of the distinction between the truth and the usefulness of the *theories* to which it subscribes.

It was therefore the dogma of the class struggle which led Marx to this irrationalist theory of ideologies which he developed in his general writing and which Engels carried on – is there an explanation of why the under-class takes at face value theories which are to its disadvantage and why the ruling class fails to distinguish between the truth and the usefulness of a theory, other than going back to Bacon's 'idols' and adapting them to the dogma of the class struggle? This leads to the proposition that 'dominant ideas are the ideas of the ruling class', which is the only one to which neo-Marxists usually subscribe.[10]

My intention is not to undertake a full survey of the Marxian theory of ideology, but I would like to make a final point to confirm that, as some of those whom Raymond Aron used to call 'intelligent Marxists' have shown, the theory is richer, more interesting and also much more confused than most neo-Marxists think.

In certain cases, Marx analyses the 'ideological process' not as consisting of symbolic action with a strategic purpose (for example bourgeois theorizing about the benefits of the monarchy), but as the result of what might be called excusable illusions or, in less normative terms, illusions directly inspired by reality and from which it is difficult to escape. Just as the stick which is half in the water seems to be broken, or the house opposite appears to be small because from where I am I cannot see the main part of it, so some social phenomena tend to be perceived as other than they in fact are. Here, we are again outside the bounds of the theory of ideology as it is formulated in the general works which I considered earlier; and in this case there is no longer any reason to speak of an *irrationalist* theory of ideology, nor to refer to the analogy of the *camera obscura*. The illusion here is not because hidden forces cloud the minds of social actors, but simply because they hear what they want to hear, or more accurately because they cannot be regarded as outside observers in that they are socially situated.

One example from this group is the classic analysis of commodity 'fetishism': economic agents see goods being exchanged in the market and think that they are being sold at their true value, at the equilibrium point of supply and demand. From the point of view of Marx, and taking the labour theory of value as valid, this is of course a mere illusion, though one which is readily understandable. The exchange of goods in the market is visible, the production process is not; the broken stick in the water is visible, the phenomenon of refraction is not. Of course, there is an important difference between the two examples, in that the theory of refraction is sounder than the theory of surplus value. However, this point does not directly concern us here, so we can disregard it and emphasize the important idea behind this analysis of commodity fetishism, which is that in society as well as in nature, reality can *in a natural way* appear distorted to the observer.

Another example in the same vein is the mercantilist illusion:[11] the merchant who becomes rich by trading readily concludes that trade creates wealth. However, when all people who engage in trade are taken together, it is a zero-sum game, though this is harder to see. This is because we are dealing not with a readily visible fact, but with a conclusion which can be established only by reasoning, and this was done only at a late stage by the physiocrats.

Another point is that Marx argues on several occasions that 'the vital process', the 'material life' as it is *here and now*, suggest categories and concepts to social actors which provide a guide for them in analysing and understanding the real world. This amounts to saying, for example, that if it had not been for the means of so-called mass communication, the concept of 'society of communication' would not have sprung up, or that, without the development of industry, the concept of 'worker' or 'working class' would not have been invented. So long as one does not give a wider meaning to the idea that 'the production of ideas [. . .] is directly interwoven into the material activity and the material interaction of people', and if materialism is defined on this basis, then this is a perfectly acceptable doctrine.

It was important to deal with Marx's theory of ideology in some detail. It is confused, diverse, and contradictory, yet has many thought-provoking ideas, and puts forward interesting theoretical ways of analysing ideological beliefs as *rational* or *meaningful* beliefs in the Weberian sense. However, we must not forget his *general* theory of ideology – the one summed up in the analogy of the *camera obscura* – and it is this theory in particular which history has retained, thanks to neo-Marxists of all shades.

There will be no difficulty in agreeing that this *general* theory should be categorized as *irrationalist*: people unknowingly adhere to false ideas because they are impelled by *unconscious* forces outside their control which make them slaves either to their own interests (if they belong to the ruling class) or to the interests of the ruling class (if they belong to the underclass).

It may come as a surprise that I would put in the same category Edward Shils's or Raymond Aron's theories of ideology, making clear two points, however: firstly, that they introduce a view of irrationality which has nothing to do with the analogy of the *camera obscura*; and secondly, that though they are much more acceptable than Marx's general theory, they too are rather insubstantial.

It may be paradoxical, in that they are two writers who have shown themselves to be sensitive to the ideological phenomenon, and have devoted much of their work to it, but one has the impression that neither has thought seriously about the reasons why it exists. Shils's interest has been in constructing a brilliant and useful typology of belief systems, which I considered in the previous chapter. Aron tried to analyse in great detail the sophistry of ideologues, to pinpoint the key words in ideologies, and the lines of strength and pseudo-consistency of ideological reasoning. Occasionally he tried to explain why some ideologies appear in certain political or economic circumstances rather than others. Neither, however, really thought about the question of why ideologies spread so easily, or why false ideas are so readily believed in. Marx gave a somewhat doubtful reply to this question, but at least he posed it.

The answer to the paradox is fairly simple. Both writers were content to attribute adherence to ideologies to feelings, fanaticism, the need for the absolute – in other words, to irrational affective forces. What is significant in this respect is the passage where, speaking of Pareto, Aron ignores the relatively complex and rather full theory of *derivations* except for the idea, which is both simple and questionable, that derivations are rationalizations of feelings. In doing this, he disregards the much more interesting analyses in which Pareto attempts to identify the mechanisms whereby derivations become credible:

> Pareto thought, with good reason, that the rational critique of *derivations* has only a slight influence on *residues*, in other words on sentiments which make human beings act, reason, and talk nonsense. The critique might possibly manage to *unmask* the sophistry of the sacred words *left*, *proletariat*, *Revolution*, *History*. In the absence of these words, the intellectual, enamoured of the absolute, and indignant at the ever-present defects in the social order, will find others to justify or rationalize revolt, hostility, physical or verbal violence.[12]

Who is right – those who propound a rational theory of ideology or those who see it as an irrational phenomenon? Aron and Shils are no doubt correct when they say that false ideas are in fact, in certain cases and by certain people, subscribed to because of passion, fanaticism, and thirst for the absolute. It is however hard to believe that this explanation can have general application. If this were the case, it would be difficult to understand why ideologies should be based systematically on scientific reasoning and scientific theories. Ordinary experience shows that although some people hold their beliefs with conviction and fanaticism, the vast majority hold them either with conviction but without fanaticism, or without both. And is the need for the absolute as widespread as is claimed?

Of course, Marx's *general* theory is not only insufficient but unacceptable. The image of the *camera obscura* which tries to compare ideology with sight is in fact merely a simple *metaphor*, even though it might seem like an *analogy*. After all, nobody has put forward even the slightest hypothesis on what might be in the ideological process the equivalent of the optical nerve or the eye as far as sight is concerned.[13]

Marx, however, usually abandons this general theory when he wants to analyse a particular ideological process. We have seen this in examples I have given, and more of these could be adduced. Land-owning aristocrats extol the monarchy because it sustains a system which gives them a social position to their liking; mercantilists think that trade brings wealth to society because merchants *as a matter of fact* become rich through trade; peasants owning strips of land have no 'class consciousness' because they are obsessed by their own boundary problems; and people from all walks of life think that the price of goods comes simply from the interplay of supply and demand in the market, since the market is visible whereas enterprise and *a fortiori* production processes are less visible. It would be absurd to expect the audience to see what is going on in the wings as well as they can see what is happening on stage.

The question of whether the theories behind these examples are true or false does not particularly interest me here. I am merely stressing that in all these cases, Marx interprets the ideological beliefs which he analyses either as *meaningful* effects (in the Weberian sense) of the actors' situation, or as optical illusions as explicable and rational as the classic perceptive illusions.

There is therefore a Marx I, applying a *general* theory of ideology, and a Marx II who, in his analysis of specific ideological processes, gives us another *general* theory of ideologies which contradicts the first one. The first theory, which merely puts sociological trimmings on the classical philosophical theory of falsehood, propounds an irrationalist view of ideology. In the second one, Marx puts forward, in line with Weber's later suggestion, a rational view of social behaviour.[14]

Marx I, Aron, and Shils therefore belong to the group of irrational theories of ideology, and Marx II to the rational theory group. It is this second class for which I will find some more members.

Any excursion into the literature of ideology has to include Karl

Mannheim, and it is important to do this because Mannheim extended and systematized the best intuitive work of Marx, which is in Marx II. Mannheim's classic book *Ideology and Utopia* amounts to a collection of articles and essays with no readily visible thread; but it has become a classic because it is the founding work of a new discipline – the sociology of knowledge, which aims to identify the social basis of thought: 'The principal thesis of the sociology of knowledge is that there are modes of thought which cannot be adequately understood as long as their social origins are obscured.'[15]

Mannheim argues that we are making a mistake if we fail to recognize the individual nature of thought; and it is indeed true that only the individual is capable of thought. On the other hand, however, the individual is merely repeating what has been said in the past: 'Every individual is therefore in a two-fold sense predetermined by the fact of growing up in a society: on the one hand, he finds a ready-made situation and on the other he finds in that situation performed patterns of thought and of conduct.'[16]

We cannot therefore take up the viewpoint of pure logic, which separated individual thought from its group origin just as it separated thought from action. We have to see that universal knowledge (such as that $2 \times 2 = 4$) is merely one kind of specific knowledge. Mannheim argues that is only because of a distortion, for which the Age of Reason was responsible, that knowledge of the mathematical sort is regarded as a kind of supreme model of knowledge. Although mathematical knowledge and images can be seen to be true regardless of any historical and 'social' situation, the same cannot be said of the totality of images from the history of ideas, manners or philosophy, or of political history. In order to be understood, most of these ideas and images have to relate to the social and historical situation of the actors: 'Even a god could not, on historical subjects, formulate a proposition of the kind $2 \times 2 = 4$, since what is intelligible in history can be formulated only by reference to problems and conceptual constructs which themselves arise in the flux of historical experience.'[17]

The intellectual constructs we are dealing with here therefore have the effect and the function of giving meaning – as far as social actors are concerned – to the social and historical situation in which they find themselves. These constructs allow them to understand this situation and to direct their actions. This idea is easily illustrated by the case of *norms*, which do not derive from absolute truths ($2 \times 2 = 4$). Nevertheless, they are not mere illusions; they can only be present within specific social situations, to which they are more or less adapted. They would be unintelligible and regarded as arbitrary in a social vacuum, which in any case is difficult to conceive. A system of norms is therefore 'valid' and possible only within a 'given type of historical existence'; and 'when the social situation changes, the system of norms to which it had previously given birth ceases to be in harmony with it.'[18] One is then likely to see the appearance of new norms.

What is true of norms is also true of 'representations': when a new social phenomenon appears, for instance a new type of productive enterprise, actors who are experts – intellectuals, journalists, economists – will try to give it a name and define it – for example, the concept of capitalist enterprise, which will be accepted because it describes a reality which exists.

In other words, one can in any society identify all kinds of mental production which, though not possessing the universal status of mathematical propositions, is intelligible only in relation to specific historic and social situations. They consist of sets of descriptive and prescriptive notions and propositions which are more or less adapted to a particular situation. Mannheim calls these notions and propositions, in a rather obscure and clumsy way, 'relational',[19] to distinguish them from representations which might lay claim to absolute truth – that is, be independent of systems of interpersonal relationships in a particular social and historical situation. However, he does not suggest that they have to be regarded as passive and anonymous 'reflections'. On the contrary, they are *produced* by social actors – by specialist producers, but also by social actors who are not specialists in intellectual activities. The concept of capitalist enterprise, for example, was no doubt suggested by economists, but it was then adopted by all kinds of actors, from the capitalist entrepreneur to workers. Similarly, legislators who want to give the force of law to a particular norm must take account of the state of opinion.

Since they are the very opposite of mechanical reflections, 'relational' representations and propositions can more or less adapt to a particular historical situation, and in this respect the phenomena of advance and retard are readily seen – some ideas may already be out-of-date, like dead stars which are still giving off light; others, like stars whose light has not yet reached us, may be in advance of their time. Mannheim suggests that the name *ideology* should be given to the former, and *utopia* to the latter. He is not certain that these names are appropriate, or that they have helped to throw light on the debate, but although the names can be challenged, the idea itself is perfectly clear.

Mannheim does not normally use many examples, but he does give some of this retard or delay which according to him defines ideology. Thus, for example, the taboo against charging interest on loans has survived so long because an outdated ethical norm became ideology. This norm was perfectly in keeping with the historical situation within which it developed – so long as economic and social relations were restricted to neighbours or people who knew each other, it was justified and quite understandable.

Person A helped person B financially, knowing that when reciprocal help was needed in the future, B would provide it. In these circumstances, where social relationships are limited to acquaintances, interest-free loans are the accepted practice and any attempt to profit from lending money is regarded as deviant and reprehensible. It therefore is easy to see why, in social systems with a reciprocal economy, actors who were experts made interest-free loans into a norm: in the history of the Western world, it was of course the Church which fulfilled this role.

However, 'the more the real structure of [Western] society changed, the more this ethical precept took on an ideological character, and became virtually incapable of practical acceptance.'[20] Of course, the Church tried to use this precept as a weapon against nascent capitalism, but as capitalism grew, it became more and more difficult, not to say impossible, and the Church had to bring the attempt to an end. As economic relations expanded, reciprocity applied only to the family unit, where interest-free loans remained the norm.

This example is a good illustration of Mannheim's theory of ideologies. The positive value attached to interest-free loans is *meaningful* in an economy based on reciprocity. No doubt the situation arises where the institution itself is no longer in keeping with an exchange economy, but the moral value associated with it can persist, especially in the mind of those who, because of their function, act as guardians of the moral order. These guardians may even try to use the authority of the former precept in their opposition to the new institutions: this behaviour is explicable in terms of the social situation of the actors, and is not irrational, meaningless, or the result of blindness or the weight of tradition. In the same way, the advent of the new practice of charging interest on loans from the beginning of the capitalist era is also understandable: in an economy where, because trade is widespread, it is rational for A, who no longer has any reason to believe that B will be able to repay in the future the service being sought now, to sell rather than give his or her services to B.

In this way, the constant change in 'historical situations' gives rise to new ideas and representations which are intelligible only in terms of this change; but at the same time, the adjustment cannot always be immediate, and certain social actors, because of their social position, will, in a perfectly intelligible way, cling to the old ideas.

This is what happens in another of Mannheim's examples, in which a landowner's estate has gradually become a capitalist undertaking without the landowner realising it. The landowner still has – or tries to have – a paternalistic relationship with workers on the estate; is aware that the number of workers has risen; and is in a position to know that any future workers will be recruited on the basis of their efficiency rather than their links with a particular person or family, as was the case in the past. The landowner is also conscious that other landowners are changing in this way. However, the systematic and convergent nature of all these changes has not yet occurred to the landowners. The concept of agricultural capitalism may have been written about, but the landowner is not aware of it and attention has not been drawn to it. The landowner still looks up on the estate as a world far removed from an industrial undertaking, and upon relationships with estate workers as totally different from those between the industrialists and their workers. Urban life is another world entirely.

For the way the landowner conceives of the nature of personal activities to change, it will first have to be realized that estate workers no longer behave towards the landowner as in 'the good old days'. Apart from this, however, specialist actors such as intellectuals and economists will have to think up new words and new concepts marking the change and identifying its nature. Even that will not be enough, since the new words and the new concepts they convey will have to come to the attention of the Junker, i.e. the person referred to, without being named, in Mannheim's example of the development of capitalist agriculture on the large Prussian estates.[21]

I accept that my survey has added slightly to what Mannheim originally said in *Ideology and Utopia*, which is a collection of rather disparate essays, but I do not think I have distorted his thought, which is that:

1 As part of the mental production supplied by history, there are two kinds of 'ideas' (in the widest sense of the word): the first includes ideas which can justly lay claim to universal validity or, to put it another way, to truth. This first kind gives rise to propositions in mathematics and the sciences generally. However, there are also ideas which cannot claim this, but which nevertheless are neither illusions nor the product of arbitrariness or fantasy.

2 The ideas of this second kind, in the form of descriptive as well as prescriptive propositions or *systems* of propositions, may be grouped according to their *adaptation* to a particular 'historical situation'. From this viewpoint, some ideas have adapted, others are either antiquated, or before their time. Thus, for example, the fact that interest-free loans are regarded in a positive light is well adapted to an economy based on reciprocity.

3 However, antiquated ideas, the only ones to which Mannheim attaches the concept of ideology, and ideas which are before their time ('utopian' ideas) should not be interpreted as irrational in origin. Generally speaking, they are explicable in terms neither of fanaticism nor blindness, but can be regarded as *meaningful* when one takes into account the situation of the actors who sustain, promote, or subscribe to them. It is understandable, for example, that the Junker still sees his estate as it

once was, or that the Church, having helped to make interest-free loans an unconditional norm, should still think it valid when the practice of loans with interest became widespread. Similarly, it is understandable that people should postulate the utopia of a classless society when commentators of all persuasions saw a link between the development of industry and working-class poverty.

In the end, objections to Mannheim's arguments stem from questions of words rather than basic questions. In applying the concept of ideology only to antiquated ideas, he raises an unnecessary problem, in that although one can often show that a particular idea is out-of-date in relation to a particular 'historical situation', this is obviously not always the case. Marxist ideas, for example, like liberal ideas, were at certain times considered to be definitely 'antiquated', but this did not prevent their being regarded later as 'surprisingly modern.'

Mannheim's linguistic distinctions are therefore not always easily applied. Although the example of interest-free loans is perfectly clear, this is an exception rather than the rule. Moreover, Mannheim's distinction between ideology and utopia suggests an evolutionist view of history which he himself has perhaps been unable to steer clear of completely. The point is that Mannheim's theory does not need such clumsy linguistic distinctions. The theory can be kept intact, and the problems caused by this distinction avoided, if the concept of ideology is applied to all of what I earlier called ideas of the second kind. There is nothing to prevent one's keeping the theory while getting rid of the distinctions.

After all, surgery of this kind was done by Clifford Geertz, a contemporary ideology theorist whom I mentioned in the last chapter. His theory is based on a distinction between two types of ideas – those which derive from the criterion of truth and falsehood and those which allow the social actor to find direction in the complex environment of social life. For Geertz, the concept of ideology covers all ideas of the second type: 'it is through the construction of ideologies, schematic images of social order, that man makes himself for better or worse a political animal.' In other words, '[t]he function of ideology is to make an autonomous politics possible by providing the authoritative concepts that render it meaningful, the suasive images by means of which it can be sensibly grasped.' Ideas of the second type, or ideologies, therefore include both prescriptive and descriptive notions and propositions. However, these descriptive propositions have a relationship with social reality like road maps have with geographical reality – that is, a symbolic one. Of course, these ideas are the 'utopias' of Mannheim, since '[i]t is in country unfamiliar emotionally or topographically that one needs poems and road maps.'[22]

I do not think that Geertz's theory adds much to Mannheim's, and I tend to think that Mannheim's is clearer and more analytical. On the other hand, however, it is useful to group under the single concept of *ideology*, as Geertz does, three kinds of ideas of the second type which Mannheim distinguishes. Geertz is less clear than Mannheim for, I believe, the simple reason that, as I stated in the previous chapter, he tries to attribute too much generality to one single idea – that ideology is metaphorical, arguing that *metaphor* is the device *par excellence* on which the construction and attraction of ideologies rest. It is true that many ideological notions (the exploitation of people by others, the invisible hand, the class struggle) are metaphors, and that many myths are metaphor systems; but the belief that charging interest on loans is immoral is not based on metaphor. Similarly, it is not in a metaphorical way that the Junker sees his relations with his workers as paternalistic.

On one point, Geertz and Mannheim are entirely at one – ideologies (the word itself, as well as the phenomenon to which it refers) have developed in modern times as a consequence of the break with Tradition which modernity represents. Geertz writes:

> In politics firmly embedded in Edmund Burke's golden assemblage of 'ancient opinions and rules of life', the role of ideology [. . .] is marginal. In such truly traditional political systems the participants [. . .] are guided both emotionally and intellectually in their judgements and activities by unexamined prejudices. [. . .] But when, as in the revolutionary France Burke was indicting and in fact in the shaken England from which, as perhaps his nation's greatest ideologue, he was indicting it, those hallowed opinions and rules of life come into question, the search for systematic ideological formulations, either to reinforce them or to replace them, flourishes.[23]

In my discussion of the problems of defining ideologies, I will not go back to the other theories of ideology mentioned in chapter 1, and I will mention only one new theory, in that I think that it is useful to state that Jean Baechler's thoughts on ideology are very close to the theoretical framework established by Mannheim.[24] This is not to say, of course, that Baechler's work – or Geertz's – should be disregarded: in both writers there is a rich picking of stimulating remarks and analyses, without there being in either any notable development of Mannheim's theory. For Baechler too, ideologies are ideas in the broad sense of the word (representations, myths, descriptive and normative propositions) set in motion by political factors, which are of course always linked to what Mannheim called 'historical situations'. Ideologies as Baechler understands them therefore correspond to those ideas of the second type which Mannheim had identified. He agrees that ideologies are responses which are more or less well adapted to historical situations, and suggests rather appropriately that ideologies should be analysed in terms of supply and demand. However, he also develops the hypothesis that, because of their *passions*, people are more or less predisposed to subscribe to a particular type of ideology. In this way there are in his analysis principles of explanation which are both rational and irrational.

Mannheim would probably not have denied the role of these irrational elements – it seems fairly clear that they play a part in adherence to a particular ideology. However, the question is to say how important or relevant they are; and reference to *passions* usually adds little to explanatory potential – for example, they hardly go to explain belief in the immorality of charging interest on loans; and in the context of Mannheim's second example, although passions may explain why some Junkers abandoned more readily than others their paternalistic view of things, this is a minor point, and the main point about how this view arose, persisted, and declined among Prussian Junkers can be explained without reference to these irrational aspects.

This case is another which gives us a clear idea of what Max Weber had in mind when he suggested that the irrational principles of social action should be treated as residual.

The theories which I have discussed in this chapter can in conclusion be put fairly simply into a two-fold classification. Some theories (Marx I, Aron–Shils) account for ideological phenomena by reference to an irrational theory of the behaviour of social actors, who may be blinded by their interests (Marx I) or by their passions (Aron–Shils).

I have already mentioned the main objection to the Aron–Shils type of theories, while accepting that they are sound – they do not help us to understand why many people subscribe to ideologies without great conviction. Moreover, they do not account for the fairly sharp rises and declines in popularity which characterize ideologies. If ideologies were essentially the product of passion and fanaticism, it would be difficult to understand why these passions could rise and fall sharply, or why so many people transfer from one ideology to another.

The theory that people are blinded by their own interest simply runs counter to personal experience, and it is hard to see what principles could refute that. It is true that social actors are capable of bad faith in the normal meaning of the word: they may make others believe that they regard as true a theory which serves their own particular interests, even if they do not believe it themselves. In general, however, they will be capable of distinguishing the *usefulness* of the theory from the matter of its *truth*. It may also happen that particular social actors take as true a false theory whose basis they have not really looked at, and which they have taken other people's word for, but which nevertheless serves their interests.

These two cases, however, are far removed from bad faith in Sartre's sense, that is, this strange mix where:

1　social actors are convinced that a particular theory is *false*; and
2　they are at the same time so dominated by their own interest that they forget the influence of this on their ideas, so that they might be convinced of the *truth* of the theory if it serves their interest.

In this way, social actors may be convinced in their heart of hearts, at one and the same time of the truth *and* the falsehood of the same idea.[25] Conundrums like this need not detain us long, I think. They are even more unacceptable than the mechanistic views of the unconscious which appear in the Marxian analogy of the *camera obscura*, and which the early Freud also developed.[26] One can almost argue, or at least hope, that progress in biology and neurology will one day allow us to decipher the physiological basis of these mental processes which lead to the inversion of images of reality, to which Marx refers. Conversely, nobody has ever undergone, and nobody ever will undergo, the kind of personal experience which Sartre's notion of bad faith claims to describe: wanting and at the same time not wanting something. One can also want something and at the same time try not to show that one wants it, thus leaving oneself open to the risk of doing or saying the wrong thing. One can of course hesitate over the truth or falseness of an idea; one can also change ideas; but one cannot at the same time be convinced in one's heart of hearts that an idea is false *and* that it is true. It would seem very hard, therefore, to make a credible psychological theory correspond to the notion of being blinded by one's interest, since the only choice in the matter is between the Charybdis of Marx I and the Scylla of Sartre.

In the second group of theories (Mannheim, Geertz), adherence to ideological beliefs is presented as behaviour which is intelligible, *meaningful*, or rational; and I take these three adjectives to be synonymous. Thus, for example, it is *meaningful* for the Junker to adhere to a paternalistic view of social relations, for the clergy to go on believing in the immorality of charging interest on loans, for the American trade unions to try to present the Taft–Hartley Act as a 'slave labour law', for the nineteenth-century proletariat to succumb to socialist ideology, for merchants to have a 'fetishist' view of commodities, and for the monarchy to be favoured by land-owning aristocrats.

To summarize the discussion, I will present this two-fold classification in the form of a table (see table 2). I have retained the distinction from the table in the previous chapter between the two traditions (Marxist and

Table 2   Types of explanation of ideology

Types of tradition	Irrational explanation	Rational explanation
Marxist tradition	MARX I: ideology as the inverted image of reality under the influence of class interests	MARX II: ideology as perspective effect or as conscious adherence to useful beliefs LENIN: ideology as a weapon in the arsenal of the class struggle
Non-Marxist tradition	ARON–SHILS: ideology as the product of fanaticism, of the passions	MANNHEIM: ideology as belief in norms adapted to a 'historical situation' GEERTZ: ideology as a road-map guiding one through a complex world

non-Marxist), which is a vital division where ideology is concerned; and I have used as the other axis the two types of explanation – irrational and rational – into which most theories of ideology can easily be divided.

There may be some leeway in the case of Lenin, whom I have put in the right-hand column (rational explanation). As has frequently been stated, his manipulatory view of social action moved him considerably away from Marx in the matter of ideology. For him, ideology is defined above all by an objective – disarm the enemy by catching them in the net of what has been called dialectic (in the Marxist sense) and which today is called 'hocus-pocus'. For Lenin, ideology does derive from what Geertz calls 'symbolic action', but he takes it to the point where it becomes caricature and intellectual terrorism. With Lenin, we are not dealing with a theory of ideology, but with the theory of a practice – his own.[27]

4

Journey around a table

We have seen that it is possible to distinguish two basic types of *definition* of ideology – one which I called *traditional*, which defines ideology according to the criterion of truth and falsehood, and the *modern* one which defines it according to the concept of *meaning*. For example, a norm can have meaning and be adapted to a certain state of society without necessarily being either true or false. This applies to the case of the positive image which interest-free loans had in an economy based on reciprocity. The fact that the norm is regarded as positive suggests to social actors behaviour which is adapted to this system.

One can also distinguish two principal kinds of *explanation* of ideological phenomena: *irrational* and *rational*. To a large extent the first kind follows in the same vein as the classical philosophy of falsehood, and claims that, like falsehood, ideology is the product of forces beyond the control of the subject. Marx, however, though he follows philosophical tradition on this point, puts a sociological slant on it: these forces for him are not psychological, but social. In his general theory of ideology at least, it is the internalization of class interests which is responsible for ideological distortions.

In explanations of the rational kind, however, adherence to ideologies can be analysed as *meaningful* behaviour in the Weberian sense. This does not of course mean that the behaviour is deliberate or calculated. It is 'without thinking about it' that people have a positive attitude towards interest-free loans in a traditional society where the economy is based on reciprocity. They think it natural, because they see that everybody has this attitude; and they have probably never thought that there is in theory another possible system, charging interest on loans, which nobody they know has ever done. However, their positive attitude ought not to be attributed exclusively to the weight of tradition. The explanation lies in the fact that it is a response which the subjects regard as well adapted to their social environment. Although it is not deliberate, it is meaningful and therefore rational.

A cross-reference of both kinds of definition of ideology with both types of explanation gives four possible combinations:

1 *Traditional* definition (ideology is falsehood) and *irrational* explanation (adherence to ideology is because of forces beyond the control of the subject);
2 *Traditional* definition (ideology is falsehood) and *rational* explanation (adherence to ideology is meaningful);
3 *Modern* definition (ideology does not derive from the criterion of true or false) and *irrational* explanation (adherence to ideology is because of forces beyond the control of the subject);
4 *Modern* definition (ideology does not derive from the criterion of true or false) and *rational* explanation (adherence to ideology is meaningful).

These four combinations are illustrated in table 3, and I have given in each of the boxes the main examples of ideology surveyed in chapters 2 and 3. The table shows up a correlation between the type of definition and the type of explanation of ideology in the authors involved. In other words theorists who have examined ideology tend to see it either as a social form of falsehood *and* the product of forces beyond the control of the subject, or as a meaningful interpretation of the world outside the criterion of truth and falsehood *and* as something which can be explained by reference to the social environment of the actor.

This is why most of the theories examined in previous chapters fall in either the first or the fourth box in table 3. However, the table also reveals two possibilities which, it would seem, are not exploited, or insufficiently exploited by the theory of ideologies – those contained in the second and third boxes.

I will look first at the third box, combining a definition of ideology independent of the criterion of truth and falsehood with an irrationalist explanation of adherence to ideologies.

It is not difficult to find examples of sociological analysis which are in this category, such as Durkheim's study of the glorification of the national flag.[1] Obviously, a flag does not come under the heading of true or false, but is a symbol of the national community. In certain sets of circumstances (Durkheim was of course writing at the beginning of the century), it can evoke the feeling that it is sacred and inspire an attitude of respect, because citizens have a *feeling* of attachment to the national community symbolized by the flag. Durkheim argues that such a feeling arises naturally; one

Table 3

Types of definition of ideology	Types of explanation of ideology	
	Irrational explanation	*Rational explanation*
Traditional definition (in relation to the criterion of true and false)	1 MARX I: the black chamber, class interests ARON–SHILS: fanaticism, need for the absolute	2 MARX II: commodity fetishism, mercantilist ideology
Modern definition (without reference to the criterion of true and false)	3	4 MANNHEIM: charging interest on loans GEERTZ: the Taft-Hartley Act

cannot choose to have it or not have it any more than one can choose tastes in food. The latter can of course develop over time: they are the product not only of a physiological make-up determined for all time, but also of experience. They can be cultivated. One does not, however, choose one's tastes, and in this sense people experience them passively. Similarly, joy and sadness are probably to some extent dependent on external circumstances. People may try to induce them, but they cannot decide to make them appear or disappear at will. To argue that one is sad because one has decided to be sad needed all the mental deceitfulness of which Sartre was capable.[2]

Durkheim's argument (my comparison with taste is obviously not his) is that the glorification of the flag is rather similar – we do not ourselves decide to experience the feeling of respect which the flag evokes in us. Just as tastes in food are the result of physiological mechanisms possibly conditioned by experience, so this feeling of respect is caused, unknown to us, by our identification with the national community. We are part and parcel of it, share its language, identify to some extent with its history.

These feelings, as I have argued, may change over time; they are not fixed once and for all. International tension such as that obtaining at the beginning of the century is more favourable to the development of 'national feeling' than a situation where there is peace and *détente*, and anti-German feeling was more widespread in France at the beginning of the century than it is today. Clearly, something like 'national feeling' depends on external factors; but this does not necessarily mean that it loses its affective dimension, without which it would hardly be a feeling.

Although Durkheim's analysis of the glorification of the flag is not very meaningful today in that there is no real feeling that the flag is sacred, it can be applied to examples more relevant to present-day situations. Nobody would argue, for example, that national feeling is not present nowadays in the context of sporting events.

Some of Max Weber's analyses can be put in the third box, such as his study of charisma. The feeling of respect and even adulation inspired by charismatic leaders may have something to do with the message they are giving: if Ayatollah Khomeini decided to repudiate Islam, it is likely that his authority would suffer. However, though for example the declarations of John Paul II on abortion and contraception upset many Catholics, it is nevertheless true that provided they keep within certain limits, charismatic leaders inspire a feeling of respect which attaches to their person rather than to their message. The followers of charismatic leaders will feel that what they say is correct or true or acceptable because it is *they* who are saying it: charisma is usually associated with a feeling that the leader in question is infallible. There therefore is no need to attribute the dogma of papal infallibility, which many non-Catholics cannot take seriously, either to the cunning of the Roman Catholic Church or to a particular propensity to superstition on the part of Catholics. It is probably impossible to explain why this dogma was adopted without reference to the specific historical circumstances in which it was promulgated, but it nevertheless illustrates the general sociological process summarized by the Weberian concept of charisma.

There is therefore no problem in finding classic sociological studies to put in the third box of table 4. Neither the national flag nor the authority of charismatic leaders derives from the notion of truth and falsehood. Both, however, inspire *feelings* – in this case respect – which are beyond the control of the social actor and whose affective dimension is clear.

Social feelings as shown by the classic studies of Weber and Durkheim undoubtedly exist and it is essential to bear them in mind when analysing ideologies: for example, some ideologies were spread by charismatic leaders, such as Hitler, Lenin, or Khomeini. It is true, moreover, that adherence to certain ideologies is often based on social feelings of the sort described by Durkheim – adherence to nationalism is more likely in somebody who has a strong national feeling; and adherence to racist or xenophobic precepts is more common in somebody who thinks national cohesion and unity are threatened. Durkheim's study of the glorification

Table 4

Types of definition of ideology	Types of explanation of ideology	
	Irrational explanation	*Rational explanation*
Traditional definition (in relation to the criterion of true and false)	1 Blindness caused by class interests (MARX) Adherence to false ideas through fanaticism (ARON, SHILS)	2 Commodity fetishism, mercantilist ideology (MARX) Magic (MAX WEBER)
Modern definition (without reference to the criterion of true and false)	3 Respect for the flag (DURKHEIM) Admiration for a charismatic leader (MAX WEBER)	4 Roman gods, the cult of Mithra (MAX WEBER) Respect of aristocracy for the absolute monarchy (MARX) Charging interest on loans (MANNHEIM) The Taft-Hartley Act (GEERTZ)

of the flag, like Weber's of charisma and the many others which could be quoted, reminds us in a timely way of the processes which we have to bear in mind when we are looking at the spread of certain ideologies.

The reason why it seems difficult to find any ideology theorists (apart perhaps from Pareto) to put in the third box of table 4 is simply that whatever definition one adopts of the notion of ideology, one point is clear: ideologies are doctrines with varying degrees of consistency combining in varying ratios prescriptive propositions and descriptive propositions. The basic component of ideology is therefore the *proposition* in the sense in which the word is used in logic. A proposition can be regarded as true or false or, if this criterion is rejected, it can be thought of as acceptable, plausible, or sound, or conversely, unacceptable, implausible, or not ringing true (in the way in which a poem does not ring true). It is however difficult to assert, without more, that one likes it or dislikes it; in other words, it is impossible to combine a proposition and a feeling, without the contribution of something else.

The objective correlates of feelings are always *objects*, whatever their physical or symbolic nature. People like (or dislike) *foie gras*; they respect (or do not respect) the flag; they like (or dislike), or respect (or do not respect) a charismatic leader.

As soon as ideology is defined (as it always is) as a more or less consistent combination of those elements we call descriptive and prescriptive propositions, we cannot see in it a mere show of feelings. Feelings may be behind adherence to a particular ideology, but even here, the affective aspect can only be one instant in the production and spread of ideologies. Take for example the influence of Marxist ideology. It is possible that adherence to this ideology sometimes reveals the presence of certain feelings in those who subscribe to it, for instance the feeling of exclusion from society. Such feelings are however, not enough to explain why Marxist doctrine is influential. Sympathizing with a theory is not the same as regarding it as true.

We must be aware, therefore, that when we use expressions such as 'X is a Marxist because of feeling excluded from society' or 'Marxism is a philosophy of resentment', we are using phrases which if taken literally amount to dangerous shorthand. The conjunction 'because' conceals a complex pattern of links; we should have said (1) X *feels* excluded from society (2) and therefore sympathizes with Marxism, and (3) *moreover*, tends to *regard it as true*, for example because people he or she believes to be trustworthy and qualified regard it as true. The shorthand expressions I quoted give the impression that a feeling can be the cause of a belief, but this casual link is in fact meaningless.

Moreover, as writers such as Mannheim and Geertz point out, positive or negative attitudes inspired by certain practices are not always purely affective in origin – interest-free loans were regarded in a positive light because they were in keeping with social systems which had an economy based on reciprocity. Conversely, priests who realised that this practice was being replaced by one where interest was charged may have had a *feeling* of regret at the passing of the old order.

Therefore, although most ideology theorists agree that collective feelings play a part in the spread of ideologies, they rightly accept that this affective aspect amounts to only one small stage in the process.

The only sociologist who placed any importance on this affective stage was, as I have stated, Vilfredo Pareto. He argued that we give credence to two kinds of propositions (or systems of propositions) – scientific ones and non-scientific ones, i.e. those which are unproved and unprovable. It is for example impossible to prove the validity of Hesiod's advice that 'people should not urinate in rivers',[3] which many Greeks, it seems, followed. Similarly, it is impossible to prove the validity of the proposition that 'one should not do to others what one would not like others to do to oneself.' In other words, Pareto's starting point is the simple observation that in any society, people give credence to precepts and value judgements which Pareto thinks can never be proved. Moreover, they believe in all kinds of descriptive propositions lacking a scientific basis, rather than prescriptive ones. Magic is a perfect example of this.[4] One must add, of course, that Pareto does not think that belief in magic is limited to primitive societies, and in fact suggests (and in many cases asserts) that the solutions to particular problems proposed by modern politicians often owe a lot to magic. He might well have regarded as magic the faith of contemporary socialists in the economic virtue of nationalization, since the essence of magic is the belief in a causal link which is confirmed neither by experience nor theory.

Pareto says that these two kinds of belief – belief in precepts and value judgements which can be neither true nor false, and belief in unproved descriptive propositions – are explained by the influence of *feelings*. Thus, for example, we have positive feelings about purity, negative ones about impurity. This is why the Greeks thought that 'people should not urinate in rivers', and why in many societies women are not allowed to participate in certain activities when they are menstruating.

However, people also need to put a 'logical gloss' on their beliefs, because the latter are often seen not as subjective truths deriving only from personal conviction, but as objective truths. There are of course *opinions* which are regarded and articulated as such, as when people are aware of the tentative nature of propositions. Sometimes, however, doubtful or unprovable propositions are regarded as objective truths, as evidenced by the turns of phrase used to express them. Hesiod did not say 'I think it would be better not to urinate in rivers', but '*people should not* urinate in rivers.' Socialists in France did not say 'I think nationalizations are a good thing', but 'nationalizations are good for the country.'

According to Pareto, therefore, people need *theories* proving that their beliefs are justified, not only to convince others but also to convince themselves. As we have seen, Pareto calls these theories *derivations*. They call into play either exegetical reasoning or rhetorical reasoning or scientific reasoning, but in the latter case scientific argument is by definition unable to prove the conclusions which are supposed to be drawn from them.

In other words, behind ideologies (derivations) there are always feelings. Ideologies themselves are merely a rationalized expression of these feelings. The whole of Pareto's theory is in fact based on a simple argument:

1 people believe in the objective truth of all kinds of propositions, both unproved and unprovable;
2 by definition, their conviction cannot be founded on the objective truth of these propositions;
3 therefore it must have its basis in an irrational act of faith;
4 which can only be based on feelings.

In fact, I think Pareto's theory rests on the dubious general application of the examples quoted and analysed by Durkheim (the flag) and Weber (charisma) to all *derivations*. In other words, he accepts too readily the idea that people may regard as true a theory which they find attractive, simply because it corresponds to their feelings. I repeat, love of the flag *is* a feeling; but one does not love a theory like one loves a flag. More precisely, being predisposed towards a theory and believing in its truth are two separate issues.

We need only refer to the famous drunkard of Aristotle to understand the difficulties caused by Pareto's general theory.[5] The drunkard justifies liking for the bottle by coming up with reasoning which in itself is perfectly consistent – we must follow the precepts of nature; nature teaches us that we have to drink to live; so drinking is a good thing.

This is a good illustration of Pareto's theory: the drunkard is a prisoner of a craving, rationalizing it by covering it with a 'logical gloss'. However, it also illustrates the difficulty of this theory: it is unlikely that the clever *derivation* of the drunkard convinced either drunkard or people he or she told. It is probable – Aristotle does not say so, but it can be assumed – that it was meant as a joke rather than a serious assertion and that it was a clever way of arousing sympathy to counter any negative reaction which might occur. In other words, the drunkard's derivation should be regarded as 'symbolic action' in the Geertzian sense, and not as a theory which the drunkard was convinced would justify the craving.

In any event, I do not think we can take very seriously the idea that ideologies are merely a cover for feelings or passions. It is not, I repeat, that collective feelings do not exist; simply that when they do, it is as feelings that they are experienced. One has respect for the flag, or not. One likes 'foreigners', or not. But people do not believe in the truth of a theory simply because they are kindly disposed to it, or *feel* attracted to it. When people say that they have the *feeling* that a particular theory is true, it is merely a way – an ambiguous way, and therefore dangerous – of saying that they *believe* in it.

The third box in table 4 therefore includes social processes which certainly exist, but which represent only short stages in the production and diffusion of ideologies. After all, ideologies never amount merely to the function of covering feelings and passions.

We now turn to the second box in table 4, which by definition deals with propositions or theories assumed to derive from the criterion of truth and falsehood, but which are in fact false. Moreover, because of the very way this box is defined, there is no question of regarding adherence to such theories as having an irrational cause: by definition, the cause of adherence is neither passions, nor feelings, nor an unconditional attachment to tradition, nor any force outside the control of the subject.

At first sight, this second box in table 4 seems to indicate a paradoxical and improbable combination, but in fact, certain examples from Marx which I quoted in the last chapter show that this is not so. Merchants have a 'fetishist' concept of commodities, believing that it is goods which are exchanged because this is what they see in the market. They think that prices derive *only* from the law of supply and demand, since they are aware that the only way they can sell something for which there is not much demand is to lower its price. Of course, the merchants' beliefs are false and 'fetishist' only if they are seen in the context of the labour theory of value, which is a *true* theory. There is every reason to believe, of course, that it was only in Marx's mind that this theory was true; but this point is not really relevant to the present discussion. What is important is that, *if* one agrees that the merchants' beliefs are in fact false and fetishist, then Marx is putting forward a *rational* explanation of a false idea: in other words he has managed to explain why merchants have false ideas without assuming that they are a prey to passions, dispositions, or forces outside their control which play havoc with their sense of judgement. In fact merchants are simply believing what they see; if their view is a false one, it is because they see only part of reality.

Similarly, observers in a position to see only one side of a trihedron are likely to regard it as a triangle. Not only can one not speak of irrationality in this case, but it is not even a case of an optical illusion. The observers see a triangle because that is what they have in front of them. The reality, however, is that it is not a triangle, as other observers could confirm, and as they themselves would see if they were to move.

As I have tried to show in the previous chapter, this kind of analysis occurs frequently in Marx. They are interesting for two reasons: firstly, because they show that adherence to false ideas (that is, ideas subject to the criterion of truth) can spring from something other than the action of irrational forces. I think this is extremely important in that it hints at a reply to the question which the theory of ideologies has always come up against – why is it that false ideas are often so credible? The second reason is, as I have said, that Marx's analyses appear to run counter to the general theory of ideology which he develops in other parts of his work and which has been the one to attract attention.

Marx, however, is not only writer to have outlined a theory of ideology which fits in the second box of the table – there are also many analyses of this kind in Max Weber's work. I will return to this issue, having first looked at those analyses of Weber which fit into the other boxes. Although Weber – and this seems paradoxical – almost never uses the word 'ideology', there is in his work almost everything needed to construct a general theory of ideologies; and of all the great sociologists he was the one who best understood the complexity of the ideological phenomenon.

I have already pointed out how some of his analyses, such as that on charisma, contributed to such a theory. Like Durkheim, Weber saw clearly the importance of those collective feelings which confer a sacred character on certain symbolic objects or authority on a particular person. Generally speaking, many of Weber's analyses could be put in the *third* box of table 4. Weber was also well aware, before Mannheim and *a fortiori* before Geertz, of the importance of the processes exemplified by Mannheim's analysis of beliefs about interest-free loans. This is the area of normative beliefs, which cannot be proved true or false, but of which the authority can be analysed in rational terms. In my classification, these analyses go into the *fourth* box of table 4.

What is true of normative beliefs is also true of those descriptive beliefs and representations which, like religious beliefs, cannot by definition derive from truth or falsehood. For example, the reason why Roman gods were so punctilious and why they presided over every minute detail of people's lives is that Roman landowners (that is, most Romans) were obsessed with boundary problems.[6] The reason why the cult of Mithra was so widespread among professional soldiers and Roman administrators was that 'apart from the promises about this life which, here as elsewhere, were linked to promises about the next life', the cult not only was confined to men, but 'contained a whole hierarchy of sacred ceremonies and religious ranks'. Soldiers and administrators were therefore on familiar ground. Furthermore, the religion of Mithra was 'essentially ritualistic'; and 'bureaucracy always claims as an absolute standard of value on the one hand a comprehensively sober rationalism, and on the other hand, the ideal of a disciplined "order" and security.' Moreover, 'bureaucracy is usually characterised by utter contempt for any kind of irrational religion, an attitude which goes hand in hand with the fact that such religion can be used as a means of social subordination.'[7] Weber argues that the attraction of freemasonry for Prussian kings and civil servants can be explained in the same way – it contained principles and values which they regarded as positive.

All these analyses and the many others which could be drawn from Weber's sociology of religion go in the *fourth* box of table 4; in all these examples, belief in prescriptive or descriptive propositions which does not depend on the criterion of truth and falsehood is interpreted as rational, that is, as meaningful in terms of the situation of the actors and their dispositions. Conversely, there are hardly any analyses in Weber which could be put in the *first* box in table 4. I have already stressed that he was extremely reluctant to accept that adherence to false ideas could be explained merely by reference to the irrationality of social actors. In a more basic sense, he thought that, although people are often irrational, sociology and economics ought, in order to be fruitful, to exhaust first of all the resources of the premises of rationality.

A final point is that many of Weber's analyses show that, like Marx, he was aware that belief in false ideas could often be explained in a rational way, which brings us back to the *second* box in table 4, the one exemplified by the Marxian analysis of commodity fetishism.

I will examine in some detail one example – that of the Weberian theory of magic. Belief in magic typifies beliefs which are subject to the criterion of truth and falsehood. Moreover, they are by definition beliefs in false ideas. In this sense they can be compared with those ideological beliefs which also have the twin characteristics of being subject to the criterion of truth and falsehood and being false. The difference, therefore, between belief in magic and this kind of ideological belief is only one of content, and not of form – the former apply to natural phenomena, the latter to social ones.

Weber sometimes has the annoying habit of sketching out an important theory in a few sentences, merely giving the main points of the argument and the conclusion to which it leads, and leaving it to the reader to fill in his reasoning. This is unfortunately true of his deliberations on magic in *Economy and Society*. These are merely given in outline, but the outline is clear enough – to allow us to see the difference between his explanation of magic and the one which Pareto, another great classical sociologist, later put forward.

Pareto, by applying the general theory the principles of which I summarized earlier, said that the reason why magicians believe in causal relationships which are false is that they are the victims of their feelings, or at least are misled by them – magicians know that people are impatiently awaiting the rain which will help their crops grow, and they want to please them and at the same time confirm their own power. Like them, the magicians end up by believing that they have the ability to make the rain come by means of a particular ritual. If the rain does not come, they can always blame the ill will of superior powers, unless they conclude privately that they have not performed the ritual properly; and although they have no clear idea of what they have done wrong, they will have no difficulty in persuading themselves that they may not have noticed their mistakes. In other words, magic for Pareto is an example of wishful thinking.

Weber's theory is the exact opposite of Pareto's: Pareto puts forward an irrational theory, Weber proposes a rational explanation of magic:

> Acts prescribed by religion or magic must be carried out 'in order to have happiness and a long life in this world' (*Deuteronomy* IV, 40). [. . .] [A]cts motivated by religion or magic are acts which are, relatively at least, rational, particularly in their original form: they follow the rules of experience even though they are not necessarily acts according to means and ends. In the same way that the piece of wood causes the spark, gesticulations will cause the rain to fall. The sparks caused by rubbing the piece of wood are effects which are just as "magic" as the rain caused by the manipulations of the rainmaker. We must not therefore exclude from the domain of everyday finalist behaviour, religious or magic ways of thinking, all the more so because the aims of magic or religious acts are above all economic.[8]

Weber is suggesting an important basic point – that it is easier to show the relationship between magical and religious practices and the preoccupations of everyday life in the case of primitive societies. At about the same time, Durkheim was also deciding to study the basis of religion by reference to its primitive forms.[9] However, since he did not share either the individualist methodology of Weber, or his rational view of action, Durkheim does not put as much emphasis as Weber does on the role of religion and magic in everyday life. His reason for studying primitive religions was that he had an evolutionist view, inherited from Auguste Comte.

The idea which Weber is expressing here is, I think, quite different: outside the field of primitive societies, religious and magic practices, ideas and representations consist of a traditional content reworked over time as a function of complex and more or less cumulative social transformations. This is why it is more difficult to perceive the relationship between religion and everyday life in a complex society than in a primitive society. Moreover, the totality of social structures can be seen more easily in the latter case.

It is also easier to perceive directly the 'relatively rational' character of religion and magic in the case of primitive societies: magic aims to bring rain for crops, and is therefore explained by an intention. It is very probable that the means used by the rainmaker appear as irrational to us as observers; but they are not so for primitive people, since, *for them* (but not *for us*), the effect of causing a spark by rubbing a stick is just as 'magical' as the rain produced by the manipulations of the rainmaker.

Here Weber is putting forward a kind of Copernican revolution. Magic appears irrational to us, and it is in these terms that we define it; it is based on a belief in false causal relationships. This belief can be interpreted in the way Pareto does or, like the early Lévy-Bruhl, we can argue that primitive people have a *mentality* different from ours.[10] Weber on the other hand suggests a quite different approach: to understand magic, attention should be given less to primitive people than to the observers, since the concept of magic appears only when the acts of primitive people are observed by people culturally different. It is not that it identifies a type of *behaviour*, but that it is based on a type of *relationship* between observers and observed.

The reason why producing fire by rubbing a stick seems to *us* different from making the rain come is that we have read Hume, we have learned to manipulate the notions of cause and effect, and we apply almost spontaneously J. S. Mill's rules of induction. In other words we have a more or less precise idea of the rules of controlled experiments. It needed Bacon, Hume, and J. S. Mill, however, before these rules became second nature to *us*. Is it not therefore unreasonable to assume that the notions and principles which Western thought took centuries to codify are present in primitive people? If one accepts that such a hypothesis is ludicrous, then one must also accept that, *for* primitive people, the acts of the rainmaker are just as rational as those of the firemaker.

A possible objection is that as a matter of fact the former are less successful than the latter, and that primitive people ought to see this. However, this too would assume that primitive people could miraculously understand the concepts and findings of statistics – a discipline which has developed comparatively recently in Western thought. It is only against the background of all the notions and ideas of this discipline that a notion such as that of frequency makes sense. The fact that a notion such as this has become familiar to us, like that of cause, does not mean that it is a natural one.

I will return to this point in the next chapter, since it is obvious that more can be said about it than these few remarks. I simply wanted to say at this stage that Weber's analysis of magic, like many other of his analyses, goes into the *second* box in table 4: the beliefs of primitive people in magic are false, but they are not irrational. As for the incomprehension of Western observers when faced with the magical beliefs of primitive peoples, this is not itself incomprehensible – it is to be expected that such observers, because of dispositions produced in their minds from knowledge of physics and statistics, find it extremely difficult to see that primitive people attribute causal power to the gesticulations of the rainmaker.

Our journey around the four boxes of the table was time-consuming, but I think it was useful.

Each of the writers I have mentioned tends to fit into just one box, but sometimes two and exceptionally, like Weber, into three. This is understandable. The language Geertz uses shows that he was irritated by Sutton's interpretation of trade union reaction to the Taft–Hartley Act, but he was also irritated by Aron and Shils's irrationalist conception of ideologies, and therefore put himself in the diametrically opposite box – ideologies ought not to be judged according to the criterion of truth and falsehood; they represent rational symbolic action with a strategic or cognitive aim (ideology as a road-map allowing one to find one's way in a complex world).

Mannheim is in the same box. Mannheim's intention of establishing a sociology of knowledge had led him to distinguish two types of theories, ideas and representations – those which can lay claim to timeless truth, like mathematical theorems or the findings of physics, and those which cannot, but which are nevertheless not absurd. These can be called *historical* truths, since they consist of propositions seen as correct and valid by actors who are historically situated. It is therefore quite natural that Mannheim should be in the fourth box.[11]

It is also easy to understand why Aron and Shils, writing soon after the horrors of the Nazi and Stalinist eras, saw ideologies as systems of false ideas which social actors adopt under the influence of irrational forces.

It should now be clear that the four boxes are useful in showing aspects or stages of ideological processes as well as the classic ways in which ideologies have been analysed. There is no doubt (box 1) that fanaticism and passions can facilitate adherence to ideologies; but this is an obvious point, which cannot provide the principle for a theory covering the whole of the ideological phenomenon. As for the theory generally adopted in the Marxist creed, that ideologies are views of the world distorted by class interests, nobody believes this any more except for a few old die-hards.

The third box does contain stages of some of the processes by which ideologies are spread. Respect for a charismatic leader can contribute to the spread of this leader's message. And when an ideology becomes institutionalized, it can base itself on symbols (swastika, hammer and sickle) which then function not only as *signals* to mobilize people, but above all as *symbols* of identification.

Moreover, ideologies usually include beliefs and representations which are not subject to the criterion of truth and falsehood, but which are nevertheless not irrational – it is quite understandable that the trade unions were not pleased with the Taft–Hartley Act, and it is easy to analyse the reasons why they preferred to express their discontent in a metaphorical rather than a direct manner. Similarly, it is easy to understand why the Catholic Church tried to resist capitalism in the early stages by saying that charging interest on loans was immoral. No theory of ideology can disregard this dimension of the phenomenon, which was clearly emphasized by Weber and Mannheim as well as by Geertz (box 4).

As for box 2, illustrated by Weber's theory of magic or some Marxian analyses (commodity fetishism, mercantilist ideology), this shows that in certain circumstances, social actors can for the best *reasons* subscribe to *false* ideas. They represent a very basic dimension of the ideological phenomenon, but unlike the others one which is often ill-perceived. It was ill-perceived by Marx himself, since he did not draw the general conclusions from the particular analyses propounded by Marx II.

In fact it is not difficult to understand why box 2 is relatively empty, since at first sight, as I have said, it seems to represent something paradoxical and improbable – how can belief in false ideas be interpreted as rational? Not only does this proposition seem contradictory, but it runs totally counter to a long-standing tradition – the classical conception of falsehood.

I would like at this point to look further at the idea that in many cases adherence to false ideas can be explained in a rational way, since I think it is essential for the analysis of ideologies in the narrow sense (which is also the normal meaning), whereas as I said in the first chapter, the concept of ideology has a wider meaning in Geertz or Althusser, and ends up by including all beliefs about social and political matters. What common sense means by ideology, however, is all beliefs about social and political matters which are based directly or indirectly on scientific authority. All ideologies, major and minor, right-wing and left-wing, Marxism and Third Worldism, Liberalism and development theory, are based on the authority of science. The word 'ideology' itself caught on because it conveniently described the new-found desire, which appeared with the Modern Age, to find a basis in Science for a social order which seemed incapable of being based on Tradition any more.

This is why a basic question of the theory of ideologies is: how can false ideas be based on the authority of science? To this must be added another question: must we postulate irrational social actors in order to understand why false ideas can be based on the authority of science?

In delineating my field of investigation in this way, and in adopting a limited definition of the notion of ideology, I am not trying to argue that other definitions cannot be adopted or that other questions cannot not asked. On the contrary, I believe that the four boxes in the table do in fact represent realities, and that they define all the important aspects of ideological processes. This is why I felt the need to emphasize the hidden dimensions of theories of ideology,[12] as well as the combinations brought about by these dimensions.

On the other hand, I do not think it would be appropriate to deal simultaneously with all these aspects. The notion of symbolic action, for instance, would, if developed to its full extent, lead to a treatise on social rhetoric. This was clearly seen by Pareto, and it is one of the reasons why he spoke of 'derivations' and not 'ideology'. It is a concept which meant that he could keep together theories based on scientific reasoning ('theories which are based on experience but which go beyond experience')[13] and those based on exegetical or rhetorical reasoning. His reason for being reluctant to isolate the former group by using a specific concept to designate it was that he thought that both groups had a common function – to rationalize sentiments. If on the other hand one does not attribute to this function of rationalization the generality which he did – wrongly, in my view – then it is proper to study as a separate group those particular derivations which ideologies in the ordinary meaning of the word are; in other words those which are based on scientific reasoning.

Part II

5

Outline of a restricted theory of ideology

In the following chapters, my main task will be to show that, in contrast to a single received idea, those received ideas which go to make up ideologies can emerge *normally* in the subject's mind, rather than being the result of arbitrary or unclear forces over which the subject has no control. In other words, we can very often analyse adherence to received ideas as a *meaningful* act in the Weberian sense of the word.

A further task is to show that even though science undoubtedly helps in creating and spreading true ideas, it also plays an important role in confirming and propagating false ideas. However, this additional result must not necessarily be imputed to the perversity or irrationality of the actors who directly or indirectly take part in the scientific process. In other words, we need to show that received ideas can be a normal product of normal science.

Of course, when I speak of science, I mean the social sciences, since ideologies are systems of ideas which relate to society. Moreover, I take the expression 'social sciences' in the broad sense to include history and economics as well as anthropology, sociology, or politics.

Given that such questions do not cover all the phenomena subsumed by the notion of ideology, I propose to take the argument in the following chapters as the outline of a *restricted* theory of ideology. In this chapter, however, using several examples, I will outline the various kinds of effects which jointly constitute the definition of this restricted theory of ideology; the argument will be developed more explicitly in succeeding chapters.

Such a theory must first of all take account of what are best called *position* effects and *disposition* effects, both of which can be subsumed in the general category of *situation* effects.

These situation effects tend, in certain circumstances which I will try to describe, to make social actors perceive reality not as it is and as others can see it, but in a distorted or incomplete way. Moreover, they will often have difficulty in realizing that what they see is affected by the viewpoint from which they see it, even though this is not necessarily due to irrationality on their part. These situation effects are particularly important in that they often serve to explain why a social actor subscribes to a wrong or dubious notion. However, in other cases, they combine with other kinds of effects which will be looked at later.

Position effects and disposition effects merely introduce, into the realm of ideas, phenomena which are regarded as commonplace in the realm of perception. It is obvious that what I observe here and now depends on where I am physically located. Looking out on to the front garden gives a different view from looking out on to the backyard; and in the latter case, what I see has a great deal to do with what I know already, such as whether the house opposite is inhabited by an attractive woman or a cantankerous couple. These *intentionalities* (which must be distinguished from the intentions of action theory) affecting the way one looks at things constitute *a priori* forms of perception. The emphasis placed on them in phenomenology, since Husserl, has been such that we can usefully dwell on them for a moment. The fact that in France, Husserl's work has been brilliantly popularized, for example by Merleau-Ponty,[1] lends further weight to this point.

The contribution of Alfred Schütz has been to show that his Husserlian analysis can be applied not only to perception in general, but also to social perception.[2] However, Schütz and his followers, particularly Peter Berger and Thomas Luckmann,[3] have applied the ideas of Husserlian phenomenology to the *symbolic* dimension rather than the *cognitive* dimension of social life. Thus, perceiving individuals as 'criminals' or 'outsiders' will have a whole range of implications for the way their behaviour is perceived or interpreted. The same act will be given a different meaning by observers depending on whether it is done by 'outsiders', by acquaintances of the observer, or by somebody perceived by observers as belonging to the same group as themselves. The 'outsider's' acts are therefore interpreted by the observer according to a frame of reference, or, using a different linguistic register, according to a kind of *a priori* form. However, this classic notion must be given a more flexible and more open meaning than Kant himself gave to it.

A further point is that the ideas of Husserl and Schütz appear without explicit acknowledgement in the work of many analysts who do not derive their approach directly from phenomenology. Linton,[4] for example, notes that people travelling in Norway will willingly entrust their luggage to a porter whom they will arrange to meet at the other end of the station platform, whereas in the same situation in Italy, they will prefer to keep their eyes on the porter. Thus, a 'Norwegian porter' or an 'Italian baggage-handler' are not mere descriptive notions as far as travellers are concerned, but indicate frameworks of thought, or forms which guide the travellers' perception and involve expectations: they would be very surprised not to find the Norwegian porter waiting for them, but not surprised to see the Italian porter disappear into thin air.

The idea that social *perception* is not contemplative but active is nowadays of sufficiently common currency that we need not dwell on it. On the other hand, no doubt because of the classical philosophical theory of truth and falsehood (to which I will return later), it is not easy to take seriously the idea that social *knowledge* is acquired not by abstract actors able to look at the real world from the outside, but by actors who are socially *situated* – that is, characterized by a *position* and by *dispositions*. Their position makes them perceive reality in one light rather than in another; even from the same position, their dispositions will lead them, or in certain cases allow them, to interpret the same reality in a different way. Thus, a banker is likely to perceive monetary phenomena in a different way from a teacher of Greek, and the interpretation would depend on whether the person in question had been, or had not been, exposed to the ideas of Keynes.

These position and disposition effects, as I call them, are in many respects commonplace notions. The fact that they are given less importance than they deserve is firstly because of the positive reason just mentioned – the classical philosophy of truth and falsehood tends to reduce knowledge to a process of contemplation of the real world by an external subject.[5] There is also a negative reason however: writers such as Marx and Karl Mannheim had, as I have already mentioned, clearly seen the importance of these position and disposition effects (situation effects) for the theory of ideology; but the discredit nowadays generally attached to the Marxian theory of ideology in its general form has made us throw out the baby with the bath water. We have failed to see that much of Marx's analysis is in no way reducible to the well-known *camera obscura* analogy. Moreover, Mannheim's writings on the sociology of knowledge have been reduced in much too facile a way to a shoddy historism.[6] It is impossible, however, as we have seen, to reduce Mannheim's thought to the notion that ideas are the product of society and history – on this matter Mannheim is much more careful than Durkheim. His view is that ideas, apart from those which by their very nature can claim to convey universal truth, cannot be understood without reference to the social and historical context in which they appear. However, this statement also implies that ideas have to be *understood*; in other words, they cannot really be interpreted as mechanical reflections of historical and social situations or as mere emanations from a hypothetical collective consciousness, but must be capable of being imputed to rational actors. They are not of course deprived of this rationality merely because they are located historically and socially.

In any case, one of the main reasons why some of the insights of Marx and Mannheim have not received the attention they deserved is that the simplified versions to which certain people believed their thought could be reduced have been discredited. This may also account for the fact that whereas the basic insight of Husserlian phenomenology has largely inspired the analysis of the phenomena of social *perception*, sociologists have not really applied it to social *knowledge*.

I will not dwell too much on position effects, several examples of which have already been given. Let us look, however, at the Marxian analysis of commodity fetishism: merchants conclude that they can raise their prices if the goods they offer are selling well, whereas if the goods are not selling, they can get rid of them only by price reductions. Conversely, they are well aware that, even for products which seem to be feeling well, they cannot raise prices beyond those of their neighbours and competitors.

It is not therefore surprising that because of their position, in the role of distributors, merchants understand that the value of their goods is determined exclusively by the interplay of the market forces of supply and demand; and they would find it rather difficult to believe in the labour theory of value (even if they had heard of it), because the market price of a given product seems to vary so much, even though the conditions under which it is produced do not change.

I have already said that Marx uses the word 'fetishism' because he thinks the merchant's evaluation is wrong when looked at against the truth of the labour theory of value. However, if one leaves aside this doubtful statement, Marx's analysis not only is acceptable, but also provides a shining example of what I have termed position effects.

I will go a little further into disposition effects, by looking again at an example from Weber, the analysis of which was deliberately held over from the previous chapter.[7] I am referring to his superb analysis of magic, outlined in a short piece in *Economy and Society*.[8] Weber argues that the reason why observers are astonished at magic practices is not that these are objectively astonishing, but that they find it very difficult to reconstruct the subjectivity of magicians and of those watching them perform. The difficulty is that observers perceive as different two relationships which the magician seems to regard as similar: what the firemaker does is founded on a true causal relationship, whereas what the rainmaker does is founded on a relationship which the observer normally sees as one of illusion, which cannot possibly be a causal one. In other words, observers find it difficult to conceive that the relationship in each case can be regarded as the same. They are therefore led to conclude that there is a 'primitive mentality'. This is however merely a vacuous phrase, devoid of heuristic content: it identifies a problem, rather than helping us to solve it; it notes the astonishment of the observers rather than explaining it.

Weber suggests that we are astonished at strange behaviour because we approach it with *dispositions* which make it unintelligible and unfathomable. In theory, behaviour is always comprehensible. For our astonishment to turn into understanding, we must, at least in this case, become aware of what it is inside us which prevents our understanding others, since it is the dispositions of observers which make them astonished at what the rainmaker does.

I have already outlined the way in which this question might be looked at. What the firemaker does is based *for us* on a true causal relationship. However, the obvious and self-evident nature of this interpretation is the result of our mobilizing all kinds of notions which are familiar to us because we belong to a specific culture – Western culture. In order to interpret what the firemaker does as being based on a causal relationship, not only do we need to have the idea of cause at our disposal, but also we need to be in a position to call on knowledge which is comparatively recent in Western thought, such as the principle of the conversion of energy. It is because we know that mechanical energy can be converted into thermal energy that we believe in a causal relationship between the sticks being rubbed together and the spark appearing. There is no reason to assume that primitive intelligence, however profound one may be tempted to think it is, necessarily has, by some miraculous process, a prescience of all the principles which Western physics took centuries to discover.

It is rather unlikely that statements such as these will be challenged; but what is more debatable is the idea that primitive intelligence has no notion of causation in the Humean sense, and therefore the examination of this point outlined in the last chapter needs to be further developed.

Firstly, what do we mean by Humean causation?[9] When we say that rubbing the sticks together produces the spark, we are introducing a way of looking at causation in which cause plays the role of an active principle: this is non-Humean causation. The rubbing produces the fire exactly like the weight of the hammer causes the nail to go into the wood. The reason why, in the instant case, we can look at causation in an active (non-Humean) way is that we are acquainted with the laws of energy conversion.

If causation is looked at in what is usually called the Humean way, a causal interpretation is really the result of repetition: we do not know why A is always followed by B, but we observe that A is always followed by B. Because of the repetitive nature of the sequence AB, we conclude that there is a causal relationship between A and B.

However, even though it is easy to see that primitive peoples cannot have a non-Humean concept of the causal relationship between the rubbing and the spark, it does not necessarily follow that they cannot have a Humean concept of it, if only an unclear one. In simple terms, is it not possible, even if one is unaware of the laws of energy conversion, to note that the firemaker manages to create a spark more or less straightaway, whereas the rainmaker fails roughly half of the time.

In the last chapter, I argued that, in order to make the distinction, statistical skills needed to be called on, which the primitive intelligence did not possess. I am willing to concede, however, that this argument may not be totally convincing: though it is clear that primitive intelligence has no foresight of the laws of energy conversion, it is less clear that it has no sense of causation in the Humean sense.

It is appropriate here, therefore, to go back to my discussion of Weber's theory of magic, and ask again whether it is reasonable to assume that primitive intelligence fails to see clearly that the spark follows the rubbing more often than the gesticulations of the rainmaker produce rain. Alternatively, to pose the question in a different way, does the perception of certain statistical differences in fact depend on the acquisition of certain statistical skills?

To answer this question directly, we would need access to data showing how far, in primitive peoples, statistical skills can exist which are independent of any formalized learning of the discipline of statistics itself. Unfortunately, as far as I am aware, we do not have data of this kind relating to primitive human beings. Moreover, it would clearly be quite difficult to design the appropriate experiments, given the problem of making them culturally neutral.

However, we can make a stab at an indirect reply, in that cognitive psychology has taken the trouble to ask the question in relation to ourselves, i.e. people belonging to Western society. Moreover, the reply it has come up with is unequivocal: people belonging to Western culture do have a preknowledge of statistics, but they will make mistakes which in the final analysis are as serious as those so frequently imputed to primitive peoples. Since this conclusion has an important bearing on Weber's interpretation of magic, I propose to look at it more closely.

Several of the experiments to which I will refer try to get the subject to solve some elementary statistical problems involving a concrete example – the distribution of births in maternity hospitals. The subjects were selected from groups with variable characteristics: sometimes, samples were comparable with those used in opinion polls; sometimes they were made up of students. In all cases, the subjects had at least secondary education, and of course none had any training in statistics.

In one of the experiments,[10] subjects were asked a question worded more or less as follows:

Suppose that in a particular maternity hospital on a certain day, six children were born, in the following order according to sex:
BBBGGG
In other words, the first three were boys, the last three girls. Suppose that on another day, in the same hospital, there were again six births and that the order was:
BGBBGG
If records were kept in the hospital over a long period of time, which of these two sequences would occur more often?

It is obvious that both sequences are equally probable. Just as when a coin is spun, there is one chance in two that the first birth will be a boy, and one chance in two that it will be a girl. The same applies to all succeeding births, with the result that any particular sequence is just as likely to occur as any other. Nevertheless, most of the people to whom the question was put thought that the first sequence was less likely to recur.

This example shows that subjects without statistical skills quite justifiably tend to think in terms of order and chance: the BBBGGG sequence seems more orderly than the BGBBGG sequence, which is closer to one's idea of chance. Thus we see that whereas legitimate conceptual associations or distinctions can sometimes be of heuristic value, they can also lead to a wrong view of statistical phenomena. 'Intuition' rightly concludes that a sequence such as BBBBBBGGGGGG is highly improbable; but it will also tend to conclude that this sequence is *less* probable than BGGBBGBBGGBG, which is wrong. So the difference between the first conclusion (right) and the second conclusion (wrong) can be clearly perceived only when one can call on certain statistical concepts.

In other words, this simple example suggests that, even if one can really speak of a statistical pre-knowledge which does not depend on having learned the discipline, this pre-knowledge can lead to wrong answers, even to very basic questions. The example shows clearly that even if people taking part in the experiment have a certain notion of what chance is, this does not lead them to a clear view of what statisticians are describing when they use the notion of independence of events. The subjects' pre-knowledge of statistics is not sufficient to make them see that either of the sequences put to them has the same probability of occurrence, since each birth in the series can be a boy or a girl.

Moreover, Weber's rainmaker would have to be capable of answering a *more complex* question than the one asked in the experiment, to be able to distinguish between what he or she does and what the firemaker does, and to perceive that Humean causation applies to the firemaker but not to him or herself. In technical language, the rainmaker's pre-knowledge of statistics would have to bring about a sufficiently clear sight of what statisticians call a correlation – the rainmaker would have to see clearly that a spark follows the rubbing of the sticks *more often* than his or her ritual acts lead to rain.

However, it can easily be shown by other experiments as well as by observations in other contexts that here again, statistical pre-knowledge can easily lead to wrong conclusions: educated subjects do indeed understand the notion of correlation, as well as the notion of chance, but they do not understand it clearly enough to apply it correctly to even the most simple questions. In other words, they understand the phenomenon of Humean causation (if B occurs more frequently when A is present than when A is not present, then A is the cause of B), but this general conclusion has no significant effect on their specific conclusions. Thus, in one experiment, a sample of educated subjects was asked questions such as:[11] 'Suppose that out of a hundred babies born in a maternity hospital, twenty were premature and were born of mothers older than thirty-five. What conclusion do you draw from this?'

Faced with this kind of question, many subjects have no hesitation in saying there is a causal relationship between the two facts, attributing premature birth to the age of the mother. This conclusion is reached in the subject's mind by the combination of three elements:

1 a statistical pre-knowledge about Humean causation;
2 the resemblance in kind between the presumed cause and its effect – the mother is older than normal, therefore the birth is abnormal;
3 the fact that the coincidence of the two facts is quite frequent (twenty times out of a hundred).

In fact, the question is incapable of being answered, except to say that no conclusion is possible from the data given.

However, to convince the sceptic of this, a formal proof is needed, to show basically that two characteristics can coincide with a certain frequency without there being any causal relationship in the Humean sense.

Figure 1 shows that we are given two pieces of information – the total number of children (100) and the number of premature babies born to older mothers (20) but that we have no information about the areas indicated by a question mark. We need these to show the existence of Humean causation, as in figure 2.

Here, twenty out of fifty premature babies are born to mothers over the age of thirty-five. Yet the proportion is the same in the case of full-term births, twenty out of fifty of which are to mothers over thirty-five. From the information provided, therefore, it is totally impossible to conclude that there is a Humean causal link between the age of the mother and premature births.

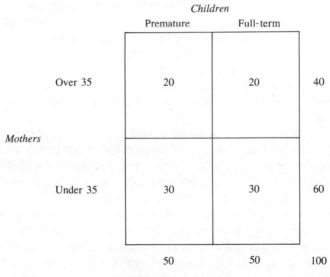

Children

	Premature	Full-term	
Over 35	20	?	?
Under 35	?	?	?
	?	?	100

Mothers (row label)

Figure 1

Children

	Premature	Full-term	
Over 35	20	20	40
Under 35	30	30	60
	50	50	100

Mothers (row label)

Figure 2

I have gone into some detail concerning this proof because it shows that the idea of Humean causation, however intuitive its basis, is nevertheless relatively complex. The combination of the two characteristics has a significant effect: the subjects do not know (because the notion is complex), but they think they know (because the notion of causation in the Humean sense has an intuitive basis). Thus, they do not know that they do not know. And their belief that the numerical data confirms the causal relationship is reinforced by their being more convinced, from other contexts, by the proposition that abnormal birth *conditions* bring about an increased *risk* of an abnormal birth.[12]

This example seems to me to strengthen considerably the plausibility of Weber's theory of magic: is it not unreasonable to assume that primitive peoples have a clearer idea of Humean causation than most of us? In any case, it shows that we have to distinguish between the prescientific know-ledge (pre-knowledge) which we might have of this matter, and the know-ledge which comes exclusively from statistical training.

To sum up, a primitive person's inability to distinguish between the fire-maker and the rainmaker may be difficult for us to grasp, but this is simply the consequence of a powerful disposition effect – we are so imbued with the laws of energy conversion that the causal relationship relied on by the firemaker appears to us as self-evident as the illusion created by the rain-maker. And the difference between the two is so great that we are prepared to insist that primitive people, even if they have no idea of the laws of energy conversion, should at least see that the firemaker is relying on Humean causation whereas the rainmaker is not. Educated people who are from an advanced society, but who have no statistical training, are often left floundering when it comes to Humean causation. However, ideas such as frequency and causation are so familiar to such people that they find it dif-ficult to admit that they are not *natural*, even though they may fail to see them clearly themselves, as was shown in the examples just given.

I think my analysis has shown sufficiently clearly what I mean by *disposi-tion effect*: because of the diffuse knowledge they have of their own culture, observers find it difficult to understand that a difference which they take to be self-evident does not appear thus in the mind of the person observed. Weber's genius was needed in order to suggest that the solution to the problem of magic lay not in the *mentality* of the magician but in the mind of the observers, whose mental dispositions lead them to misinterpret magic and to see it as irrational behaviour. However, these dispositions are not themselves incomprehensible or irrational. On the contrary, it is easy to understand why the Western observer is amazed at what magicians do.

These disposition effects seem to me to be an essential element in the theory of ideologies, since they often give rise, in an almost unnatural way (and in any case in an understandable way) to misinterpretations which are diffi-cult to shift.

In the previous example, I referred to dispositions of a *cognitive* kind:

because of the *knowledge* at their disposal, Western observers find it difficult to understand the magician's behaviour.

There are also dispositions of an *affective* or *ethical* kind, which obviously play a part in explaining ideologies. We have seen that Pareto, Aron, Shils, and others have rightly stressed their importance; but I will nevertheless leave them out of my limited theory.

Finally, I have already said that it is convenient to put position and disposition effects together in a category of situation effects. What I see in the backyard of the house opposite depends on my position and my disposition. Similarly, what observers see in the magician's behaviour depends on their own positions in relation to the magician and to the latter's dispositions: the misunderstanding arises from the fact that observer and magician are thus in a different situation.

Communication effects are another category of effects essential to the analysis of ideological phenomena. To bring them into the analysis we can take a well-known argument by Habermas, and turn it on its head.

The German sociologist and philosopher Jürgen Habermas, sometimes regarded as one of the most outstanding of his generation, developed a rather strange theory in several of his works.[13]

He argued that sociology could not be regarded as a neutral science, dedicated primarily to improving our understanding and knowledge of social phenomena. Its main inspiration is in fact a normative one. It ought to help societies to move in the right direction, though not by simply influencing history, because societies do not contain within themselves their future pattern: Habermas argues that the normative inspiration of sociology lies in the kind of objective which Habermas gives it – the main task of the sociologist is to interpret the conflicts and discontent from which societies are suffering. Habermas's view is that this discontent could in principle be reduced if people could express their opinions and wishes without hindrance and in a totally egalitarian manner.

Habermas deduces from this argument that the degree of legitimacy of a society can be measured by how close it is to the model of a pure and perfect society of communication, since conflict and discontent are in proportion to the difference between a society as it is and the society which its citizens would build if they could engage in untrammelled debate on what was needed to improve it.

Habermas recognizes that his pure and perfect society of communication represents an ideal model: it must be regarded as a point located in infinity which can be reached only in an asymptotic way. He argues, however, that this model has the advantage, on the one hand, of providing a principle for redefining the meaning of the conflict or the discontent, and, on the other hand, if I can use the language of geometry, of marking out a curve and a tangent to this curve. In short, it gives us a better perception of the direction and meaning of social change at any given time.

However interesting it may be, Habermas's ideal model seems to me so far removed from what we know of the phenomena of communication that I do not think that it has any chance of being considered in the same way as other idealized models – for example, perfect competition, which has all kinds of interesting implications, and represents, even if in a very simplified way, certain processes in the real world. By contrast, the perfect-communication model seems to be literally impossible to conceptualize: firstly, because it assumes that everybody is equally competent in all areas; secondly, because it assumes that there is no time-lag at all in acquiring and circulating information; thirdly, because it assumes that within the communication group there is no question of manipulation, coalition, or strategy; fourthly, because it assumes that everybody has clear and discernible opinions and wishes on all matters; fifthly, because it blithely ignores the classic problem of how individual preferences and opinions are transformed into collective preferences and opinions; and finally, because it obscures the distinction, even though it has been a classic one ever since Aristotle, between topics of debate which stem from opinions and those which are raised by proof or experiment.

Habermas argues that his model of pure and perfect communication can be validly used for complex societies, or for what Durkheim called *society*. I tend to think that it is applicable only to small communication groups which are discussing very specific subjects. If a practical use needs to be found for the model, I suggest that it represents, for example, what happens in a small seminar group of mathematicians. Here, clearly, each participant is regarded as being able to take part freely in the discussion. Moreover, the nature of the subject allows us to assume that there is total agreement by the participants on the aims and ground rules of the discussion. Finally, the nature of the discussion rules out in theory any strategic behaviour or attempt at manipulation. It is, therefore, a pure and perfect society of communication, but it is achieved only because the mathematicians are indulging in a rather abnormal activity, where the rules can be defined with total clarity: it is only because he is dealing with *mathematics* that what each participant says is fully accessible to all the others.

Apart from such an exceptional case, however, communication systems in the real world tend to contradict Habermas's model in almost every aspect. In fact, the model of total accessibility which Habermas postulates does not cover, because of their very nature, the processes of communication, circulation, and diffusion of information in social life as it is (rather, perhaps, than as it should be) because social actors, through their role, their position, and their dispositions, very often regard ideas not as – if I may put it in this way – white boxes, but as black boxes.

In a mathematics seminar, ideas are in fact white boxes, in that all participants are assumed to understand clearly and distinctly what others are saying. They are assumed to be capable of following all the stages of a proof, of judging whether the path followed is the right one, and of evaluating the importance of the result. Participants could have said what the seminar leader said, if they had set their minds to it, if their research interests had been in the same area, and if they had had the same intellectual skills. Apart from these reservations, each participant at the end of the seminar can reproduce for him or herself the seminar leader's proof.

Let us look now at any law of physics, for example, e = mc². The reader is very likely to take this as true, as I myself do. However, the fact that we both take it as true is not because we are capable (I am assuming the reader is not a physicist) of reproducing for ourselves the complex process of deduction, induction, and (to use Pierce's term) abduction, which led Einstein to this formula; it is rather because we note that physicists generally seem to take it as true, and we consider physicists to have, rightly, a monopoly of the truth as far as physics is concerned. This truth is of course always contingent – today's truths, as we are quite aware, can become tomorrow's errors. Moreover, while we know that physicists can at any time disagree about any set of circumstances, physicists as a body are in the best position to say what the truth is on a question of physics.

Of course, instead of accepting the *authority* of physicists, and regarding the formula e = mc² as a black box, it would in theory be possible to learn enough about physics to be in a position to reproduce for ourselves how Einstein arrived at the formula; but would that be rational? Yes, if we could assume that the assimilation of knowledge is an immediate process, as Habermas implicitly argues. No, if the opposite is true, which seems to be a more realistic and more useful assumption.

In short, it seems *rational*, if one is not a physicist, to regard ideas in physics as black boxes which can be right or wrong not because one has reproduced the process allowing this evaluation to be made, but because people skilled in this area take them to be right or wrong. Put another way, certain ideas will be regarded as white boxes or black boxes, depending on one's social location. Of course, to social location are linked disposition – one cannot hope to be considered a physicist if one has no idea of physics.

Basically, Habermas's theory of true and perfect communication rests on a prenotion which is surprising coming from a sociologist, because the 'democratic' model which it proposes excludes, in principle and by definition, phenomena of *authority*. It is easy to see the feelings, as Pareto would have said, which might inspire a negative attitude to these phenomena; and, in this regard, Habermas is revealing an attitude which is fairly widespread nowadays. The main argument to understand, however, is that such a theory leads to the quite absurd conclusion that everybody can have the same level of competence in all subjects.

The objection will be raised that Habermas implicitly excluded from his consideration the particular institutionalized disciplines of the natural sciences, and moreover, that these do not directly involve social problems. This statement is true, but I took the example of physics because it is particularly striking: I could have taken the case of other institutionalized disciplines which do involve society directly.

It is therefore clear that, as Keynes said in a well-known aphorism, bankers themselves often regard economic theories as black boxes: they do not try to find out whether they are right or wrong. In other words, they do not try to reproduce in their own mind the more or less complex process by which a particular economist arrived at a particular theory. It is much more likely that they will look at the theory and then perhaps adopt it, firstly because it seems likely to clarify the problems they are facing as bankers, and secondly because they can readily see that it is an authoritative one in their area. Moreover, a more or less complex process will influence the way they perceive it: perhaps the economist who put forward the theory in question is a Nobel Prize winner, or considered as a future candidate; perhaps the theory has attracted the attention of professional economists, or at least of those whom the banker thinks are respectable.

I am well aware that economics is not physics: general agreement on theories and results of experiments is less frequent among social scientists than in the field of physics; and there is hardly need to stress that the scientific world seems much more fragmented and conflict-ridden in the case of the social sciences than in the case of the natural sciences.

These distinctions, however, have no direct bearing on my present argument: in rejecting Habermas's utopia, I simply want to stress that ideas are often (and, I would say, *normally*) regarded by social actors as black boxes, and that it is sometimes rational for them, because of both their social locations and the dispositions which go with this location, not to try to see what there is inside them, but rather to rely on authoritative arguments and judgements.

This is not to say that Keynes's banker should do no more than look towards the authority principle. Such a person may also quite legitimately understand the theory being adopted and even have a critical attitude towards it. However, in this case, the way the banker examines it will usually be different from the way an economist would look at it – the former will look at it in a mostly unsystematic way, limiting his or her examination to partial testing or to questions about how far the theory fits in with personal experiences.

In other words, adopting an idea can be a bit like choosing a complex

technical object. Consumers, when buying television sets, would not contemplate checking to see whether the parts were of the right quality or
correctly installed; they would simply check the quality of the picture, and
perhaps take the maker's name as a guarantee of quality. Obviously,
merely checking the picture and being reassured by the name will not be
enough to make them absolutely certain that the sets will work as they
wished over a long period of time: a more careful and methodical check,
however would not only be more expensive, but would assume knowledge
which the consumers are not likely to possess.

The consumer who regards the television set as a black box is therefore
neither more nor less rational than the banker. The main difference is that
it is easier for the former to check whether the set is working than it is for
the latter to check the forecasts of the economic theory which he or she
intends to use.

However, the authority principle is not the only one which may enter
into play when it is impossible or too expensive to subject the validity of an
idea to direct examination. To put it more clearly, this principle may
combine with others. Axiological rationality, as Weber would have called
it, can also be brought in, at least in the first stages, when a critical
examination proves too difficult or impossible; and of course Weber's use
of the word *rationality* in this phrase is both deliberate and very relevant.

Let us take the case of communist activists who know something about
Lenin's theory of imperialism. In the normal course of events, they will
regard it as a black box, because it is likely to be irrational for them to
submit it to methodical examination; for this they would need to go back
to the sources of the theory – to Hobson and Hilferding, whose arguments were largely taken up, summarized, and condensed by Lenin. But
Hilferding's *Finance Capital* is a difficult technical work, written by a
professional economist. Even that would not be enough, because they
would have to look at the critical literature on Lenin's views and perhaps
try to find out directly whether his arguments are really credible and
consistent with known facts. It follows that this critical examination
would require considerable preparation, similar in nature (though different in degree) to what would be needed for non-physicists to verify for
themselves the laws of Newton or Einstein. Thus, instead of looking
closely at how the transistors are installed, activists would probably limit
themselves to checking the quality of the picture; and in the event they will
no doubt feel that the theory confirms certain values which they consider
themselves as espousing. However, even though this *Wertrationalität* is
very likely to arouse his interest in Lenin's theory, it will certainly not be
enough, without more, to lead them to adhere to it. They will also have to
be in a position to apply the authority principle, a task which will be made
easier in this respect when they learn, by reading the works of, or being

told by, those whom they trust, that they are dealing with a 'classic'. So we
see that an authority effect will develop normally in all cases where there is
a one-way communication between an idea or a theory and a public
(information-technology jargon would speak of a non-conversational
relationship) and where the public in question does not have *at its disposal*
enough time or skill to regard the theory as a white box. Moreover, since it
would appear far-fetched (except in a society where the division of labour
had been abolished) to try to eliminate this difference in resources, positions, and dispositions, it is impossible to see how these authority effects
could not be present. In other words, therefore, Habermas's theory also
assumes that the division of labour has been abolished.

I have been dealing here, by way of introduction, with a particular kind of
communication effect; there are others, to which I will return. It is however necessary to stress the importance of these effects for the theory of
ideologies, which can be done by taking a quick look at the commonly
held view that the influence of ideas is often a question of fashion. It has
frequently been said that ideas, or at least certain categories of ideas, seem
subject to what are usually called fashion cycles. The conclusion has been
that, just as with fashion in clothes for example, these cycles should be put
down to *imitation* phenomena, as Gabriel Tarde would have said, or,
what amounts to the same thing, that they are explicable in terms of a
tendency by social actors (certain ones at least) towards conformism.

This kind of explanation certainly has some truth in it, but I think its
importance should not be exaggerated, for the simple reason that ideas,
unlike clothes for example, are not experienced as if they were a matter of
taste or preference – they are true or false, or they sound right or 'wrong'
(in the way in which a poem sounds wrong).

It is, rather, that ideas go in cycles because many of them are regarded
by various groups of the public as black boxes. It is understandable that
many people, because of their position and dispositions, have an interest
in an idea but at the same time neither think they can nor want to evaluate
its basis; so they rely on the judgement of those they regard as experts on
the question.

However, there has only to be an open attack on the fashionable idea
for its authority to be undermined, and as a result for it perhaps to sink
rather suddenly into obsolescence. To account for these cycles, one does
not necessarily have to conceive of a social actor who is either irrational,
according to the imitation argument, or constrained, according to
Habermas. An actor who is rational, but *located*, does the job better.

There is a problem which has not yet been dealt with at this stage in our
discussion, and which can be formulated thus – why do some ideas, and
not others, seem to be subject to fashion? Thus, for example, theories in

physics seem to be less susceptible to fashion than those in sociology or economics. The conventional reply to this question is to argue that there is a difference in nature between a science such as physics and the social sciences. The former is supposed to be more scientific than are the latter. Even though there may be some truth in this argument, I do not think it deals with the whole problem, because there is another difference between the two kinds of discipline which is vital to my viewpoint – namely, that few people apart from physicists themselves are interested in what physics has to tell us. Of course, the public is interested in the applications of physics, and explanations offered by physics provoke some curiosity, but this has no significant social implications. Moreover, it is clear that in general the public is more interested in the applications than the explanations of physical phenomena – an example is that of the laser.

The relationship between the producer and the consumer, or to use a different register, the one who propounds and the one who receives, is quite different in the case of theories advanced by the social sciences, where, for example, economists will tend to modify their theories of unemployment or inflation in circumstances in which these phenomena constitute social problems in need of urgent solutions. As a result, their theories will be likely to attract the attention of various sections of the public, from unemployed people or basic economic actors to political leaders.

By combining the two kinds of effects to which I have referred – effects stemming from the natural exotericism of the social sciences, and black box effects – I think one can arrive at a simple and credible explanation of the cyclical nature of ideas on social matters. This explanation enables us in any case to avoid the difficulties inherent in theories which are clearly tautological, like that of imitation.

I will conclude these preliminary remarks on communication effects by a consideration of a general nature. The fact that the theory of ideologies has not attached to these effects the importance they warranted is in large part because it often uses two models of the social actor, both to my mind inadequate.

The first, which can be seen in Habermas's work, is that of the rational person of classical philosophy – as a repository of truth, all such a person needs in order to distinguish what is correct from what is false is to apply the light of his or her reason. Of course it is easy for wrong or dubious ideas to become accepted, but this is either because of the irrational forces which are present in social actors (passions) or, as Habermas argues, because of the constraints imposed on them by society, which is why Habermas emphasizes that the right to free expression should be available to all.

The second model is that of the irrational person which sociology, in some of its perspectives, has helped to establish. Here the social actor is depicted either as an essentially mimetic being, or as a passive being whose mind is like a sensitive plate on which fashionable ideas are imprinted, or again as someone fired by exclusively social passions – in other words, people who subscribe to the ideas of Keynes or Milton Friedman out of conformism or self-interest, provided that they see in such adherence a symbolic means of showing they belong to certain groups, or of asserting themselves.

By evoking position and disposition effects, as well as communication effects, I argue that there is a third model, which can be summarized in the notion of 'located rationality'. In this model, social actors are assumed to be rational; and *because* they are rational, they see clearly, for example, that if they tried to judge for themselves the validity of Einstein's laws, it would involve them in considerable expense.

Therefore, when observers see a social phenomenon, for example magic, they are subject to various kinds of position and disposition effects. When the attention of the social actor is attracted by an idea or a social or economic theory, he or she is exposed to all kinds of communication effects, as well as situation effects. Moreover, those who propound these theories are subject to a third group of effects which, because I have failed to come up with a more refined term, I will call epistemological effects. I will however abbreviate this and make it easier by using the term *E effects*.

To understand what these are, we can start from two theories of knowledge which are the result of a long tradition of theorizing to which both philosophy and the social sciences have contributed.

The first can be called the *contemplative* theory of knowledge. To use a rather unrefined image, this theory argues that the subject acquiring the knowledge would be located in a panopticon from which he or she could discover reality by doing various things – moving around; taking different perspectives; cleaning one by one the windows separating him or herself from reality; paying sufficient attention to what is seen; and trying as carefully as possible to make the various images and impressions offered by reality consistent with each other. One can refine the model by introducing several subjects instead of just one, where each describes personal experience to the others; moreover, these subjects might be there at different times rather than all at same time.

The second theory can be called the *active* theory of knowledge.[14] Its starting point is the straightforward statement that many notions, and more generally many symbols and basic expressions that we use when speaking of reality, even when we say that we are merely describing it, have no counterpart in reality. Thus, for example, there is no objective correlate in reality of the negative 'not' or the word 'nothing', any more than there are correlates of addition or multiplication signs, or of the mathematical symbol for integration. These signs and symbols indicate not bits of reality, but mental processes. Similarly, there is nothing in reality which corresponds to the notion of 'zero'.

Historically speaking, the active theory of knowledge of course goes back to Hume. The theory argues that knowledge is produced when subjects decipher reality using tools provided by their own minds. For Hume, this activity is apparent in our use of the simplest and most ordinary notions to speak about the real world – for example, that of *cause*. Reality may provide repetitive sequences (for example, that A is always followed by B), but it never lets us observe directly the effect of A on B; so a statement such as 'A causes B' must be regarded as an interpretation (by means of the notion of cause) of a reality which we see as a simple repetitive sequence.

Over the last 200 years, right up to the present, Hume's classical analysis has been taken up, systematized, and refined by Kant and the neo-Kantians, and I do not propose to go into its history, even briefly. I will simply say that the work of somebody such as Popper[15] belongs directly to this tradition, in that the main underlying idea, going back beyond the way Popper's thought developed, is that knowledge comes about when the subject acquiring the knowledge addresses to reality *questions* which are more or less well formulated, more or less relevant, and more or less central. The fact that these questions may be divulged to research scientists by reality itself is principally because of the questions which their predecessors have already put and the answers which reality has already provided. Popper argues, of course, that a scientific theory is really a question formulated in such a way that reality can reply 'yes' or 'no'. In any event, one thing is clear: those questions which make up the texture of the history of science are not directly made available to the subject by reality itself.

It is of course the same tradition which Kuhn[16] is following when he stresses that research scientists, even in the most obdurate sciences, formulate their questions and theories within a linguistic framework which they will usually accept without demur, unless their discipline seems to them to be going through a crisis. Kuhn tells us[17] that he was for a long time obsessed by a problem which he could not solve: how could a mind as powerful and incisive as Aristotle's have developed perspectives on physics which cause modern-day physicists merely to shrug their shoulders, when he had worked out in so many areas – politics, ethics, rhetoric, logic, and many others – analytical perspectives so sophisticated and advanced that even today they are often regarded as definitive? Kuhn relates that the answer came to him suddenly when, pondering on the question for the thousandth time, his eye happened to land on a tree visible from his window. He realised that the reason why Aristotelian physics seemed unintelligible to modern physicists is that the word *movement* relates to two entirely different concepts in Aristotelian physics and in modern physics. Whereas for the modern physicist, the movement of a body is defined by extrapolating from the nature of the body, for an Aristotelian physicist the movement is conceived as a property of the body itself. This is why Aristotle took a tree growing to be as much a movement ($\kappa\iota\nu\eta\sigma\iota\varsigma$) as a sphere rolling down an inclined plane.

However, the modern meaning of the word 'movement', or the meaning given to it by modern physics, has become so well known for physicist and non-physicist alike that it is almost impossible to understand how the same word could have applied to phenomena which to our modern minds are so *obviously* different.

In any event, our argument shows that a research scientist is located within a linguistic framework which tradition provides, and which as a general rule the scientist does not question. Of course, it is not only a lexical corpus which is inherited, but also a syntax, and at a still higher level of abstraction, what might be called theoretical and methodological perspectives, or, more appropriately, paradigms.

I myself tend to see Kuhn's work principally as a refinement of the classic ideas of Kantism and neo-Kantism, in that both Kuhn's paradigms and Kant's *a priori* forms follow closely the same basic idea. Kuhn's originality lies in the emphasis he puts on the historical and social nature of these forms and paradigms, as Durkheim had also done.[18] The paradigms become established within specific scientific communities, providing them with a kind of provisional constitution which will survive, as political constitutions do, as long as it can solve problems which scientific research is bringing up all the time. Further, just as a political constitution is likely to be revised to cope with unforeseen problems if these become numerous, just as after a certain time it will be regarded as outdated and out of step with politics, and just as major constitutional revisions coincide with and reflect periods of political crisis, so agonizing reappraisals of paradigms coincide with periods of scientific crisis.

From Hume through Kant to Kuhn, therefore, what I have called the *active* theory of knowledge has been developed through infinite variations, some of which are philosophical in nature, others more connected with history or sociology. However, because of an unfortunate effect of the division of labour, the unity which is there throughout the development of this thought has often been difficult to see.

However, hypotheses stemming from the *active* theory of knowledge seem to me to be relevant and centrally important from the point of view of the theory of ideologies. After all, if one adheres to the realistic or contemplative theory of knowledge, false ideas have to be ascribed to passion, precipitate action, or prejudice – in other words, regarded as the effect of irrational forces. On the other hand, the perspective offered by the active theory of knowledge makes it easier to understand how false or dubious ideas not only make their appearance but also at the same time are so readily accepted.

Since ideologies attach themselves to theories in the political and social fields, it is from these areas that I now intend to take an example, in order to show the importance of what I have called the active theory of knowledge for the analysis of ideological phenomena.

During the last thirty years, economists have established an extensive body of research and theory which can be collectively referred to as *development economics.* In parallel to this and as a complement to it, sociologists have amassed hypotheses and research data referring to what is called the *sociology of modernization.*

Mention of these labels shows immediately how the researchers in question, merely by using them, have taken on a linguistic framework, or, if one prefers, a paradigm or a collection of *a priori* forms: unlike the way in which one would apply, for example, the idea of 'dog' to certain well-known animals, it is not possible to associate readily identifiable phenomena in the real world with concepts such as *development* or *modernization*, which are the product of a mental construct with complex causes. At the basis of this construct are perfectly ordinary impressions – certain countries are poor, their people seem not to be engaged in much activity, their economies are primitive; they are *underdeveloped* compared with other countries which display the opposite characteristics. However, the concept of development is not only based on descriptive impressions, it also has normative objectives (development is normal, underdevelopment is not), and it outlines an evolutionist perspective – all societies will in due course reach the normal state called 'development'.

Similar remarks could be made about the concept of modernization, which also contains a normative aim, and potentially it has within it a whole philosophy of history.

What I have to say on these points is of course widely accepted, and I would certainly not claim to be in any way original. It is simply meant to illustrate that the basic vocabulary of social sciences, far from merely describing a particular fragment of reality, is in fact the result, as here, of choices made more or less consciously by the researcher.

The analysis, however, must be taken further. A phrase such as *development economics* also betrays an *a priori* form in that the use of *development* in the singular assumes that there is something in common between the development of Great Britain from the eighteenth century onwards and that, for example, of Prussia from the nineteenth century. Similarly, use of *underdevelopment* in the singular assumes that it has a common cause in, say, Zaïre and Nicaragua. The use of the singular therefore becomes a declaration of principles asserting, as if no confirmation were needed, that the analysis of states of underdevelopment and processes of development can lead to a general theory which is simply there to be discovered. At the same time, it rejects the idea that development phenomena are the preserve of the historian; it does not accept that one need go no further than emphasize the particular conditions which have given rise to more or less spectacular changes in the economic system in specific cases.[19]

Finally, to speak of development economics implicitly assumes that economic development and underdevelopment are for the most part explained by factors of an economic nature.

One therefore has merely to mention the phrases *development economics* or *sociology of modernization* to conjure up a whole range of *a priori* forms or, putting it another way, to bring into play a paradigm.

Even though paradigms are necessary for research, since they define the ground rules or the constitutional framework without which it cannot get started, they also constitute a kind of two-headed Janus, in that they can be bearers of wrong or dubious ideas, as my example suggests: can underdevelopment really be used in the singular, and are the causes of development or underdevelopment largely economic? We are well aware nowadays that the answers to these questions have to be worded very carefully.

As Kuhn rightly argues, paradigms, like constitutions, tend to be overthrown only when a surfeit of problems has built up: it is then that doubts begin to appear, and one begins to question what before was undisputed.

However, before there are serious questions raised about a paradigm, it will often have had time to produce theories which will widely accepted by the scientific community, which will have unquestioned scientific authority and which consequently might well exert considerable social and political influence. I think that this example adequately shows how important it is to look at what I call *E effects* in analysing ideological phenomena.

The theoretical outline just established can be conveniently summarized by a diagram in the shape of a triangle (see figure 3). One of the corners represents reality (R). The second (PROD) indicates those who produce ideas and theories in the political and social fields – for example, economists or sociologists. The third (PUBL) represents the public.

The relationship between PROD and R is one of observation. It is

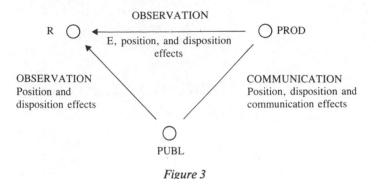

Figure 3

subject to E effects, but also to position and disposition effects. Because he has a certain role, the economist will naturally interpret the underdevelopment of Zaïre, for example, from the perspective defined by development economics.

The relationship between PUBL and R is one of observation, subject to position and disposition effects. In this way, the Western observer is usually disconcerted by the activities of magicians.

The relationship between PROD and PUBL is one of communication: it is subject to communication effects but also position and disposition effects. Thus, it is likely that the 1930s banker is interested in Keynesian theory, but unlikely that the banker has read the 'General Theory' in any detail.

If we look at all the phenomena briefly outlined in this diagram, we see that although wrong or dubious ideas sometimes stem from irrational forces, they can also be quite normal in the way in which Durkheim considered crime to be a normal phenomenon. Position and disposition effects, communication effects, and E effects correspond not to abnormal social phenomena which need to be looked at because they are strange, but to normal everyday phenomena of social life – examples of which are readily observed. When these effects are combined, when the attempt is made to see them in conjunction, the conclusion is that they can easily lead to collective belief in ideas which are weak, dubious, and false.

6

Ideology, social position, and dispositions

It is open to the sociologist to regard social actors as rational, and according to Max Weber, it is advantageous to do so. At the same time however, there is a need to be aware of all the implications inherent in the fact that social actors are socially *situated*, in the sense that they have social roles, and belong to certain social backgrounds and certain societies, that they have access to certain resources (particularly cognitive), and that because of the socialization process which they have undergone, they have *internalized* a certain number of skills and representations. For these reasons, they are subject to what I have called situation effects (position and disposition effects).

On the matter of internalization, it is vital to be aware of certain distinctions and not get carried away into an untenable theory of consciousness. There is no objection to asserting that one has *internalized* Pythagoras' theorem, or that one has internalized a particular habit or value. Conversely, when novelists can justifiably suggest, as Faulkner does with *Sartoris*, that their heroes have killed themselves *because* they have internalized their fates, an explanation of this nature is usually regarded as unacceptable in a scientific context.[1] The *dispositions* which I will deal with here are of a cognitive kind. They are *internalized* by social actors in the same way that school-children internalize Pythagoras' theorem. If it is limited to this kind of usage, I do not think the notion of internalization should present any great difficulty.

It would be wrong to try to draw up for present purposes a comprehensive taxonomy of these situation effects. My aim in this chapter is simply to give an idea of their diversity and their importance from the standpoint of the question with which I am dealing – how do received ideas come about?

The social *position* of social actors involves first of all the appearance of what might be called perspective effects, to which I have already referred. They are what Marx has in mind when he looks at why the proletariat seems to agree so readily to exploitation by capitalists:[2] workers agree to being paid less than their work is worth, knowing as they do so that a true wage is what they would get if they worked in complete isolation.

Let us take the case of workers in a shoe factory. The division of labour leads to productivity gains; as, for example, when a pair of shoes can be made in n hours, whereas it would take $n + h$ hours for each worker alone. By putting several workers on the same job, the capitalist therefore saves h hours' work for each pair of shoes. However, it does not cross the workers' minds that the saving comes from their own efforts: if they think that ten loaves of bread can be made in the same time as a pair of shoes, they will regard their wage as acceptable if they can buy ten loaves of bread with it, after $n + h$ hours' work. Since during this time, however, they will have produced not one pair of shoes, but $(n + h)/n$ pairs of shoes, they are allowing the capitalist to keep the productivity gains accruing from the division of labour.

Whether or not this analysis is correct,[3] I think it has considerable methodological scope and is particularly useful. It suggests that the workers are incapable of perceiving the real value of their work, since this would imply an ability to analyse the complex system of production to which they belong, to estimate accurately the capitalist's production costs, to allow for the depreciation of equipment, and so forth. Of course, not only do they not have the information to do these calculations, but they also lack the analytical tools, which is why they are content with a more straightforward assessment – they know that they make shoes, have a rough idea of how long a worker on his or her own would need to make a pair of shoes, and therefore agree to being paid on this basis.

Another classic example is that of the Luddite movement, which is one more illustration of what I call perspective effects. The development of mechanization in eighteenth-century Britain allowed manufacturers to make significant productivity gains. From the worker's point of view, however, what was important was that it increased unemployment. The reaction of the Luddites was to attack the machines and occasionally to wreck them.

The Luddite movement has aroused considerable interest among historians and sociologists. Some see it as a resistance to change, irrational in nature – a protest against the perceived threat posed by mechanization to long-established traditions. They see the destruction of machines by the Luddites as a desire to extirpate evil, to block a kind of progress which was regarded as the manifestation of evil forces.

In fact, what this irrationalist interpretation shows perhaps most clearly are the observer's prejudices. The observer is greatly tempted to regard the Luddites' behaviour as irrational because of a conviction that the higher productivity and standard of living made possible by machines is to everybody's advantage.

Lewis Coser, in rejecting this irrationalist interpretation, suggested an interesting alternative of a strategic kind:[4] the Luddites did indeed understand the advantages which mechanization would bring, but, he argued, their machine-wrecking was an attempt to show the owners of the new textile mills that they were a force to be reckoned with, that they had a 'nuisance value'. By acting in this way, their main objective was to gain concessions from the employers.

This strategic interpretation of the Luddite movement is confirmed by the fact that the workers often destroyed only those machines which were turning out faulty goods. It was still true, of course, that a worker who went on strike could easily be replaced by somebody from the army of unemployed people willing to be strike-breakers, at a time when nascent trade-unionism was harshly suppressed. Since machine-breaking brought the factory to a halt, it was not only a functional substitute for striking, it was also much more effective.[5]

We see that, if Coser's line of argument is followed, the Luddite movement was perhaps the first example of a kind of social action which is very familiar to us nowadays. The argument is that Luddite machine-breakers were roughly equivalent to the left-wing trade-unionist electricians who cut off the electricity supply to a whole urban area. Their aim is not of course to harm people, nor to oppose increases in the consumption of electricity, but to take advantage of the nuisance value of their situation and strengthen the negotiating position of their trade union.

Coser's interpretation is interesting: he argues that the irrationalist explanation of the Luddite movement, no doubt the most common one, is the product of a disposition effect. Just as the Western observer, being removed from 'primitive man', finds it extremely difficult to fathom the rituals of magic, so the modern observer, being convinced of the benefits of mechanization, finds it difficult to interpret machine-breaking at the beginning of the industrial age as anything else than irrational behaviour.

There is however a third possible interpretation of the Luddite movement – as an example of perspective effect. Thus, the worker who loses his or her job sees unemployment as the starkest and most immediate effect of the introduction of machines. The same is true of the worker who keeps a job, but who nevertheless is well aware that it is at risk because of the absence of job protection and the growing pool of rural migrants looking for jobs. In other words, *from the workers' point of view*, there is a causal link between mechanization and unemployment, and on a general level between the introduction of machines and the deterioration of their life-style, the difficulty of finding work, the greater risk of losing their jobs, and the increase in competition between workers. *As far as they are concerned*, machines are responsible for the worsening of their situation and that of their peers, just as machines are responsible for the deterioration of solidarity among workers.

Clearly, the validity of this causal relationship is purely on the individual level: at the general level, the relationship is the opposite. Here, mechanization has positive effects: by being a factor in rising productivity, it contributes to growth, to an increase in everybody's living standards – or, to be accurate, in average living standards – to increased job opportunities, to greater worker solidarity, and to an increase in the resources which workers' organizations are able to call upon.

In other words, as Alfred Sauvy forcefully points out,[6] it is not true that at the general level mechanization leads to unemployment. A certain number of hours of work are needed to produce the machine itself, so if the machine destroys jobs, it helps at the same time to create more. Of course it does not automatically follow that the number of jobs created in this way is greater than the number of jobs lost, a fact we are well aware of today. Only observation will tell what this figure is and whether it is positive or negative; this depends on the circumstances. The only certainty is that in the medium and long term, mechanization creates more jobs than it destroys. Intuition tells us, without recourse to statistics, that the number of French people employed in production is higher today than it was a century ago.

It is well known that Sauvy had great difficulty in getting his argument across, partly for intellectual reasons (I will return to this point), because proof that mechanization had beneficial effects on employment relies on abstract reasoning – it assumes that the economic system is perceived as a system, and that one is in a position to analyse this system in all its complexity.

However, another reason why many people have difficulty in perceiving this causal link is that at the individual grassroots level, one is more likely to see a link which gives a negative result. *For workers*, viewing matters from their own standpoint, it is the machine which is often the direct cause of unemployment, the reason why they and their fellow workers are laid off.

This perspective effect therefore suggests a third explanation of the Luddite movement which has the virtue of simplicity: Luddite workers tried to oppose the introduction of machines because they were a clear threat to their jobs and the means to live. From their own viewpoint, machines seemed to be a undisputed cause of unemployment. Naturally, machines could be regarded as creating jobs in the long term and in the wider context, but they were unlikely to see matters from this *point of view*.

I am undecided as to which of these interpretations of the Luddite movement is the best. It may be that each of the three has some truth in it, and it is up to the historian to pronounce on the matter. What is important is that the commonest interpretation, the irrationalist one, reveals the presence of disposition effects on the part of the observer, and the third interpretation discloses a remarkable perspective effect – from their own viewpoint, the workers see the *negative* effect of mechanization on jobs whereas the observer from a distance perceives a *positive* effect.

This kind of perspective effect is quite common: for example, employers often think that any increase in taxes must be inflationary, even though it is quite clear that this is not always so. By reducing purchasing power, a rise in taxes can cut overall demand and lead to a fall in prices, though again (contrary to what a cursory glance at Keynes might suggest) an anti-inflationary effect is not inevitable. The only certainty is that *under certain conditions* an increase in taxes can slow down price rises.

However, so long as employers stick to the perspective which their location leads them naturally to adopt, there will be a tendency not to perceive this possible effect. Just as Luddite workers could see at their level the effects of mechanization on unemployment, employers can also see directly the effects of an increase in taxes. They are well aware that if their fixed costs rise, their production costs will increase. If they want to keep their business on an even keel and not cut back too much on investment, they will try to pass on increased production costs to the customer, unless this would reduce sales. In any event, they will consider tax increases to be a source of inflation, a belief which is simply the result of direct observation – it is what they see at their level. They would have to adopt a standpoint which is not naturally their own in order to see that the causal relationship might be the opposite at the general level.

Perspective effects therefore constitute a significant class of position effects. They can be defined as follows (it is a definition which simply generalizes a classical notion of the psychology of perception by giving it a more abstract meaning): there is a perspective effect when the same object can be perceived from different viewpoints and when the images corresponding to these viewpoints are themselves different.

It is clear that actors are never riveted to a single viewpoint; they can break free from it. Employers can read, understand, even agree with Keynes and appreciate that tax increases might be deflationary. Similarly, Luddite workers might understand that mechanization can create jobs. But these general points of view are foreign to both. Moreover, they would be persuaded only if things were explained to them. In other words, not only have there to be theories which make clear and support this general viewpoint, but they must be sufficiently apparent to come to their attention. Further, even in this case, they might have difficulty in reconciling the general viewpoint with the facts which they perceive directly themselves, since, to use an evocative expression, workers and employers are *in a position* to know all about the effects of mechanization on unemployment or tax increases on inflation.

Because many social and economic actors are 'in a position to know', certain ideas which set a general perspective against particular perspectives are often difficult to accept. The example of Sauvy's ideas is a telling one.

Apart from perspective effects, a second category of effects ought to be mentioned. As with ordinary phenomena of perception, they establish a distinction between the foreground and the background, and, as with ordinary perception, they tend to stress the foreground. In an excellent book on India, to which I have referred elsewhere,[7] the following example occurs. The peasants in the Indian villages studied have access, as is often the case, to a well which is reserved for them, while the untouchables, living on the outskirts of the village, have their own well which is more inconvenient, harder to get to, and with fewer facilities.

A Member of Parliament from the nearest town wanted to lower the social barriers of the caste system and tried to get the untouchables to demand that they be allowed to use the peasants' well. He was politely told to go away, and the untouchables tried to explain why: they are tied to the peasants by complex contractual relations of clientelism which stem from common law. In return for the work they do on the peasants' land and for the various obligations to which they are subject, such as attending wedding and funeral ceremonies, they can count on the peasants when they are ill, for example, or when they need money for emergencies. These services and counter-services are subject to complex rules, the stability of which is ensured by being handed down from one generation to the next. Despite their stability, however, they are subject to interpretation, and the peasants often tend to find pretexts for asking the untouchables to do more than the latter think they are obliged to do. If the peasants let the untouchables use their well, the latter would be exposed to recriminations and disputes, since the peasants would exploit their presence at the well to increase their claims and demands.

Of course, the *viewpoint* of the Member of Parliament was justified; and what he was trying to get the untouchables to demand would have been in their interest in the medium and long term. However, the strategy he was proposing involved immediate costs which the untouchables were not prepared to accept. This is not surprising, since it is not often that social actors willingly lay themselves open to costs which are inevitable and immediate (and which can be avoided by simply adhering to normal ways of behaviour) when these costs offer only a vague hope which will materialize in the future, if at all. Gaining access to the well was not advantageous in itself, and in fact would have brought only disadvantages to the untouchables. The only advantage was that it might have been the first step in a long process of 'liberation'.

It is quite understandable that the untouchables should perceive the foreground rather than the background, just as it is understandable that the Member of Parliament should have been unaware of the considerable disadvantages which the untouchables would have suffered if they had followed his suggestion.

There is a similar case in point in Sombart's book *Why Is There No Socialism in the United States*?[8] Sombart explains that members of the working class in the United States who want to improve their social status prefer to do this by themselves rather than rely on a possible improvement in the lot of their class as a whole. At the time that Sombart was writing (the turn of the century), social mobility *was perceived* in the United States as relatively important, and no doubt was important in reality. By applying oneself to it, one could hope to move away, by one's own means, from a situation thought to be unenviable. If it succeeds, the advantage of the 'individual' strategy is immediately obvious. Conversely, a 'collective' strategy of joining a socialist movement and waiting until socialism improved the lot of the disadvantaged offered the prospects of results which were not only uncertain, but were also going to take a long time to materialize. In other words, to paraphrase Sombart's explanation, a collective strategy of this kind is likely to be successful only in situations where class barriers are (or are perceived as being) difficult to cross, and where social mobility is uncommon or at least perceived as such.

By stressing the foreground instead of the background, members of the working class in the United States, like the Indian untouchables, are not serving their long-term interests. And the relatively rudimentary nature of social welfare in the United States today, compared with Europe, is certainly the result of the kind of processes studied by Sombart at the turn of the century. However, the foreground very often has an immediacy and a significance for social actors which the background lacks.

An example of a totally different kind would be that of business people who, as is well known, have over the years exerted pressure on the Prime Minister's office to bring about a devaluation of the franc. Devaluations of course bring immediate benefits to firms which export, even though these benefits are only temporary and in any case cannot save a business which is ailing.

Distance or removal effects are another important category of situation effects. They involve position and disposition effects, and an example of them has already been given in the anecdote recounted in chapter 1. This is about a group of people from a country where if one has a large family a high standard of living is more or less impossible and where a reasonable standard of living for one's children is unthinkable. These people went to a country where a high birth-rate is one of the causes of poverty, to study the way birth control is promoted. Extrapolating from their own experience, they unhesitatingly diagnosed a basic 'irrationality' on the part of the Indian peasant. If the object observed appears *remote* from the *observer*, it is likely that the behaviour of the former will seem unintelligible to the latter. The observer will (paradoxically) cling all the more readily to personal experience to analyse the behaviour of the observed, the more the latter appear remote. It is on the basis of this kind of process that Lévy-Bruhl came up with the idea of primitive mentality, and the people in the anecdote proposed the explanation of irrationality.

Examples of these removal effects crop up frequently. Chinoy, in a classic article,[9] was intrigued by the fact that workers whom he had observed in the American car industry seemed optimistic about the future and content with their lot, whereas objectively they were in a dead-end situation, with no hope of promotion or of changing their lot. Despite this, they had the impression – or at least they said as much – that they could 'succeed in life' or improve their position significantly.

However, 'succeeding in life' meant for them earning a few more dollars, doing things to their house, buying better furniture, getting to a point on their remuneration scale earlier than they expected, or going out to enjoy themselves more often. Chinoy concluded that when these workers spoke about succeeding in life, it was for them a kind of play-acting done unconsciously though with sincerity: so that they did not have to accept the obvious fact that they were in a dead-end situation, they attached an importance which was artificial, or at least exaggerated, to the slim advantages they could hope to obtain.

In fact this interpretation is a typical example of a distance effect. Just like the people analysing the case of the Indian peasant, Chinoy had the impression that he was dealing with unintelligible behaviour – how can one speak of succeeding in life when one is in a dead-end situation? Since he could not understand the reason why the workers say that, he put it down to irrational causes. When he said that the workers 'rationalized' their situation, this meant for him that they had chosen to close their eyes so that they could not see the reality which surrounded them.

If one thinks about it for a moment, one is aware of the extreme complexity and at the same time the low credibility of an interpretation whereby not only do the workers shut their eyes but they do not know they have their eyes shut – if they did, they would not allow themselves to be hoodwinked. After all, if the 'rationalization' is to be effective, it must remain unconscious. Chinoy regards the behaviour of the workers as so unintelligible that he does not hesitate to call on the resources of psycho-analysis to explain it.[10]

Just as in the previous example, the remoteness which observers experience regarding the behaviour of the observed leads them to take themselves as the point of comparison, and to infer the irrationality of the observed – how can earning a few dollars more, going up a few points on the scale, or improving one's material comfort possibly be 'succeeding in life'? This definition of succeeding in life, however, is incomprehensible only if observers take an egocentric position and measure the other person's definition against their own.

When something is in the distance and its shape is not clear, the tendency is to use a well-known object as reference. Similarly, with actions which are remote, the tendency is to measure them against one's own. Conversely, with actions which are less remote, more attention is paid to the circumstances which might have given rise to them, and the explanation of irrationality is less likely. If Chinoy had given the matter some thought, he would readily have concluded that for some of his academic colleagues, 'succeeding in life' or 'success' was also measured in steps which were quite 'trivial' – having a few more citations in academic journals, or becoming a member of a slightly more prestigious academic body. There is nothing objective to say that the criteria of success to which the academic attaches importance are *objectively* important, while those which are important to the worker are simply a figment of the imagination. It is quite likely, however, that academics will *understand* why colleagues will move heaven and earth to get a favourable review of their latest book. They may find it conceited or bad form, but they will regard such behaviour as neither incomprehensible nor irrational. Conversely, the same academics have no hesitation in describing as irrational workers who think extending their house is proof of succeeding in life.

In the same way, many writers attribute to irrationality the fact that with regard to their children's education, the ambitions of the lower classes are not as strong as those of the middle classes, the argument being that the lower classes 'internalize' the idea that academic qualifications are not for their children. Here again, the researchers are projecting their own experience (that academic qualifications are necessary for somebody doing research) and putting forward irrationality as an explanation.

We therefore see that remoteness can often suggest to the observer a socio-centric or egocentric interpretation of the behaviour pattern – attitudes, beliefs, and so on – of the group or person being observed. This tendency of observers to refer to their own categories and personal experience is all the greater because of the apparent difficulty in understanding the behaviour pattern of the observed. As suggested in several of the examples I have given, even though social scientists are skilled in analysing behaviour, they are not, as Herbert Spencer pointed out,[11] immune to faulty perception.

Mention must be made of other types of position effect, such as role effects. Certain roles direct the attention of social actors towards certain theories. If these theories are, or are almost, the only ones available, the actor is likely to subscribe to them. Thus, for example, if all economists agree that the only remedy for underdevelopment is to inject foreign capital, it will be difficult for actors whose role involves them in the 'fight' against underdevelopment not to endorse this view of the problem. I will however return to these questions in the next chapter, since position effects are in this example becoming mixed up with communication effects.

In previous chapters I have already given many examples of what I call disposition effects. Let us recall the interpretation of the actions of the rainmaker by Western observers: they find it difficult to disregard their own knowledge of physics and statistics; they also tend to regard what the magician does as irrational, but have no difficulty in understanding the firemaker. Because of this knowledge, they approach the phenomenon of magic with mental *dispositions* which, in the event, will hinder rather than help their understanding of the phenomenon.

It would be even more difficult to try to classify disposition effects than it would be to classify position effects. Their form is infinitely variable, even though they exemplify an obvious fact – that in interpreting any phenomenon, we call on previously acquired knowledge and experience, which can just as much hinder as help our understanding of the phenomenon. This is why, instead of trying to draw up or even sketch out a classification, as I did for position effects, I will emphasize one particular aspect of disposition effects which seems to me very important.

When we have a problem to solve or an objective to achieve, not only the nature of the problem or the objective but also our dispositions can be such that we know how to solve the problem or achieve the objective. Nobody who has elementary notions of algebra, for example, would find it difficult to solve the equation $3x = 2$. One knows how to solve this problem, and one knows that one knows. Classical philosophy, from Averroes to Schopenhauer, has struggled with the question of whether 'I know' can be taken to mean the same as 'I know that I know.'[12]

More interesting for our purposes are the examples obtained by introducing a negative in one of the elements of this phrase, and by building more complex variants of this classic reflex expression, which allow us to show types of dispositions where social actors seem to be particularly liable to adopt received ideas. Faced with a problem, and depending at the same time on the nature of the problem and the state of their cognitive resources, actors may:

1 know that they know – this is the classic case;
2 know that they do not know and that it is difficult to know;
3 know that they do not know, but see a certain number of alternative solutions to a particular problem;
4 not know that they do not know and think that they know;
5 not know that they do not know and be convinced that they know.

As will be seen, the dispositions of types (2) to (5) inclusive all open the door to beliefs and received ideas, and it is therefore necessary to look at them in some detail. They are not philosophical hairsplitting, but perfectly normal examples from social life. They appear, as it were, at the intersection of the *nature of the problems* with which social actors are faced and the *resources* available to them to solve them. The first example does not concern us and will be disregarded.

In the second example, actors are aware of the complexity of the problem they face. They know that they do not know and that they are dealing with difficult questions. They will however have to think of possible solutions, particularly if they are pushed by what is usually called the need to act. Often, in a case such as that, they will rely on what one might call the extrapolation method, provided this expression is given a very general definition. I will therefore define extrapolation as relying on the known to explain the unknown. A common form of this sort of extrapolation method is to refer to what is commonly called 'the lessons of the past.'

A book by Ernest May gives a host of examples of this,[13] and I will simply quote one of them. In 1943, in one of his fireside chats, Roosevelt said that 'the elimination of the Japanese empire as a potential aggressor is vital for peace and security', that German military power should not be allowed 'to rise again in the foreseeable future', and that the United States and the Soviet Union were destined to get along and to get along very well: in any case, 'the tragic mistakes of the past' ought not to be repeated. It has been established that this speech was carefully prepared and that it was intended not just to boost the morale of the armed forces: it was not in other words *symbolic action* in the way Geertz meant it. Roosevelt was indeed convinced that his analysis was correct; but he did not realize that, while making another war impossible, he was 'preparing the last peace'. He was of course wrong about relations between the United States and the Soviet Union; but these relations had never been cordial and the Soviets had said on several occasions that they wanted to keep some of the Polish territory which they had seized in 1939. Moreover, in mid 1943, before

Roosevelt's Christmas speech, they had started setting up a communist regime for Poland which would take over after the war.

Roosevelt's prophecies about the continued threat of German and Japanese militarism were also wrong, but he was so convinced of the importance of the 'lessons of history' that a repeat of the past had to be avoided and above all the mistakes of Woodrow Wilson's 'Fourteen Points'. The opposite course had to be taken – there would be no armistice with Germany, but unconditional surrender; there would be no 'escape clause', German courts would not be allowed to try war criminals, and Germany would be demilitarized by the Allies. Since in the case of Japan there could be no extrapolation from the lessons of history, a similar policy would be applied as in the German case.

In economic policy also, Roosevelt's principles were defined by the extrapolation method. Since it was clear that economic nationalism and the barriers erected against investment and trade were responsible for the Depression, which had led to Fascism, Nazism, and the Second World War, the International Monetary Fund and the World Bank were set up, and restrictions on trade were removed, to prevent a recurrence of these unfortunate events.

Ernest May never says of course that these policies were wrong, simply that they are inexplicable unless one sees that they were based, more or less consciously, on what I call the extrapolation method. In any case, this analysis illustrated an example which is at the same time simple, fundamental, and extremely common. When we lack an effective method of deciphering the future, the simplest thing is to start from the present or the recent past which have a reality, a solidity, and a 'truth' which the future could never claim to have. However, since the future is never a repetition of the past, and is rarely a simple continuation of the present, the extrapolation method, though a powerful means of legitimating beliefs and received ideas, is at the same time always likely to be refuted. One never completely believes in the 'lessons of history', even though it is at the same time difficult to dismiss them totally. This is why forecasts, even short-term ones, can seem so outlandish as soon as the future becomes the present.[14]

In the third of the five examples mentioned above, one knows that one does not know the solution to a problem, but one has an idea of the possible solutions, though one is unable by demonstrative reason to choose between them. This case is also very important for the theory of ideologies. When there is an *ambiguity* of this kind, social actors are likely to resort to adventitious beliefs. In other words they choose not the solution which seems most valid objectively, but that which for a variety of reasons seems to them the most desirable.[15]

This can be illustrated by a example taken from education policy. Since the mid-1950s, most governments in France, as in other countries, have wanted to reduce educational inequalities. Even though social inequalities are generally regarded as compatible with democracy, inequality of opportunity is, rightly or wrongly,[16] frequently regarded as incompatible with the fundamental values on which democracy is based. Even though what social actors get out of life may depend on what they put into it, it is more difficult to concede that privilege should depend on accidents of birth, as in the case of differential access to higher education. It is easy to understand why many people find this fact shocking, and why educational achievement which gives access to the most interesting jobs should depend on birth. The strength of feeling about this issue has been proved by the amount which has been written about it over the years.

Around the middle of the 1950s, the increase in demand for education and concomitant economic growth meant that equality of opportunity became an aim of all governments, including very right-wing ones. The problem, however, was how to establish the means whereby this aim could be achieved. It is a case where two totally different solutions immediately spring to mind, both based on sound argument.

It is possible to argue that by putting children in the same educational mould for as long as possible, one will come near to achieving the desired aim. By not letting them choose options and specializations too early, the situation is avoided where weaker children, who are more likely to be those from modest backgrounds, are put from the beginning in lower streams where they make little real progress. The argument is that by abolishing selection and streaming – that is, by removing, in theory at least, differential treatment of children – no inequalities between them will be created.

The opposing argument, however, is that by introducing streaming, each child is given the opportunity of finding his or her own level. Many children of modest backgrounds would be alienated by being forced to follow an academic curriculum. Conversely, they would be more likely to make progress if they could follow from early on a curriculum more in keeping with their expectations.[17]

A counter-argument could be found for each of these arguments, which are simply given in outline here. Those in favour of streaming have always stressed (not without some justification, it would seem) that teaching the same subjects to all children would make classes difficult to manage, and would force a mainstream curriculum on children whose minds work differently; it would simply be storing up a whole range of problems. The defects of this approach would be even worse if it were carried to its logical conclusion and, to smooth out differences, grading, punishments, and rewards were abolished. The non-streamers replied that differential treatment would simply condemn children from modest backgrounds to the lower streams; increases in educational opportunity would for them simply mean being shunted into second-rate education. From the mid-1960s the non-streaming argument won the day, but the consequences of this policy were so disastrous that the wind is now blowing in the other direction.

The example of education is interesting from the viewpoint which concerns us here: a single objective can apparently be achieved in two different, even totally opposite, ways. Nobody can claim that the first method is unquestionably better than the second, or the second better than the first. The point is that it is because of the impossibility of deciding between them that the two viewpoints arose. For, as Aristotle stressed, when a question cannot be decided in a demonstrative way, resort can be had to the dialectical method. He also made it clear that this method is inevitably based on opposing positions to which it allows the means of expression.

In a situation of this kind, support for one or the other of these positions often comes about through beliefs and convictions which are tangential to the actual question. This is what has happened in education. 'Left-wingers' have made up the majority of the non-streamers – at least until the consequences of this approach became apparent – and 'right-wingers' formed the majority of the opposing camp. The former tend to believe, though in differing degrees, that social differentiation and distinctions are incompatible with human dignity. In a general sense, equality is for them a value which is more unconditional than for right-wingers. On the other hand, the latter often urge that equality cannot be bought whatever the price.

In any case, it is clearly the very nature of the problem and the ambiguity of its 'solutions' which have given rise to a dialectical process (in the Aristotelian sense) involving position and disposition effects. There is no doubt that this process has shown that it has the virtues which Aristotle attributed to it. It seems that today we are better able to see both the complexity of the effects created by the two kinds of 'solution' and the impossibility of carrying equality of opportunity beyond certain limits.

To illustrate the fourth example – 'one does not know that one does not know and thinks that one knows' – I will draw from the corpus of the experimental psychology of knowledge, as I did in chapter 4 in initiating a discussion on magic. It is a valuable source of information and thinking on the theory of ideologies. The experiment to which I will refer is of the same kind as those I have already used; what it tells us, however, is different, even though it might appear at first sight quite similar in spirit and presentation.[18]

It is another case in which psychologists put an apparently innocent statistical question to a sample of people who had a reasonable educational level without being skilled in mathematics or statistics. As in the previous case, instead of asking the question in an abstract or artificial way (they could have used, for example, the 'heads or tails' approach), they made the question an everyday one about the statistical distribution of births. The question was more or less as follows:

> Suppose there are two maternity hospitals, one large and one small. In the large one, there are on average fifty births a day, and in the small one, about fifteen. On certain days in both hospitals, more boys are born than girls. Do you think that days when out of ten births there are six or more boys born but only four or less girls born will, over a period of several months, occur more often in the large or in the small hospital? Or will the number be roughly equal in both hospitals?

A reader whose cognitive dispositions are perhaps similar to those of the people asked might be tempted to pause and answer this question.

In any event we can learn much from the range of answers given: about half of the group said that the event in question (six or more boys out of ten births) would occur as often in the large hospital as in the small one, the other half was more or less roughly divided – that is, a quarter of the whole group thought it would happen more often in the large hospital and a quarter chose the small hospital.

This breakdown offers ample evidence that, contrary to what Feyerabend and Habermas have suggested, certain questions ought not to be asked of the whole populace. The correct answer is the last one – it is in the small hospital that the event in question (six or more boys in ten births) will happen most often over a period of several months. This however was the answer of only a quarter of the sample.

I find this experiment fascinating because it shows that the response group saw the question as simple, whereas in fact it is relatively complex. It is an example of what we said – the people answering the question did not know that they did not know. They were fooled by the apparently innocent nature of the question, which at first sight seems to be no different from one to which an intuitive answer can be given, such as whether an order of births BBBGGG (B for a boy, G for a girl) is more common than BGGBGB.

It is clear that those who gave one of the two wrong answers did not realize the complexity of the question, though this might have been the case with those who gave the right answer – many of them may have done so by chance. This could only have been checked by asking them how they arrived at their answer – something the psychologists did not do. What this experiment shows particularly is that it is impossible in some cases to have a clear awareness of the *complexity* of a question if one does not know the answer. It is as if the complexity of a question is apparent only in retrospect, when details of the answer are known.

In the example, the question is in fact complex. If we assume that in the small maternity hospital there are *exactly* fifteen births every day (we are already simplifying the question, which said that the *average* was fifteen births a day), we must then determine the frequency of days when out of these fifteen births nine or more are boys. The question can be put differently: assume a particular order of the fifteen births, for example

BGBBGGGBBGGBGGG

How likely is such a sequence? Obviously there is one chance in two that the first birth will be, as here, a boy. Similarly there is one chance in two that the second birth will be, as here, a girl. There is therefore one chance in four that the first birth will be a boy and the second a girl, since for two births there are four possible outcomes: BB, BG, GB, and GG. Similarly, with three births there are eight equally possible patterns, so that there is a one in eight chance of BGB, which starts our sequence. For BGBB there is a one in sixteen chance, and one in thirty-two for BGBBG. A particular sequence of n elements has a one in $1/2^n$ chances; if n equals 5, then $1/2^n$ equals $1/32$.

For a sequence of fifteen elements as in our example of the births on one day in the small maternity hospital, there is one chance in 32,768 ($1/2^{15}$). The same would be true of a different sequence of fifteen elements, for example

GBBBBGGBBGBGBBB

How many possible sequences of this length are there? Obviously 2^{15}, since each of the elements can be either B or G. This follows, because the number of possible sequences must equal 2^{15} if the chance of each appearing is $1/2^{15}$.

However, in the first of our sequences it will be noticed that less than 60 per cent of births are boys, whereas in the second one, it is more than 60 per cent. The initial problem, therefore, is to decide how many of these 2^{15} sequences will have 60 per cent or more boys. It would take an enormously long time to check directly, since the number of sequences is considerable. The task would be even more impracticable in the case of the large maternity hospital since with fifty births a day, the total number of possible sequences is 2^{50} or $1,125,809,906,842,624$.

The question in the experiment therefore boils down to asking if the proportion of sequences where there are 60 per cent or more of Bs is greater, smaller, or the same in the case of sequences of fifteen elements as compared to those of fifty elements.

Fortunately, we do not have to go through each sequence to answer the question, and it can be shown that in the small hospital the proportion of days when births will be more than 60 per cent boys is

$$\sum_{k=9}^{15} \frac{15!}{k! \, (15-k)!} \left(\frac{1}{2}\right)^{15}$$

The term 15! ['15 factorial'] is the product of the fifteen whole numbers between one and fifteen inclusive. On a more general level, k! ['k factorial'] is the product of all whole numbers between one and k inclusive. In the large hospital, the proportion is

$$\sum_{k=9}^{50} \frac{50!}{k! \, (50-k)!} \left(\frac{1}{2}\right)^{50}$$

The question is then which of these two quantities is the greater. The calculations show that the first (0.3036) is larger than the second (0.1013), and so it is in the smaller hospital that births of 60 per cent or more boys in a day will happen more often. Moreover, as the figures show, this occurrence will be three times more frequent in the small hospital than the large one. The very complexity of the formulae used show the complexity of the question; but it was only by setting them up that one could see this complexity.

There are of course other methods, less direct and of a heuristic nature, of answering the question, and some of the people who gave the correct answer may have applied them. The gender of births can be compared with a game of heads and tails, played fifteen times in the small maternity hospital and fifty times in the large one. Here the question comes down to asking whether throwing heads six or more times in ten is more likely in a short game than in a long game. An easier way to the answer would be to take an extreme case and compare a very short game of, say, four throws with a very long one of, say, a thousand. Here the answer is intuitively apparent, since it is obvious that four throws of heads are very likely in the short game, whereas it is extremely unlikely that all the thousand throws would be heads. This extreme case suggests that one is more likely to diverge from the probable result (heads and tails appearing in roughly the same proportions) in a short game than in a long game.

This gives a hint of the correct answer in the case of the hospitals – the distribution of births between boys and girls is more likely to diverge from the average in the small hospital than in the large one. However, the application of this heuristic process involves moving away from the example given and thinking of an extreme case – what would happen in a *very* short game and in a *very* long game. However, this heuristic process is likely to be invoked only if one is aware of the complexity of the question before one tries to answer it. Another, more simple, method of proceeding would be to bring to bear on the question the inkling which we get from knowledge of opinion polls. We are well aware that a sample of 2,000 people gives more accurate results than one of only a hundred, and this awareness could be applied to other questions.

It is now clear why the maternity hospitals experiment gave such strange results. The sample group was quite willing to answer the question, but 75 per cent of them gave the wrong answer: the question seemed simple to them and they were aware of its complexity only when they knew the answer. There can be no simpler or easier game than heads and tails, but this can lead one to think that questions which seem like a game of heads and tails are also very straightforward.

The experiment which I have recounted is of course rather artificial; but it is a case in point which I regard as basic to the analysis of ideologies, since it is quite frequent in social life for the complexity of a problem to be apparent only when analysis of the problem has revealed it. This condition is, however, not sufficient in itself – the analysis must also have been perceived and have spread beyond 'specialist circles'.

This case in point is illustrated by some of the examples which I have looked at in the first part of this chapter. The reason why it was long thought that the coming of machines caused unemployment was, as I have said, because of a perspective effect – people who have lost their jobs because their firm has decided to modernize are very likely to regard machines as destroyers of jobs.

However, the strength of this conviction is not only an example of these perspective effects. It is also brought on because the effects of mechanization on jobs are complex: the best method of grasping this complexity is to look at the theories of economists who have studied the matter. Similarly, the best way to become aware of the question put by the psychologists in our example is to master the intricacies of binomial theory.

People who have lost their jobs will quite rightly think that they are *in a position* to conclude that mechanization destroys jobs. Moreover, they will find it difficult to believe that a causal link which they think is empirically proved at the personal level can be turned on its head at the general level. For this, they would need to be aware of the *complexity* of the link between mechanization and jobs, which would assume a familiarity with analyses which are themselves relatively complex. The slave in *Menon* may have found out by himself how long the diagonal of a square is, but it has to be recognized that Socrates did help him a bit.

The example of the link between mechanization and jobs leads me into a final case in point which I would like to deal with, and which illustrates two kinds of attitude. Workers who like their jobs are subject to a perspective effect; moreover, they are unlikely to see the complexity of the link between mechanization and unemployment – they do not know that they do not know and they are convinced that they do know. Those who are not concerned by questions of unemployment and are therefore not subject to perspective effects may not have any clear thoughts on the matter. Either they will know that they do not know, or they will not know that they do not know. In the second case, however, there is no reason to think that they are convinced that they know.

We see that the *nature* of the problem (here, the link between mechanization and unemployment) does not in itself lead *all* social actors to believe they have the answer. This belief will be more apparent among those who, having lost their job, are particularly prey to the perspective effect I have been describing. In other cases, the very nature of the problem leads most social actors to think they have the answer. The psychologists' question on the maternity hospitals was a trap: it was apparently simple, yet in reality extremely complex. It was not however the very nature of the problem which suggested the answers.

There are questions, however, which not only conceal their complexity but also suggest possible answers. I would like to illustrate this by an example which brings us back to the question of social inequality. It has long been regarded as obvious that equality of educational opportunities leads to an equality of what Max Weber called *opportunities in life*. The reason is, firstly, that the causal relationship can in this case be based on direct social observation – those who have a high number of educational qualifications are more successful in general than those who can merely read and write; secondly, that this relationship seems based on apparently unexceptionable logic which can be expressed as follows:

1 people's level of education has a considerable bearing on their social status – the higher the level, the higher their social position, at least on average;
2 therefore, differences in social position are explicable to a great extent by differences in educational achievement;
3 if educational achievement becomes less a function of social background, in other words if there is a democratization of education,
4 there will be less of a correlation between people's social position and their social background. Therefore, equality of opportunity in education will lead to equality of opportunity in life – in other words, greater social mobility, or a less strong social tradition.

We see immediately that this example is different from the previous one. The nature of the problem posed by the psychologists was such that people found it easy to regard it as a simple problem which amounted to a straightforward application of the law of large numbers. They did not know that they did not know, but they thought they knew. They had correctly identified the nature of the problem, but they were not aware of its complexity, and that is why they answered so readily. If, however, the psychologists had attempted to measure the degree of certainty with which they answered (which they did not do), they would no doubt have seen how uncertain people were, since the question in no way calls for one answer rather than another.

This is not so in the present example. The question about the effect of the democratization of education on social tradition can easily be perceived as a simple one. Moreover, it suggests immediately a particular answer – yes, the one does have a bearing on the other, and the outcome is a weakening of social tradition. This is so because the question immediately calls into play both the social perceptions I have mentioned and the argument I have outlined. The person who was asked the question would very likely not only reply without *difficulty* but also reply with *conviction*. Here, it is not just a question of thinking that one knows, but of being *convinced* that one knows.

At the same time, one is likely to miss the complexity of the question: one is convinced that one knows, and one does not know that one does not know. Here again, as with the previous example, awareness of the complexity of the question can appear only with the answer itself. Moreover, it is a complex question, even if it is likely to be seen as simple.

I have dealt with this question elsewhere[19] and I do not want to go over it again: I will simply give my conclusions and the main thrust of the analysis. My conclusion is in the form of a theorem: in general terms, greater educational opportunity does not bring about greater social mobility. In other words, even if one assumes that level of education has an important bearing on social status, it is quite possible to observe, in a society, a *weakening* of the link between social background and educational achievement, and a *persistence* of the link between social background and social status.

It is likely that this conclusion will appear paradoxical; but it would be paradoxical only if the opposite statement were itself seen as self-evident, which is not the case here. Moreover, this paradoxical conclusion is in keeping with the facts: it is true that in most Western countries there has been in recent decades not only a gradual growth of educational opportunity but also no real change in social mobility. By this, I do not mean that social mobility is insignificant: on the contrary, it is considerable, as shown by the fact that in many Western societies, it is rather more likely that those born in the upper class will leave it than stay in it. There is no change only in the sense that while links between social background and social status are weak, they appear to be stable over time.

It seems, therefore, that the theorem which I have set out is more consonant with the facts than one stating the contrary. However, it is not surprising that these facts have been no great help in destroying the received idea which is contradicted by the theorem; it has after all considerable intrinsic strength, for the reasons I have stated. Moreover, the facts to which I refer are complex; in effect, they are known only to specialists, and are not likely to be meaningful to other groups.

To set out the theorem we need, we have to find a way of showing individual behaviour patterns which produce the figures shown in those statistics on social mobility which indicate social background and present social status. This model assumes:

1 that people have varying levels of academic achievement and that social background has a bearing on the level likely to be reached;
2 that families, and children themselves, bear this level of achievement in mind when they make choices throughout their educational career;
3 that when they make these choices, they also bear in mind the family's social position;
4 that, over time, this influence of the family's social position is progressively declining (which leads to a progressive democratization of educational opportunity);
5 that academic achievement is a kind of priority ticket for a socio-professional status in the jobs market. Therefore academic achievement does play an important part in acquiring this status.

A close look at these statements shows that they are all very commonplace. They merely reproduce in an abstract way observations which are straightforward and which are confirmed by all research. When these five statements are recast to make a model – that is, a deductive mechanism, the consequences of which can be drawn automatically – it can be asked all kinds of questions, and particularly the question which interests us here, about social mobility over a period of time. The answer is the one I have mentioned – under general conditions, there is no distinct change over time in the pattern of mobility. Any changes are slight, erratic, and not necessarily in the same direction. However, the model assumes in its fourth proposition a reduction over time in inequality of educational opportunity, and in its fifth proposition that educational attainment plays a decisive role in determining social status. The model therefore clearly shows that the received idea with which we started is a false idea.

Parenthetically, we can say that the argument that there has been a progressive reduction in educational inequality in Western societies has not gone unchallenged.[20] It is true that this reduction can remain hidden in the short term, but it is certainly observable in the long term. In any case this discussion has only a marginal importance for the question we are looking at – whether the reduction in educational inequality, *assuming* that it in fact happens, is likely to increase social mobility.

The model gives an unequivocal answer to this question: contrary to what one might expect, greater educational opportunity does not, under general conditions, bring greater social mobility. Moreover the paradox is not totally absurd: a rough summary of a host of complex effects which only a model can illuminate suggests that it is because greater educational opportunity inevitably brings what economists call congestion effects – there is a tendency for educational qualifications to lose value simply because they are more common. There is no need here to resort to what Popper calls conspiracy theory and to refer to the invisible hand of a ruling class that wants to keep its position. All we need do is to state the obvious by saying that a priority ticket loses its effectiveness when it is given out to many people.

The important point is that the falseness of the received idea that education is a powerful lever to equalize opportunities in life is perceived only when one becomes aware of the complexity of the elementary mechanisms linking these two phenomena. This complexity is itself revealed only when it is illuminated by analysis. Moreover, the analysis has itself to be socially visible.

Here, then, is a case in point similar to the one I have often evoked – the relationship between mechanization and unemployment. The difference is that the received idea is often the result, in this case, of a perspective effect to which certain people are directly exposed. In the instant case, the received idea stands out because of its significant *intrinsic strength*.

I do not claim in this chapter to have examined fully the questions which I have raised in it. Types of effect other than the ones I have looked at could of course be mentioned; but I think I have done enough to signal my intention, which is to show that certain questions are such that when they are looked at by people with certain positions and certain dispositions, they are very likely to lead to received ideas without these being attributable to perversion, blindness, passion, or any other form of irrationality.

At the same time, I think I have opened up certain avenues for research; but even though the main thrusts are clear, I admit that the details remain to be filled in. This can only be done, I think, if the barriers which the division of labour has unfortunately built between disciplines such as philosophy, psychology, and sociology can be broken down.

7

Ideology and communication

As I indicated in chapter 4, it is only in very specific conditions that a theory, whether scientific, exegetical, or of any other kind, is perceived by social actors as a white box, in other words as a collection of totally clear statements. For theologians, the works of Hans Küng are no doubt crystal clear, but they are not for many people who can nevertheless agree with particular conclusions in them. Similarly, the theory of relativity is really only clear to physicists, but that does not stop most people being prepared to accept that it is true.

This second example presents no problem – since we cannot be at the same time physicists, chemists, biologists, doctors, or agronomists, we are prepared to trust specialists on a range of matters and to regard as true all kinds of statements which we cannot submit to critical analysis because we lack the time and the necessary cognitive skills. This straightforward example does not interest us directly regarding our restricted theory of ideology, because these black-box effects taken from the field of natural sciences seem to be of limited scope.

The position is different when we move either to the area of the social sciences or to theories which are not *stricto sensu* scientific – for example, exegetical theories. Here, it often happens that we are interested in a theory in so far as it seems to be in accordance with certain position and disposition effects to which we are in the nature of things subjected, and that precisely because of this we subscribe to it.

Thus, for example people whose jobs involve them in development policy will pay particular attention to theories of development put forward by economists. If they are not economists, however, these theories are likely to be black boxes as far as they are concerned. They will therefore be led to subscribe to a particular theory less because they have checked its truth for themselves than because it is propounded by a reputable economist.

The characteristic of a theory, whatever it is, is that it has two dimensions which do not necessarily have to be in accordance with each other. As Pareto said, a theory can be true without being useful, and useful without being true. There are also theories which are both true and useful, and theories which are neither. However, rather than talking about the usefulness of a theory and thereby adopting an instrumental point of view, I prefer to take a more general point of view and speak about its *interest*, in the intellectual and not the utilitarian sense of the word. If a theory can be true or false, it can also seem interesting or uninteresting to us, without its interest being necessarily linked to its validity or limited to its utility. More precisely, when we require of a theory which we find interesting that it be true, we are attributing these two characteristics to it by different means. We will usually be relying on the authority principle to accept the truth of a particular theory; but it is of our own accord that we find it interesting or not. We are quite prepared to commit ourselves to somebody else's opinion in the matter of the truth of a particular theory, but when it comes to its interest we rely on ourselves.

Let us imagine for a moment a theory which is false or dubious. Let us assume that this theory has been propounded by a group of researchers who are scientifically authoritative, that it is regarded as a black box by a particular group of people, and that by a position or disposition effect, this group finds the theory interesting. It is likely that the theory will be regarded as true by the group in question.

Another effect is also likely to be present in this case. It is the one discussed at length at the end of the previous chapter, namely that very often, one is unaware of the complexity of a problem so long as one does not know the answer to it in any detail. It is clear that people who regard a theory as a black box are likely not to be aware of the complexity of the problem which the theory is trying to solve, and for this reason also, will tend in certain cases to accept readily its conclusions.

To summarize, belief in false ideas often comes from a readily understandable combination of communication effects and situation effects.

It is not difficult to imagine examples in which a theory, by its very nature, is likely to attract the attention and arouse the interest of certain people. Further, when this interest is the result of a coincidence between a particular feature of the theory and a particular situation effect characteristic of a group, there is likely to arise what Durkheim called a 'collective belief'.

Let us cite a most commonplace example: a theory can arouse the interest of social actors if they think it may help in fulfilling their social role. I have already referred to this case in point: the official of the World Bank who has to implement a development policy in Guatemala will naturally be interested in economic theories of development; but unless this official is an economic theorist temporarily attached to the Bank, he or she will not have the time to look at such theories in detail, nor the necessary skill to evaluate them in depth. The official will treat them therefore, at least in part, as a black box; and will tend to assess their quality according to who has propounded them, almost like somebody who buys a case of Bordeaux wine by mail order or a washing machine on the strength of the maker's name. The conclusion is that it is likely that the theory of the maker's name. The conclusion is that it is likely that the theory will *interest* the Bank official if the person propounding it is reputable, because a decision can then be based on something 'objective'.

Similarly, to return to an example I referred to earlier, bankers in the inter-war period were quite prepared, as Keynes notes with irony, to rely on Keynesianism. Whatever their reservations about him, he did at least offer them a theoretical framework to put some degree of order into a situation which was new, confused, and elusive, in that the New Deal had begun to break down the tradition of state non-intervention in the economy.

A theory can therefore interest social actors by offering a cognitive framework to fulfil a role more easily; but the use made of the theory may be only remotely connected with the use which an engineer makes of a particular theory in physics. A theory in physics is not normally useful to an engineer if it is wrong. Conversely, an economic theory can easily help the task of a politician even if it is dubious or wrong.

A theory may be of *interest* to social actors not only because it offers a cognitive basis for action, but also because it helps solve ethical or deontological problems which are encountered in the normal course of fulfilling the actors' role. On the more general level, it may be of interest because it leads actors, in their view, to a better definition of the limits of their role, of the aims which can legitimately be achieved within this role, and of the means used to achieve them.

Several examples of this can be given. The significant rise in educational demand at the end of the 1950s and concomitant changes in the social composition of groups taking up education led to what is usually called an 'education crisis'. This crisis was exacerbated by the fact that to cope with it, methods of recruiting teachers were introduced which consisted to a large extent of improvisation, where teachers were appointed who were less qualified than their predecessors. Moreover, to allow educational establishments to cater for increased demand, reforms were introduced without sufficient thought being given to their implications. The result was that the traditional image of the teacher became less distinct: teachers no longer knew what was expected of them, what aims they should try to achieve, or what their rights and duties were.

The result was that certain pedagogical or psychological theories aroused considerable interest among teachers: on the basis of laboratory research and method analysis, they suggested ways of eradicating academic failure, of *stimulating* the minds of children, of holding their attention without coercion, of imparting knowledge in a happy and relaxed atmosphere. These theories attracted experienced teachers, who perhaps thought that traditional teaching methods were no longer suited to new generations of children. However, they were also of immediate interest to younger, less qualified teachers: because their role was now defined less as imparting knowledge than as opening children's minds to the world around them, having undeveloped skills was less important. The psychological and pedagogical theories in question not only gave them a definition of their role which was scientifically based, but in addition confirmed them in their belief that they were perfectly able to fulfil this role.

In the same way, when opinion about how to tackle crime and criminals is in flux, those social actors whose role obliges them to take a position will usually pay a great deal of attention to philosophical or sociological theories on crime and justice. The reason is that such theories at the same time give them a clearer perception of the 'meaning' of their role, and help them to fulfil it, by offering 'scientifically' based cognitive and ethical principles. Foucault has adequately demonstrated[1] the considerable interest in the many criminological and penological theories propounded from the middle of the eighteenth century onwards in response to the demand created by social developments.

The common characteristic of all these examples is that they involve theories of interest to people belonging to *specific* groups – specific because easily identifiable. In the examples up to now, the groups are defined by the social role played by their members. A specific group, however, can be identified by many other criteria. Certain groups, for example, can be defined by the social position of their members, a criterion which fits in with the idea of role but of which the meaning is broader. The group constituted by businessmen is clearly a specific group whose boundaries may be clear, but it is less easily definable by role than the groups cited in the previous examples. Despite this, a specific group of this kind can also, because of the social position of its members, be attracted by certain theories – all that is needed is for the theory to confirm certain common values held by the group members because of their common social position.

To illustrate this, I will take the example of a theory (already referred to) which is not scientific but exegetical, in order to underline the fact that the communication effects which we are discussing in this chapter can be grafted on to theories which vary in nature.

Erasmus, in his book *The Praise of Folly*, one of the most influential and widely read in Western history, undertakes among other things an exegesis of certain aspects of the Bible. This exegesis, however, is presented in the form of a tract against priests, monks, and the representatives of established religion in general, which is no doubt why it was so widely read. This cannot however be the only reason why it had the influence it did. All it could do was to make more people read it and direct their attention to the central message; at the same time, presenting it as a tract helped to conceal its exegetical nature and fend off the wrath of the Church.

Erasmus' message was that the glory of God is better served by the honest and effective management of one's worldly affairs than by good works or submission to the Church: internal piety is better than ostentatious piety. One should pursue one's vocation in this world rather than trying to secure a place in the next one by deference to priests and monks who mouth incomprehensible gibberish.

This clever message found instant acceptance, and Erasmus' work attracted immediate attention in commercial quarters.[2] The increasing numbers of businessmen, traders, and financiers in early sixteenth-century Europe – in the north particularly, but also in southern Germany and northern Italy – helped to make Erasmus a success. This was not from interest – a utilitarian interpretation would be inappropriate in this case – but simply because Erasmus was offering a vision of the world which could not fail to please them. The current Catholic ideology was hostile to business: it had a preference for the poor and the noble, who were both part of God's scheme, rather than for the bourgeois ('It is easier for a camel to pass through the eye of a needle than for a rich man to enter the Kingdom of Heaven'), whose place in the worldly scheme of things was far from clear.[3] Moreover, earning money, however honestly, and changing one's social condition – that is, rising above the common herd but without achieving noble state – was regarded as suspect by the Church. All trading and banking activities, which were expanding rapidly, had always been seen as rather sinful by Catholic ideology and would continue to be so regarded for a long time afterwards.

Erasmus' message was therefore received favourably by the business world: not only did it seem to them 'modern' in that it accorded with changed social conditions, but it also fitted in with what businessmen thought – that their money was well earned, and that above all the success of their business was proof that it catered for a demand and was being conducted efficiently. Erasmus was suggesting for the first time that this success was deserved, that it was not contrary to God's glory and that perhaps the best way to serve God was to fulfil effectively one's role in this world. It is not therefore surprising that Protestantism made easy inroads into the mercantilist bourgeoisie, and that a link between Protestantism and Capitalism was established which has been the subject of so much study by sociologists. Many of Erasmus' themes were of course taken up by Luther (who criticized 'good works') and by other reformers.

The important thing from my present point of view is that Erasmus' exegetical theory was successful because it immediately attracted the attention and aroused the interest of a *specific* group – that of business-men. Moreover, they subscribed to Erasmus' message all the more strongly because, although it was published as a tract on Madness, its exegetical nature was clear: into the mouth of Madness were put the words of Authority – the undisputed authority of the Bible.

The example of Erasmus, however, suggests a third case in point, distinct from the second one – the case in which specific groups which subscribe to the theory are groups of *intellectuals*. It is very often surprising how conformist intellectuals are, and how they seem to subscribe to modish theories or to rather fragile systems of ideas. In this context, Julien Benda spoke of 'la trahison des clercs', and this phrase has been evoked many times. Milton Friedman offered a simple explanation of this phenomenon: to paraphrase Friedman, bankers have to be careful about fashionable ideas, since if the latter are wrong and the bankers apply them, they have to suffer the consequences. Conversely, the intellectual who strongly asserts a false idea will only rarely suffer the effects.

My view is that an alternative explanation of this phenomenon is possible. Very often, because of the role they play, intellectuals regard themselves as the guardians of certain values or certain traditions of thought. The appearance of a theory which seems to give fresh support to a particular value or tradition is likely to be endorsed by specific groups of intellectuals who subscribe to this value or tradition.

I will give a few examples of this case in point, which is important because although the *specific* groups through which certain theories become current may well vary and correspond to all kinds of social positions, these are often groups of intellectuals. In other words groups of people whose function is to work with ideas.

The first example is that of Eric Voegelin, who in 1952 published *The New Science of Politics*.[4] This book had a significant impact in the United States and was the subject of considerable discussion in circles whose interest in it is on the surface rather surprising. Voegelin's book begins with a strong attack on positivism: he argues that it is distorting and 'destroying' contemporary political thought, by getting it to elevate *method* to the status of an absolute value and to forget the relevance of its subject matter, with the result that it tends to accumulate often trivial facts and to interpret important facts wrongly. He argues that, generally, contemporary political science, in moving away from all reference to values, has paid over the odds to try to reach the inaccessible goal of objectivity.

Voegelin's view is that Max Weber is responsible for this emphasis on positivism, in that he took too seriously Hume's idea that judgements of fact, which alone are amenable to scientific enquiry, must be carefully distinguished from value judgements. The argument is that because Weber adhered to this principle, the source of inspiration represented by Greek and Christian political thought became taboo. The rest of Voegelin's book shows the path which 'new political science' should follow; and at the same time, extending his attack on positivism, he endeavours to show that it is in fact the last manifestation of something deeper and longer established – 'modernity'. This, he says, can be traced right back to the efforts of theologians who, in trying to make transcendence intelligible, started a process of thought which led to a situation in which the transcendental could only be reduced to the immanent, and in the end became out and out secular. It is the gnostic movement, therefore, which, the argument goes, is responsible for the appearance of modernity, and for the neglect of transcendence and, in the end, of values.

Voegelin argues that the gnostic movement began with the work of Joachim of Flora, who said that history should be interpreted in the light of the dogma of the Trinity: 'In his speculation the history of mankind had three periods corresponding to the three persons of the Trinity. The first period of the world was the age of the Father; with the appearance of Christ began the age of the Son [which] will be followed by a third age of the Spirit', which Joachim thought would dawn around AD 1260. He was thus showing the way to all the millenialisms and philosophies of history. Not only were the Hegelian triad and the Marxian triad direct descendants of Joachim's gnosticism, but so was Hitler's Third Reich.

It is easy to see why Voegelin's speculations attracted so much attention and were the object of so much comment. As Coser points out,[5] it was even frequently chosen as the theme of conferences by political science associations in the United States. How was it that this book was taken so seriously, when it was really a work of theology rather than political science, and when it was regarded as nothing short of curious by political scientists and political philosophers whose intellectual values it impugned? Coser is perhaps correct in attributing the success of the book to what can be called a *ricochet effect*. Voegelin had left Austria to escape the Nazis: he became Professor at the University of Louisiana, and then at the University of Alabama. By their very nature, the themes of his teaching and research in these universities were such that they attracted the attention of groups who were conservative in politics and fundamentalist in religious matters – groups which were more common in the southern United States than in the North. In this way, Voegelin's though aroused first of all the *interest* of a specific group, which partly explains why it was regarded as an important development in seminaries and Faculties of Theology in the South, but also in the North. It gave new intellectual impetus to discussions on modernity, and allowed a link to be established between certain ancient theological deviations and modern philosophical movements widely held to be misguided (such as Marxism), or even between recent historical convulsions (Nazism) and the history of theology. Voegelin's thought therefore again provided theology with an historical dimension, at the same time as giving theologians philosophical tools and a framework for systematic thought which were of direct use to them. In a word, it re-established a direct link between theology and the modern world. This is why it was quickly endorsed by all those whose function made them responsible for showing the importance of Christian tradition and for adapting this tradition to the modern world. Voegelin's thought was therefore taken up by a specific group which operated at the national level.

From then on there developed the ricochet effect which I mentioned earlier. Political scientists, and all those whose function was to analyse political phenomena in a scientific way, could no longer ignore *The New Science of Politics* because *everyone* was talking about it, and also because they were attacked by the book. Of course, conferences on Voegelin's theses usually came to a negative conclusion, but they merely served to disseminate his thought.

I will return later to these ricochet effects, but what I want to stress is that the extensive reception accorded to Voegelin was mainly because his book was seen as being of immediate interest to theologians as a group, since it coincided with their basic role, and with the dispositions normally attaching to this role. However, it is not surprising that the primary consideration of this group was not to subject Voegelin's thought to detailed critical analysis – not only were theologians apt to accept his conclusions but also the book was for them, at least in part, a black box, in that in general they had not the same knowledge of Hume, Weber, or the methods, findings, and theories of modern political science and philosophy which Voegelin was attacking.

An idea or a theory can therefore become influential when, for perfectly understandable reasons, it attracts the positive attention of *specific* groups of *intellectuals*. Their favourable attitude often arises from a coincidence between the theory, and dispositions and role specifics which characterize the group. To show that this case in point is typical, I will refer briefly to a second example, where the specific intellectual group responsible for the process of dissemination is more easily identified.

This second example is that of Karl Polanyi's *The Great Transformation*,[6] which was also a widely discussed and translated book, and one which gave rise to much research. There was even a voluminous doctoral thesis on it just after it was published in 1944; and even today it inspires academic comment and research. In other words, it has survived on the academic scene for more than forty years, which does not happen often – few books from the immediate post-war era have become 'classics'.[7]

The main argument of Polanyi's book is that market capitalism has failed. Having read widely in economic history, the history of economic ideas, and anthropology, he tried to show that it is possible to distinguish in history three main forms of organization of exchanges: the *reciprocal* economy, as in the famous Kula trade of the Trobriand Islands; the *redistributive* economy, particularly important in the Roman Empire, but also in modern socialist systems; and the *market* economy.

The reciprocal economy is based on two or more well-defined groups whose relationship is characterized by reciprocal gifts and ritual ceremonies. The redistributive economy tends to lead to bureaucracy, where not only domestic redistribution but also imports and exports are taken over by the government. Polanyi argues that these two traditional ways of organizing exchanges reinforce the feeling of solidarity and community:

> exchange, the most precarious of human ties, spread into the economy when it could be made to serve the validation of the community. In effect, economic transactions became possible when they could be made gainless. The peril to solidarity involved in making selfish gain at the expense of the food of one's brother had first to be removed by eliminating the invidious element inherent in such exchanges. This was achieved through the declaration of equivalences in the name of the representative of the godhead itself.[8]

The big turning-point came in the eighteenth century with the market economy. I will not go into detail on the reason for this change, which Polanyi attributes both to specific events in British political history (he stresses the significance of the Speenhamland system) and to the development of ideas, particularly in Britain, towards an 'individualist' and mechanistic view of society: it is therefore not seen as inevitable, but as a combination of chance events. Moreover, history showed that it was possible to organize exchange in other ways. A final point was that the whole thing failed when societies based on the market economy not only lost their sense of community and solidarity by reducing individuals to a mere *Homo œconomicus*, but also developed – the 'great transformation' – into something which according to Polanyi contradicted the principles of liberal thought: far from there being an 'invisible hand', the market economy now made the state more powerful and led to a finely meshed net of regulations and constraints in which the autonomy of the individual was increasingly caught.

I will not dwell on the obvious counter-arguments – that the 'invisible hand' theory does not postulate a withering away of the state, since in a complex market economy, the state, as Locke clearly saw, has a significant part in defining and regulating the rules of the game: as this becomes more complex, there is a more or less inevitable increase in the role and power of the state. Moreover, the state can make the rules stricter only after it discovers whether or not they are being obeyed: the onerous and complex nature of this process tends to increase as the market economy becomes more complex. In this way the main argument of *The Great Transformation* is fundamentally flawed. The strengthening of the state's role in liberal societies does not prove that liberalism is a failure or is unviable.

Furthermore, on another point which Polanyi stresses, it is doubtful whether exchanges in reciprocal and redistributive economies always have a religious significance and are always subordinate to a collective 'will' to affirm group solidarity.

The important point from my own perspective, however, is that Polanyi's theory was so immediately successful in many intellectual circles mainly because it sustained a view, which was and still is widely held, that market societies crush and maim individuals, reducing them to an isolated state by severing their links with the *community*. This isolation is all the more intolerable because societies based on a market economy ignore all other values and place the highest value on individuals, thus putting them in a state of moral confusion while professing to revere them.

These commonplace statements, which explain the later success of Marcuse and the writers of the Frankfurt school, were touched on by Polanyi in a discreet and very indirect way. Although his book is a contribution to the philosophy of (economic) history, his arguments are backed up, as I have mentioned, by extensive learning. The intellectual who shares Polanyi's 'feelings' can easily be led to think that the book can be used as a framework of reference and that his analyses can be *extended* in a particular direction. For this reason, the book gave rise to an 'invisible college', more or less permanent and scattered throughout the world, of followers of varying degrees of orthodoxy.

Polanyi's ideas seem not to have been persuasive enough to establish him in the academic world. After temporary posts in the Universities of Oxford and London, he taught for a time at Bennington College and the University of Colombia, but although a doctoral thesis was written on his work at Colombia, he was offered only a junior teaching post there.[9]

Many other instances could be found to illustrate this case in point, where a theory gains currency by being accepted initially in a fairly well-defined group of intellectuals. Althusser's success, for example, can be explained only by realizing that *Reading 'Capital'* was seen in many Marxist-leaning intellectual circles as a book which put the life back into Marxist theory: at a time when it seemed less and less to be a 'final horizon' (in Sartre's memorable phrase), Althusser's book made it again capable of interpreting the modern world.

Similarly, the past and present success of 'dependency theory' is in large part due to the fact that it not only breathed new life into the old Leninist theory of imperialism, but it also led to research in a variety of areas – history, economics, sociology, and political science. I will return in Chapter 9 to this example, which I believe to be very important in analysing ideologies.

We see that the influence of a theory is often determined initially by the fact that it is seen to be *interesting* by one or more specific groups, because of the social position, the social role, and the dispositions of the members. In this case, the theory is likely to be seen as not only interesting, but also *valid*. The reason is, firstly, that authority effects and black-box effects will appear, and secondly, that, even for intellectuals, the first consideration of the groups in question will not be to look critically at the theory to establish its validity. Black-box effects can be present even in the case of groups of intellectuals – the theologians who subscribed to Voegelin's theories were in general not in a position to evaluate them in detail.

Groups of other kinds frequently do not have detailed knowledge of the theories which gain currency through their support. An example is that of Rousseau's *Social Contract*, which, according to historians, was hardly read by anybody when it first appeared.[10] This is not surprising, given the austere, intensive, dry, and difficult nature of the book. Nevertheless, *everybody* was acquainted with its conclusions – that the only legitimate authority was that which came from the 'people', and that authority stemming from tradition could not be legitimate. Moreover, *everybody* knew that these conclusions were based on the authority of science, or, as was said at the time, on *Reason*.

It is quite easy to identify who *everybody* is in this case, since it corresponds to specific groups. As Augustin Cochin has shown,[11] it was lawyers, apothecaries, and members of other 'enlightened' professional groups who, in 1789, tried to implement the ideas of the *Social Contract*, usually without having read the book.

At this point, I will mention a hypothesis which merits closer analysis but which cannot be examined in detail. I have briefly described the method of analysing dissemination processes, and there is an important consequence of these: when a theory is endorsed by one or more specific groups and is regarded, at least partly, by these groups as a black box, very often the conclusions reached are simplified, diluted, or distorted. This is why Marx said – and he probably meant it – that he was 'not a Marxist', because he had many reservations about how his idea later became the Marxist creed. Other examples are the vast difference between Darwinism and the pompous pronouncements of 'social Darwinism', or between Spencer's thought and the political conclusions drawn from it. We can also look briefly at the case of Mannheim, whom I mentioned earlier. He is famous as the author of the proposition that ideas are 'socially determined', which gave rise to a vast amount of writing on the famous 'Mannheim's paradox' – how can we be sure that ideas are socially determined, since Mannheim's theory is itself socially determined? We need only recall what was said in chapter 3, however, to realize that the paradox is there only because Mannheim's thought has been popularized. The very existence of 'Mannheim's paradox' shows the influence of books about his thought. The important point is that these distorted popularizations are the normal consequences of the communication processes by which some theories achieve their authority and influence.

The theories of which I have just given examples are of varying kinds – exegetical, scientific, and, in Polanyi's case, a mixture of the scientific and the interpretive characteristic of the philosophy of history. However, the example of Polanyi brings us to an important point which I have only been able to touch upon in the previous discussion.

In the case of the natural sciences, the normal process of dissemination of a theory is that, initially, it is evaluated by the scientific community – those who, to use my imagery, can analyse it in detail and treat it as a white box. Then, if their evaluation is positive, the theory is likely to reach a wider audience: applied research may well put it to practical use. Moreover, if the theory is thought important enough, it may come to the attention of the 'educated reader' by means of scientific journals aimed at the general public.

The process can be shown in a diagram: the person producing the theory submits it to the scientific community. If it is favourably received, it is considered by mediators who in turn bring it to the attention of specific groups – for example, people who read popular scientific journals or listen to serious radio programmes.

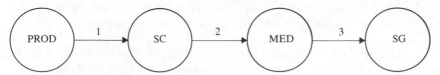

As the first part of this chapter suggests, the dissemination process may be structured differently in the case of theories in the social sciences. A theory may often come to the attention of mediators because it has first been taken on by certain specific groups and the mediators pass it on to other specific groups – for example, the readers of a particular daily newspaper – as in the second diagram.

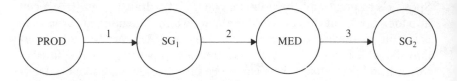

Erasmus' 'exegetical theory' was disseminated in this way. It caught on in business circles, then it was discussed much more widely, and it ended up by interesting and influencing 'groups of learned people' who were engaged in analysing matters of religion.

Of course, Erasmus' theory was not a scientific one, but in the case of theories which are scientific, these are by their very nature open to inspection by the particular scientific community. This is what economists and economic historians did when Polanyi's *The Great Transformation* appeared, and, as I have pointed out, they had reservations about it, though this did not diminish the influence it had. Polanyi's case can be illustrated as in the third diagram.

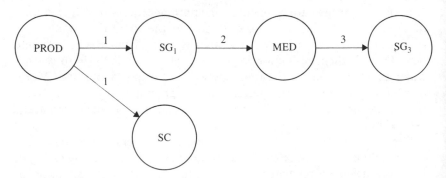

The scientific community declined to disseminate the theory, but it spread through other channels – groups of intellectuals attracted by Polanyi's message brought social confirmation of the significance of his theories and caused them to be disseminated in other groups.

In the second part of this chapter, I would like to take a closer look at the dissemination processes which are characterized by what might be called a *short circuit* of the scientific community (I use 'scientific community' in the sense in which Kuhn uses it). These processes are in fact vital in analysing ideology, because it is in this way that a weak, wrong, or dubious theory can be disseminated and possibly be taken as having the authority of science.[12] These short circuits are however present not just in the field of the social sciences; they can also appear, though less frequently, in the natural sciences.

The most obvious case is that of Lysenkoism, which deserves some attention in that the short-circuit effect which gave it the temporary status of 'truth' in genetics (at least in the Soviet Union) is more subtle than is generally thought. It is certainly not true that it was imposed merely by Stalinist intimidation: people's consciences cannot be brought into line by simple police action. In fact there was only one point where Stalinism imposed its will, and this was the quite normal one of how scientific conferences were organized. In the Soviet Union, these are the responsibility of the state, which provides the money for them and which, through authorized agencies, gives people permission to attend them.

According to Medvedev,[13] the authorities made it impossible for Soviet geneticists to attend conferences outside the Soviet Union and confined all discussion of Lysenko's theories to Soviet citizens. Another point was that conferences on Lysenko's theories were packed with a majority of people from various sciences – agronomists, physiologists, botanists, and the like, whose knowledge of genetics was limited but who outnumbered the real geneticists. These latter made it clear that they thought Lysenko's theory was false; but the others, most of whom had no specific opinion on it, realized that the authorities' view was that Lysenko's theory, inspired by Lamarckian environmentalism, was nearer to Marxism than one which stressed genetic determinism. Any waverers sided with Lysenko who, as an agronomist, hardly gave the appearance of a charlatan.

It may be that some non-geneticists found it difficult to subscribe to Lysenko's theory, though history gives us no hint of this. Obviously people's motives differed, just as their opinions and authoritativeness in debate differed. The result, however, was that conferences came down rather heavily on the side of Lysenko's theories.

The most important point is that as far as the educated public, journalists, and everybody interested in the debate were concerned, these conferences were attended by skilled people – specialists in life sciences. Most outside observers would have found it impossible to distinguish between different positions in the life sciences, and therefore they accepted in good faith the pro-Lysenko conclusions of the experts: the fact that Lysenko had many qualifications and signs of scientific respectability made it easier for them. This example can be summarized in the accompanying diagram.

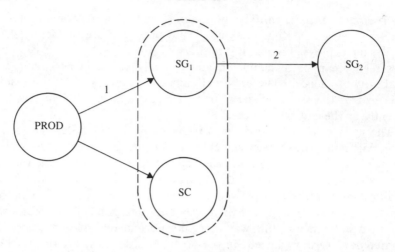

Here, the scientific community is short-circuited by the opinion of a specific group, in this case biologists who are not geneticists, which is regarded by other specific groups (journalists, educated readers, and the like) as being equivalent to geneticists. Of course, manipulators such as these were possible only because the authorities had a tool which was effective but which had to be used properly – the power to decide who went to conferences. It was well known, however, as I have mentioned, that the state reserved the right to decide in every case who went to conferences. The breakdown of participants according to specialization was not really evident to an outsider, so the manipulation was unlikely to be spotted except by a small group of skilled observers. This example is intended to show that short-circuit effects such as these can be present even where there is no manipulation: although they may not be very frequent in the natural sciences, they are much more common in the social sciences.

A case in point which is very simple but frequent is where specific groups, because of the interest (in the intellectual sense) which their members have in a theory, do no wait for its validity and its limitations to become clear – do not wait, as it were, for the sugar to melt. This suggests that *properly scientific* theories can also give rise to false ideas.

Thus, for example, Max Weber's book *The Protestant Ethic and the Spirit of Capitalism*[14] is well known and very popular. The reason is that the subject he deals with is vast and 'interesting' – he covers the mammoth theme of the conditions which led to the upheaval of the birth of the capitalist system. It is also because the theme has a philosophical and metaphysical dimension: instead of the 'materialist' interpretation of the origin of capitalism associated particularly with Marx, Weber subtly suggests an 'idealist' theory in which *values* can help to determine the relationships of production rather than being determined by them. The comprehensive nature of this question, its 'universal' interest, and the 'subversive' nature of a reply which runs counter to accepted theories, were all calculated to attract widespread attention.

Nevertheless, this theory is merely a hypothesis: it may be scientific, but it is weak. The argument of *The Protestant Ethic* is well known: because they believe in predestination, Protestants (or more accurately Calvinists and other Protestants in the Calvinist tradition) are led to look in this life for signs that they will be chosen for the next one. They try to find success in activities undertaken in this life and interpret such success as a sign that they are among the elect. This attitude leads them to invest rather than consume, and to be obsessed with the desire to be enterprising, to make their mark, to be successful.

Of course Weber presents his argument in a more subtle way than in my simplified summary. He makes it clear that he is not putting forward a theory of the origins of capitalism, but stressing the coincidence of Calvinist and particularly Puritan values with 'the spirit of capitalism'. However, as Weber himself recognized,[15] *The Protestant Ethic* presupposes that the capitalist mentality in fact influenced the development of capitalism; moreover, the theory was put forward to explain the important role of Calvinists in this development, at a time when no existing theory, not even Marxism, contained such explanation.

From the beginning, Weber's theory gave rise to numerous objections. Sombart, for example, pointed out that many capitalist entrepreneurs in the sixteenth century were Jews or Catholics. Other writers said that there had been many capitalists in the fifteenth century, before Protestantism appeared. Weber had of course tried to anticipate this objection by arguing that the Fugger family, who were famous fifteenth-century Catholic entrepreneurs with an extensive industrial and trading empire, were adventurers, to be treated as an exceptional case.

On another tack, writers were quick to point out that Weber's link between belief in predestination and entrepreneurial spirit was far from *intelligible*. It would be more *meaningful* for the desire to succeed to be present in those for whom grace was not irrevocable. In any case it is difficult to say whether belief in the irrevocable nature of grace fosters, or is more consistent with, entrepreneurship, than the belief that grace depends on merit. There is also the question of whether Weber's link between belief in predestination and entrepreneurial spirit is a prime example of an *ad hoc* hypothesis created to account for the preponderance of Calvinists among sixteenth-century entrepreneurs; and it has to be remembered that Calvinist theologians from Bèze onwards tried, through pastoral letters, to mitigate the effects of doctrine and teach that believers had the absolute right to ensure, by effective and successful works, their election to the next world.

Weber's theory nevertheless seems weak with regard to its psychological propositions: they do not satisfy the criterion of *meaningfulness*, which is vital in the individualist conception of explanation. The reconstruction of the Calvinist's mental states is not really convincing and gives rise to a feeling of arbitrariness. The theory is also weak in that the facts it seeks to explain are scanty and somewhat vague, though this did not stop Weber being impressed by one answer to the puzzle: in fifteenth-century Florence, the dominant doctrine still regarded business activities as sinful even though some nominalists tried to justify them; conversely, in eighteenth-century Pennsylvania, capital accumulation was regarded with favour since there were no banks or big businesses and without money the economy might have reverted to barter. It is obvious, however, that comparing these two cases does not amount to an experiment, and therefore no conclusion can be reached. Moreover, many facts do not really fit in with theory, which is why Schumpeter, who otherwise holds Weber in high regard, strongly attacked *The Protestant Ethic*.[16]

Weber's interpretation is nevertheless properly scientific. It raised an important new question, and it opened up and extended the materialist paradigm which had up to then been used overwhelmingly in the analysis of economic processes. It proposed that 'values' and 'cultural factors' can play an important part in economic change. It presented a radical challenge to traditional ways of thinking, and it gave rise to a debate which, while it restricted the scope of Weber's theory, could not have taken place without it.

It only remains to be said that the debate on Weber's theory increased not only our perception of its limited validity, but at the same time, because of the questions it raised, our understanding of why Protestantism influenced the development of capitalism. Calvinism, particularly in its Puritan version, certainly played a part in social changes in Europe from the sixteenth century onwards, but this was especially because the *political* climate in Protestant countries was more favourable to certain political and economic changes than in countries where the Counter-Reformation held sway.[17] There were dynamic bankers everywhere, but whereas in Catholic countries banks were under the control of the state, they had less difficulty in achieving independence of action in Protestant countries. Another point was that Protestant countries attracted those businessmen who found the climate of the Counter-Reformation uncongenial – many emigrated, for example, from Antwerp to Amsterdam. Migration of this kind helps to explain both the economic vitality of Protestant countries and the fact that economic elites were often Calvinist.[18] Businessmen were attracted by Calvinism not only because it conferred dignity on activities in this world but also because it was implacably hostile to the Counter-Reformation. We see here that the facts turn Weber's theory on its head: they show that businessmen felt close to Calvinism, not that Calvinists preferred to go into business. The conclusion is that the relationship between Protestantism and economic modernization is better explained by *political* factors rather than by *cultural* or *economic* factors.

The interest aroused by Weber's theory, however, immediately gave rise to a short-circuit effect: it was seen by many specific groups as confirmation of the idea that 'values' play a decisive role in economic change, and that a casual link could be made between Protestant culture and economic dynamism. In this way, a hypothesis which was authentically scientific gave rise to a received idea. Moreover this received idea was not subsequently corrected since the process of evaluation by the scientific community was not only interminable but also led to a conclusion which was particularly complex, as illustrated in the accompanying diagram.

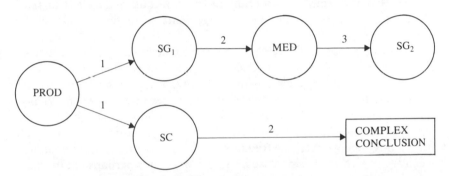

These short-circuit effects can also help to confer scientific authority on theories which deviate from 'normal science', as we have seen in the case of Lysenkoism. However, although the appearance of these effects in the natural sciences depends on particular conditions, the same is not true of social sciences, where frequently a dubious theory finds easy acceptance.

In all cases the process is the same: one or more specific groups endorse a theory because it corresponds to a latent demand on their part – a demand which may be due to position effects, to disposition effects, or to both at the same time. For these reasons, the groups have an *interest* in the theory. Furthermore, if the theory is at least partly a black box for these groups, authority effects can appear. It is very likely that dissemination of the theory among other groups in society will be facilitated by mediators, some of whom because they go along with its conclusions (while still regarding the theory itself as a black box), and some because they simply believe that it is part of their role as mediators to inform the general public of an idea or a theory which is being 'talked about'. If the process is quick enough, the theory can become a 'collective belief' even before it has been evaluated by those who are in the best position to treat it as a white box.

To illustrate this case in point, I will refer to Michel Foucault's *Surveiller et punir*, published in 1975 (*Discipline and Punish - the birth of the prison*, London, Allen Lane, 1977). It puts forward the masterly theory that since the eighteenth century, the punishment of criminals has become less severe. Criminals are imprisoned instead of being broken at the wheel, burned at the stake, or impaled. Foucault asked why prison had become the norm when it was so unsatisfactory, as all expert observers since the middle of the nineteenth century had shown: it was a school for criminals, it produced professional recidivists, it created an alienated group intent on tormenting law-abiding citizens as soon as they were released. Toqueville[19] had already come to such conclusions in his writing on the American prison system, even though this was 'modern' and took account of all 'advanced' thinking on criminology. Foucault makes it clear that since Toqueville the same harsh judgements have been consistently made.

As to why prison still survives when it is condemned by all the experts, the obvious answer - and it is no doubt an acceptable one - is that nobody has found anything better. Clearly, prison contributes to re-offending, but it also has a deterrent effect: because of prisons, many crimes which would be committed are not committed. Obviously, this statement cannot be verified directly, but it can be indirectly, in that, all other things being equal, the frequency of certain crimes tends to go down when the punishment is increased.[20] Imprisonment is perhaps not the best solution, in that it involves social costs of which the rate of re-offence is the most obvious, but it is difficult to argue that its disadvantages are greater than its (social) advantages, or that its negative effects are greater than its positive effects, looking at it from the law-abiding citizen's point of view.

One of the points where Foucault's theory goes off the rails is his radical reworking of the view that imprisonment involves social costs by saying that its effects are purely negative (from the point of view of the general public) Foucault says that 'prisons do not bring down the crime rate: even with bigger, more or different kinds of prisons, the number of crimes and criminals stays the same, or, worse still, increases',[21] and in support of this he quotes the view of a writer in 1842 who noted the increase in crime during that period despite hanging, hard labour, and straightforward imprisonment. However, it is clear that this statement does not confirm Foucault's assertion that not only does prison have no effect on crime, but contributes to its increase. It is an assertion which accords neither with common sense nor with the findings of criminological research, but he comes back to it several times. An example is when he says: 'If the law defines offences, if the penal system is supposed to reduce them, and if prison is the instrument of this repression, then the conclusion is that they have failed'; and he goes on: 'or rather – since in order to establish it in historical terms we would have to measure the effects of the penalty of detention on the overall level of criminality – the surprising conclusion is that for a hundred and fifty years prison has been regarded as a failure but it still survives.'[22] This second quotation reveals methodological concerns – that the specific contribution of imprisonment to the *increase* in crime needs to be measured. This concern goes only one way, however. Foucault never seems to contemplate, for a balanced picture, the need to measure the deterrent effect of imprisonment and take account of its contribution to *reducing* crime.

In this way, imprisonment is presented as having only disadvantages from the social point of view. Following this assertion, Foucault goes off the rails again, this time in a much more spectacular way. He wonders, on the basis of his first assertion, whether 'the question should not be turned round so that it becomes a matter of the purpose which the failure of prison serves.'[23] If prison has only negative effects, the reason is clear: '[it is to] keep crime going, encourage re-offending, make an habitual criminal of the occasional law-breaker, set up a closed milieu of delinquency.' If imprisonment still exists, it must be assumed that it serves some purpose. With some care, Foucault then puts forward the hypothesis to which the whole book is moving:

> One must therefore assume that the prison, and no doubt punishment in general, is not intended to eliminate offences, but rather to distinguish them, to distribute them, to use them [. . .] And, if one can speak of a class justice, it is not only because the law itself or the way of applying it serves the interests of a class, it is also that the whole differential question of illegalities through penalty forms part of those mechanisms of domination.

Prison therefore serves neither to prevent nor to limit crime; it serves to reinforce the 'mechanisms of (class) domination'. How does it do this? In the first place by 'helping to establish law-breaking which is conspicuous, distinctive, irreducible at a certain level, and *secretly* useful',[24] i.e. the criminal behaviour characteristic of the lower classes (theft, for example). The fact that such law-breaking is made 'distinctive' by prison and is nurtured by it 'means that one can ignore those [types of law-breaking] which one wants to tolerate and which must be tolerated' (presumably economic crime). In this way, the thief is put in prison so that the white-collar criminal can operate more freely. Even though prison creates a body of criminals, at the same time it confines them, singles them out, and keeps

them under control, so that 'law-breaking of this kind, being concen-
trated, controlled and rendered defenceless, is of direct use.' This direct
usefulness is obvious: if there are no prisons there are no grasses, police
spies, or informers. So no police. So no social order. So no domination:

> After the French Revolution, this practice [the use of informers etc.]
> acquired totally different dimensions: the infiltration of political parties
> and workers' associations, the recruitment of thugs against strikers and
> rioters, the organization of a sub-police – working directly with the legal
> police and capable if necessary of becoming a sort of parallel army – a
> whole extra-legal functioning of power was partly assured by the mass of
> reserve labour constituted by criminals: a clandestine police force and
> standby army at the disposal of the state. [. . .] It can be said that crime,
> solidified by a penal system based on prison, represented a diversion of
> illegality for the illicit circuits of profit and power of the ruling class.[25]

Here, then, is the answer: the ruling class keeps prisons to enable it to
have a pool of identifiable criminals from which the police can recruit its
spies and informers.

Clearly, Foucault's theory is constituted in such a way that it does not
stand up to serious analysis. In the first place it is based on a hypothesis
for which there is no evidence (prison leads to an absolute increase in
crime); then comes a scientific pseudo-enigma (why do we keep prisons
when everybody agrees – though this does not follow from Foucault's
evidence – that they do not help to bring down crime?) Finally, he solves
the enigma by recourse to a method not normally used in scientific writing –
explaining cause by unintended effects. Prison is useful to the police, and
the police are useful to the ruling class.

Since this epistemological point is of vital importance, we will have a
closer look at it: where it is clear that an actor wants to achieve an aim, the
consequences of this act can in fact be interpreted as the cause of this
act – the pleasure I get from drinking a glass of wine explains why I empty
it. Conversely, when an act leads to an unintended consequence, this
cannot always be regarded as the cause of the act. A friend persuades me
to go to a concert; I go in order not to disappoint my friend, but I
unexpectedly enjoy the concert. My enjoyment obviously cannot be
regarded as the reason why I went to the concert.

Here two cases in point may present themselves:

Either the act leads to consequences which were unintended but
which are felicitous for the actor. Here, the act may be repeated even
though initially the consequences were not the cause of the act. Having
discovered that I enjoyed the concert, I may want to go again.

Or the act has consequences which were unintended and are infelicitious
for the actor. Here, the consequences will never, then or subsequently, be

the cause of the act. If the concert is, as I had expected, not enjoyable, I will not go there again unless it is not to disappoint a friend.[26]

Many sociological studies are based on the first example. They have found, for instance, that it is not uncommon in a firm to divide the job of an employee who cannot produce enough to satisfy demand, and give it to two people. If these two people, rather than doing half the work, divide the actual tasks between them, it is likely that they will eventually get through more work because of a *division of labour*. Possibly the difference between the two new jobs will be confirmed and institutionalized. Here the positive effects of the division of labour can justifiably be regarded as the cause of the job split. Writers such as Adam Smith or Spencer used this kind of model – the 'invisible hand' model – to explain why the division of labour made progress.

If one is willing to interpret Foucault's thought in a generous way, it can offer an illustration of this case in point: because the ruling class sees imprisonment as serving its own purpose, allowing it to recruit informers and diverting attention from white-collar crime, the consequence is that it keeps the institution. If however one is less kindly disposed to Foucault, objections will be made to this interpretation. It assumes not only that the ruling class has absolute power, but also that it can conceal this power. If the underclass realized not only that prison increased the risks it faced but also helped to keep it in check, it might begin to object. Moreover, how can these hypotheses, which are weighty and extreme, be reconciled with the fact that, as Foucault himself says, criticisms of imprisonment were usually made by the ruling class? Foucault in fact relies on reports drawn up for governments to assert that imprisonment was frequently criticized. Must we then pose an adventitious hypothesis and say that the ruling class has not kept a tight enough rein on its intellectuals, even though they are, according to modern neo-Marxism, the underclass of the ruling class? But why in this case would they have had numerous reports on imprisonment drawn up? Or is the conclusion that the ruling class saw the advantages it derived from imprisonment only in the depths of its collective unconscious?

The rhetorical precautions employed by Foucault's ('perhaps the question should be turned round . . .', 'perhaps we ought to look for . . .', 'can one on the other hand not see . . .', 'we ought therefore to . . .', etc.)[27] get weaker as he progresses, and are perhaps a sign of doubt about his frenzied imagination.

How could a theory such as this purport to be not only original but also academically respectable, scientifically based, and socially instructive? The first reason is that it is based on historical research which, though it has sometimes been criticized, is certainly extensive.[28] In this way, Foucault's book fulfils one generally accepted criterion for a scientific work, in a way which everyone, expert or not, can judge, though in different degrees. From a purely historiographic viewpoint, the book *is* clearly a scientific book. It may be that it is clearly not so at the level of interpretation, but to see whether it is scientific, we need to examine closely the logic of the argument. This assumes a level of application which can be expected of an article in a learned journal, but not for example of a newspaper article. Moreover, once the logic of the argument has been looked at closely, it must be evaluated, which presupposes methodological preparation. It is not for example obvious to the ordinary reader that Foucault is putting forward – though in a totally unjustified way – the hypothesis that keeping imprisonment as a punishment is due to the presence of a 'composition effect' – in other words, the kind of effect of which Adam Smith's 'invisible hand' is the classic example.

Moreover, composition effects frequently bring into play a complex logic which an untrained reader – for instance, one who knows nothing about game theory – is unlikely to perceive. It was likely, therefore, that Foucault's book, being full of historiography, was going to be regarded by many 'educated' readers as scientifically significant. It was less likely that the logical weaknesses of the argument were going to be spotted. A black-box effect could therefore easily be created.

The second reason is that Foucault's theory was consistent with a perspective effect: it is easy to state and to prove that prison is 'a school for crime', that it leads to re-offending, that it 'stamps' offenders and can turn them into professional criminals. Conversely, though the deterrent effects of prison are certainly present, in the nature of things they are less obvious – it is easier to show real facts than hypothetical ones. It is only, as I have said, by indirect methods such as comparing crime rates with severity of punishment, and showing that the relationship can be given a causal interpretation, that this deterrent effect can be, and has in fact been, proved.

That is not the end of it, however; for to see how complex is the problem of determining the *net* effects of imprisonment on crime rates, it must be realized that lenient penal policy is also a significant cause not only of crime but also of re-offending – criminals who run only a small risk of being caught, and if they are caught of being punished, will naturally be prepared to commit further crimes.

To return to Foucault: since his theory is consistent with a powerful perspective effect[29] which applies to those whose role brings them into daily direct or indirect contact with crime, it aroused the immediate interest of many of these people, whatever their beliefs or ideologies. Furthermore – though this point is so obvious that there is no need to stress it – it also encountered fairly widespread *dispositions* (in the ethical sense) of hostility to 'repression'.

A final point – Foucault must be given credit for having brought brilliantly to our attention the point (though it was not this that interested him) that imprisonment is a failure *if* we regard its primary function as one of 'rehabilitation' or 'reintegration into society'. By doing this, he helped to move penal policy towards the prevention of crime. This sound idea of his does not of course confer the authority of truth on his theory. On the contrary, it is extremely weak and scientifically unacceptable, though it is easy to see how it won over specific groups, by pointing to *one* effect which cannot be contested and to which many social actors could not, because of their role, be indifferent.

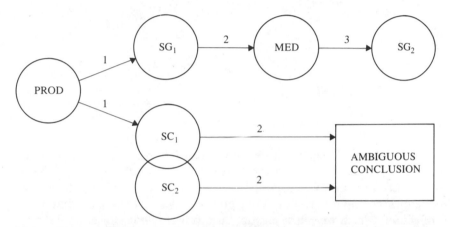

The book was therefore regarded by many people as *interesting*. Moreover, it seemed to be a scientific work because the historiographic research on which it was based seemed comprehensive and accurate. This is why it was well received: there seemed to be no need to wait for a fuller evaluation of its scientific worth, since it appeared to be immediately clear. The book was not addressed to one clearly defined scientific community, but to several – historians, sociologists, criminologists. If it was scientifically satisfactory in some respects, it was not so in others – opinions were divided and frequently expressed with circumspection.

Reference must also be made to a third type of short-circuit effect, in which the author addresses himself directly and explicitly to specific groups who are not in any scientific community. By setting off position and disposition effects, he may get ideas accepted which may run counter to established knowledge. This was the case with MacLuhan[30] who went on putting forward the idea that the media were all-powerful, when the whole of the sociology of communication stressed their limitations –

receivers of messages are *actors*, and not screens on which messages are printed; as such, they are in a position not only to select incoming messages but also to interpret and evaluate them, which is why the media do not have the power and influence sometimes attributed to them. MacLuhan's ideas, however, depended on a powerful perspective effect – although television viewers are aware that they themselves are casting a critical eye on a particular message, they may fear that the television message being relayed to millions of homes is being received mechanically by many people. This case in point, where the scientific community is quite simply ignored, can be shown in the accompanying diagram.

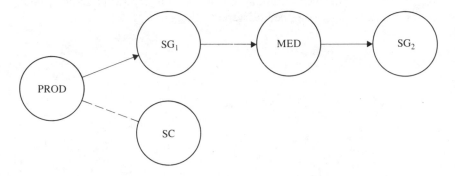

Something which goes without saying is often best said, so I will now make it clear that the definition of *scientific community* which I have been implicitly using may well correspond to reality only imperfectly. Ideally, a scientific community is subject to a body of rules characterizing that form of activity which we call scientific. Such rules exclude, for example, certain types of explanation regarded as scientifically unsound: they require all theories to be submitted to methodical examination, their consistency verified, their compatibility with existing knowledge established, and so on. However, like any other community, a scientific community may function properly or not: it may, or may not, stick closely to the rules and objectives according to which it functions and from which it derives its legitimacy. The degree to which it does this depends on several factors, particularly the institutions on which it is based and the way in which it reacts with its environment. Given that these conditions are many and varied, it is not surprising that a scientific community may not live up to the ideal I have postulated here.

By going into such details, I want to stress that the analyses I have outlined represent models which, it must be realized, tend to simplify matters. Cases in point which are more complex than those I have given as examples may exist in the real world. Thus, for example, when a scientific community in a particular discipline or covering several disciplines departs from the ideal I have postulated, because of institutional upheavals for instance, and is no longer in a position to fulfil a critical role, communication effects can then be so strong that the most absurd theories may be taken seriously and be accepted as the truth. There may then be a kind of institutionalization, more or less permanent, of the right to say absolutely anything. It is as if the court of rational criticism ceases to exist or make itself heard, and the only condition a theory still has to fulfil is to be *interesting* (to certain categories of the public). It is then only a matter of the effective formulation of this right to say absolutely anything, of its presentation as one of the basic rights of human beings in general and intellectuals in particular, or as a necessary condition of scientific creation in its (supposedly) higher forms, for us to come full circle and for the terrorism of the false idea to become established. It was thanks to a scenario of this kind that in France in the 1960s and 1970s, for instance, there became established certain philosophical, psychological, or sociological theories which made it difficult to know whether one should admire their absurdity or their simplicity.[31]

In this way, there are also situations in which truth and, more modestly, methodical thought, can assert themselves only through mavericks on the edge of the pack or excluded from it, just as mavericks can be indispensable to wake a scientific community from the slumber of dogma.

In the last part of this chapter, I have tried in summary form to show that certain non-scientific theories can, because of a short-circuit effect, be regarded as scientific, and thereby confirm received ideas. However, properly scientific theories may also have an ideological influence through a combination of communication and situation effects, as is shown by several examples in this chapter. However, in order to be fully aware of the decisive role of scientific theories in the origin of ideologies, account must be taken of *E effects* (epistemological effects) to which I referred in chapter 5, and these will be considered in the next chapter.

A final point needs to be emphasized. The previous considerations allow us to establish a rough typology of intellectuals, or at least of intellectual activities. Although the problem of the sociology of intellectuals is not of direct concern to me here, I will make some brief concluding remarks.

Firstly, intellectuals can have the function of producer or mediator: for example, the theoretical economist is a producer, while the journalist specializing in economic matters is a mediator.

Secondly, they may address different sections of the population: the exegetes are by definition addressing those who believe the truth and the unconditional authority of the texts of which they are setting out the exegesis. Conversely, scholars are in theory addressing everybody: what they have to say is, because of their function, applicable to all. As Max Weber said, a scholar ought in theory to be able to be understood by the Chinese.

Finally, an intellectual can put to use different linguistic registers – science, rhetoric, and exegesis are probably the most notable examples. In combination, these three dimensions allow us to define types of intellectuals; or rather, ideal types, since in reality all kinds of derogations and combinations are possible. Rhetoric may mean that dubious scientific reasoning is accepted and becomes influential in particular sections of the population. Exegesis may present itself as a science. One may act as though one were addressing the Chinese and yet be addressing a corporation, a sect, or a specific group. On the other hand, a theory may be directed to a universal audience because of its form and to specific audiences because of the interest in its content and conclusions.

In this chapter, I have taken all my examples from the social sciences, so I must make it clear in a postscript (to go into it in more detail would take me outside the framework I have established for myself) that the communication effects discussed here are produced not only in the *social* sciences but also more generally in the *human* sciences. One has only to think of the case of medicine, or psychology, or pedagogy. Because of the inevitably public nature of these disciplines, it is not uncommon for a partial or fragile scientific truth to be transformed – through the communication effects which I have tried to describe – into 'truth set in stone'. Thus, for example, people will swear by a particular diet or teaching approach 'whose positive effects have been proved by science', until the time when science, because its internal or external situation has changed, emphasizes their negative effects.

8

Science and ideology

I am well aware that up to now I have merely been putting down markers. My analysis of position and disposition effects, as well as that of communication effects, could have been and ought to have been taken further. The same is true of the third kind of effects – epistemological effects or *E effects*. With so little space at my disposal, I will have to limit myself to a certain number of indicative remarks.

It is vital to look at this third kind of effect in a theory of ideology, since as soon as one adopts an active conception of knowledge, one immediately concludes that scientific knowledge is not only not protected from beliefs which are not proven, it could not even exist without them. This idea is fairly commonplace today, thanks to the writings of Kuhn[1] in particular; but as I have already said, what Kuhn did was to offer historical examples for a proposition which was easy to establish and which had been established on the theoretical level long ago by Hume and the Kantians and neo-Kantians. Is it not obvious that the idea of cause cannot be drawn by induction from experience? To simplify even further, let us take any scientific theory. It is clear that it always has a vocabulary and basic statements which one is obliged to accept without justifying them. Otherwise one would inevitably fall into what Hans Albert amusingly called, after Schopenhauer, 'Münchhausen's trilemma',[2] where the choice would be between three equally unsatisfactory solutions: either enter an impossible infinite regression; or stop the regression at an arbitrary point; or, at a certain point, begin to turn in a vicious circle.

Münchhausen's trilemma has not prevented progress in the natural or social sciences, but the beliefs on which scientific study is based, in both areas, do not have the same effects everywhere, principally because of the communication effects discussed in the previous chapter. This is why it is crucial in a theory of ideology to analyse also what I have called E effects.

Given the proximity to the observer of objects in the social sciences, the beliefs which are indispensable to scientific study often take on a significance, for the theoretician as well as for the various audiences, which is very different from the case of the natural sciences. Not only is it possible that they will not be derived exclusively from the state and demands of the discipline in question, but also greater faith may be put in them than they warrant, for complex reasons which I will try to explain.

In other words the aim of this chapter is to show that ideology develops also at the very heart of scientific study; and here I have in mind not just those pseudo-scientific theories which of course are deplorably common in the social sciences, but also authentically scientific theories. In any case, pseudo-scientific theories are often badly controlled skids on the normal road of science.

I will not look very closely at those beliefs located at the level of vocabulary, since I have referred in chapter 5 to an example of this which I think is sufficiently telling. This was that accepting the framework of 'development economics' amounts to accepting that the idea of development has a clear and distinct meaning. However, it also amounts to accepting that, since the word 'development' is in the singular, it is a single phenomenon. The final point is that, in speaking of development economics, there is the inevitable assumption that the causes of development and underdevelopment are essentially economic. Although they appear harmless, these three words contain within them a large stock of beliefs.

The same analysis could be made of many notions which are current in the social sciences and which are generally accepted, by the public at large as well as the scientific community, as 'self-evident'. To speak of *the* Third World is not only to put into the same basket societies whose history, structures, institutions, customs, and social organization differ greatly, but also assumes that there is a hierarchy such as in pre-Revolutionary France (third world = third estate). This is a far-fetched analogy, to say the least.

Other phrases which seem even more harmless are vulnerable to beliefs: for instance historians of ideas who are planning to write books on 'the thought of Karl Marx' might be led to postulate the unity of this thought, trying to show that Marx throughout his career as philosopher and economist attempted to solve certain problems, and that his books are stages towards the solution of these problems. It will be sufficient to wave the magic wand of this concept – 'the thought of Karl Marx' – to produce in the historians' minds a complex world of '*a priori* forms' providing a framework for sifting and analysing material. Without these forms, historians would not know where to start or how to continue. At the same time, however, they can send them down false trails and make them forget facts which are obvious to other historians – for example, that the *Manifesto* and *Capital* were not written for the same audience; or that Marx was much more familiar with political economy in 1852 than he was in 1842. If the historians are philosophers, they will interpret Marx's thought as the result of an imaginary dialogue with Hegel, whereas if they are economists, they will see signs of a dialogue with Adam Smith or Ricardo. One thing is certain: it is impossible to rediscover *the* thought of Marx as it is or was. This is why certain writers have made their reputation by suggesting that *the* thought of Marx does not exist and that a distinction has to be made between the younger Marx and the older Marx. In the same way, Lukács looked only at 'the early Hegel',[3] and Lucien Goldman only at 'the early Lukács'.

To take another example, saying that one is going to undertake a *sociological* or *economic* study of a specific phenomenon is presuming a great deal; in particular, it amounts to saying that the concepts of 'sociology' and 'economics' are as easily definable as the concept of 'dog'. It may be easy to recognize those quadrupeds which can be called 'dog', but it is much more difficult to define 'sociology' or 'economics'. Some people argue that these disciplines have existed since time immemorial. Others, who are more naive or acting from the barely concealed concerns of a privileged group, are prepared to say when these disciplines began, and if pushed to give an Aristotelian definition of them – economists look at rational behaviour, sociologists study irrational behaviour. Or is this categorizing in too systematic a manner?

Certain concepts which were originally created to meet analytical requirements have themselves been transformed into ideological pillars. This happened for example to the well-known pairing of community-society (*Gemeinschaft – Gesellschaft*). Originally, Tönnies[4] used it to describe obvious sociological distinctions: social relationships between members of a family are not of the same nature as relationships in a post office between counter-clerk and customer. The conversation between father and son is wide-ranging; the clerk asks the customer only specific questions. The relationship of father and son is one of emotion, which is not as a rule the case between the clerk and the customer. The analysis need not be taken further; it shows that by comparing the idea of community with that of society, Tönnies was trying to *give names* to distinctions which were not only real but obvious. Also, he was at pains to emphasize that in every society and even in every social system, even the smallest, there are at the same time relationships of a community kind (those in families, for instance) and relationships of a societal kind (those in a post office). Even in a post office there can be relationships of a community kind (between employees, for example), and it is not uncommon for there to be arguments about money within families. The words 'community' and 'society' cannot therefore be applied to specific social objects in the way that the words 'invertebrate' or 'vertebrate' can be applied to living things.

Despite this, the conceptual distinction between community and society was quickly applied in a realist way, forgetting that the words indicated ideal types in a complex relationship with the real world: people saw in it a classification equivalent to zoological ones. Some writers, for example, began to divide all known social systems into two categories – 'primitive' societies, it was argued, were warm-hearted *communities* with no selfishness or conflicts, and where individuals were so much part of the group that they no longer had a separate identity except in the physical or biological sense. Modern social systems, on the other hand, were *societies* where social relationships were characterized by coldness and calculating selfishness, and where the individual had lost the feeling of belonging to a group. Although there is no reference to Tönnies, these arbitrary distinctions are present in the work of Karl Polanyi, Marcuse, and many others.

I think I have said enough on this point – the examples show adequately not only that the vocabulary of the social sciences is full of '*a priori* forms', even in the case of phrases such as 'X's thought' or 'development' which appear harmless, but also that some parts of this vocabulary have sometimes been enough to confer a scientific basis on ideological representations.

Of course, a scientific theory is not merely a succession of words, and a scientific discipline is not reducible to its vocabulary. It also contains what tend to be called, since Kuhn, *paradigms* – that is, frameworks of thought and theoretical or methodological orientations on which there is a certain degree of agreement in the scientific community, because they are regarded as useful and fruitful. These frameworks are a guide to scholarship, offering a language, even a way of thinking, and principles of explanation. I accept that phrases such as these are rather vague, but I do not want to embark on a prolonged discussion of the notion of paradigm. The reason why nobody has been able to come up with a satisfactory one is that frameworks of thought can vary considerably in form and content. The easiest course of action is therefore to give some examples – logicians would speak here of deictic definitions – to give an idea of the importance of the notion.

What is the connection between these paradigms and a theory of ideologies? It is simply that, like the vocabulary of the social sciences, they tend in normal conditions to be accepted without demur in scholarship. This is understandable, in that no person engaged in research wants to get bogged down in Münchhausen's trilemma. However, more credit than warranted may be given to a paradigm which is found to be useful, even though its basis has not been checked. In the case of a useful paradigm, its epistemological status of '*a priori* form' may be forgotten by the scientific community as well as the general public, and it may be seen on the contrary as the faithful image of reality *as it is*. Paradigms, like vocabularies, naturally give rise to E effects.

To begin with, I will take a simple example – the paradigm which nowadays is designated by the notion of 'utilitarianism'. According to utilitarianism, in the modern meaning of the word,[5] all that is needed to understand the behaviour of individuals is to perceive their *interests* (in the material and not the cognitive sense of the word). Every act depends, to borrow Bentham's famous phrase, on a calculus of pleasure and pain.

This paradigm has a very specific form: it limits itself to stating what might be called a principle of behaviour. It tells us that, if we want to explain why an actor chose X rather than Y, we need to show that for the actor in question, X was preferable from the point of view of the calculus of pleasure and pain, or in more modern terms, from the point of view of cost–benefit analysis.

It is clear that this paradigm is both very productive and very straightforward and that it is commonly used not only by economists but also by historians and sociologists.[6] This shows that, although it offers an interpretive framework for analysing *individual* acts, it can also be used to analyse social or collective phenomena, whether of an economic kind or not.

To illustrate this point, I will quote a simple historical example. When the Bolsheviks came to power in Russia, they tried to abolish that hated institution, the bourgeois family. Their mentor, Engels,[7] had taught them that for women marriage was merely a legalized form of prostitution characteristic of capitalist society. Since there was going to be a break with capitalism, marriage might as well be abolished as well. This is in fact what happened. Marriage solemnized by somebody representing the authorities was replaced by a free union based on mutual consent. Some time later, the Bolsheviks faced a severe housing crisis – suddenly, demand outstripped supply in a way which had never happened before. One possible solution would have been to speed up house-building; but there was hardly enough government money for this, and in any case this solution would have taken time to work through. The housing shortage had to be solved as quickly as possible since it affected the popularity of the new regime.

As good sociologists, the Bolsheviks saw that they could adopt a much simpler solution which was more immediately effective, and involved no

economic and very little political cost – reintroduce 'bourgeois' marriage. This entailed very little political cost, since it was only Bolsheviks
who regarded bourgeois marriage as degenerate: the public at large had
nothing against the institution. The biggest risk which the new government ran was giving the impression that it had no clear idea of what it
wanted. The Bolsheviks had in fact realized that the abolition of bourgeois marriage was the direct cause of the housing crisis – since people
could not be sure of having somewhere to live with their 'bourgeois'
spouse, they saw that it was in their *interest* to keep their own
accommodation in case the free union they entered into broke down. This
was the reason for the *collective* increase in demand for housing.

This anecdote can be told in language suggested by the utilitarian
paradigm, at least from the point where marriage is abolished. Young
'married couples' are fully aware of where their interest lies; and governments also indulge in a cost-benefit calculation, then choose the solution
which is least expensive and most advantageous from the point of view of
their political interests. Only the first part of the story does not come
within the utilitarian paradigm – it is obviously not for considerations of
self-interest that the Bolsheviks abolished marriage. The rationality of
this decision is neither utilitarian nor teleological; it is axiological.

As I have stated, a great deal of research and writing in sociology,
history, or economics calls implicitly or explicitly on what I call the utilitarian paradigm. Thus, for example, it has been applied in the area of the
sociology of crime, by trying, with some justification, to explain that
criminals indulge in cost–benefit analysis when they seek weaker victims, easier jobs to do, more advantageous circumstances, or types of
crime where punishment is supposed to be more lenient.[8] It has also been
applied to politics by developing models where all people in politics are
assumed to be motivated by just one factor – their own interest.[9]
Although the application of the utilitarian paradigm to politics has
recently become popular again, it is in fact long-standing: it is common in
political philosophy, and Rousseau, like Hobbes, uses it in a systematic
way. We read in *The Social Contract*: 'In the person of the magistrate, we
can distinguish three wills', but 'the private will of the individual tending
only to his personal advantage'[10] comes first.

The very effectiveness of the utilitarian paradigm has always produced
significant ideological distortions. After all, saying that it can inspire a
great deal of research into individual behaviour and provide an explanation of collective phenomena, and also declaring that 'social actors are
motivated by material interests', are two separate issues. In the first case,
the paradigm is taken for what it is, an '*a priori* form' which can very
often inspire fruitful hypotheses and correct analyses. In the second case,
people are being represented as *they are*, and scientific creativity then

becomes responsible for an ideological concept.

As Simmel was well aware, Marx's 'materialism', which postulates as a rule that not only the acts but also the ideas of social actors always boil down to questions of interest, is a perfect illustration of this ideological distortion.[11] I think that another example of this distortion can be seen in what is nowadays called 'law and order', in that the view that people *essentially* require the police and judicial system to guarantee their *safety* – that is the integrity of their persons and that of their relatives and property – is obviously false. It has been recognized since Aristotle (and Durkheim followed him closely on this) that although people are concerned for their safety, they also have a feeling of what is fair and unfair which is in no way reducible to utilitarian considerations. This feeling is manifest in the fact that people need to know that criminals have been caught and punished, even when they have not been attacked or threatened by the criminals in question, or even when there was no possibility that they could threaten them. Moreover, if they want to see the criminal punished, this is not because they expect the punishment to have a deterrent effect from which they would *benefit*; it is simply that they want the crime to be properly paid for. This is why lenient treatment of petty crime gives rise to feelings of *indignation* out of proportion to the damage caused. Even though the thief who snatches the old lady's handbag is no threat to me, I will feel *indignant* if I think that the thief can get away with it. Moral indignation is therefore never reducible, either directly or indirectly, to considerations of utility. The utilitarian ideology, however, is so widespread that, as we see from politicians' speeches – and often their policies – people's moral feelings are either ignored or reduced to considerations of utility.

If it were not for the remarkable scientific creative capacity of the utilitarian paradigm, I do not think that one could so easily – and, as it were, so naturally – produce utilitarian interpretations of behaviour which, like the indignant reaction to crime, has nothing to do with utility. What I have said about crime could also be applied to other kinds of phenomena. The all-pervading nature of utilitarianism means that there is nowadays a tendency to confuse equity and equality. It is not true, contrary to what many of those responsible for 'social policy' think, that social actors are utilitarian and that they want either more than or at least as much as their neighbour. As all the research on the subject shows, what they want above all is that there should be a certain proportionality between what they contribute to society and what they get from it. This is why they may have a strong feeling of *indignation* if they have slightly less than their neighbour when they are convinced that they have actually done slightly more. This is also why equality and equity should not be confused, any more than the feeling of envy or desire should be confused with this feeling of indignation.

Nowadays, of course, the idea of 'equity' has virtually disappeared from the political vocabulary, to be replaced by 'equality', which seems to interest certain intellectuals more than ordinary people. The reason is that in social philosophy as in moral philosophy, a utilitarian ideology reigns supreme, no doubt largely based on the interest in, and the scientific success of, the utilitarian paradigm. It is easy for a productive paradigm to suggest that it is putting forward a realistic representation of the world as it is; and in fact politicians and journalists, just like many sociologists, historians, or economists, often seem to think nowadays that people are guided only by their interests. It is after all difficult to accept that a paradigm which 'works' does not represent the world as it is.[12] It can also - and many examples of this could be given - be transformed insidiously into a *vision of the world*, though this transformation is really complete only when the scientific origin of the paradigm is collectively forgotten.

I will now consider another paradigm which is also an *ism* - functionalism (it is significant that paradigms used in the social sciences often end in *ism*, like ideologies).

Like utilitarianism, it defines a framework of thought which is not only acceptable but which has also proved extremely creative scientifically. And like utilitarianism, it has given rise to several ideological distortions, which are given the scientific seal of approval because of the creative capacity of the paradigm. Apart from these general similarities, however, the two cases differ sufficiently in their details to make an examination of the second one worthwhile, especially as certain ideological variants of functionalism are worth looking at because they are so quaint.

Let us assume that I am examining a particular political institution in a society. Two questions can very often be asked about such institutions - how they began and how legitimate they are. In other words, the question of their origin and their function: why were they set up and why do they survive?

Historical anamnesis is often not sufficient to answer these questions. Origin is not usually enough to explain function. Moreover, historical data is often lacking, which is why Western political philosophy has had to resort for a long time now, and certainly since the seventeenth and eighteenth centuries, to what might be called in modern parlance functional analysis. Assume I want to explain the institutional fact D: if I can show that people probably freely consented to the setting up of D, then I would have gone some way to explaining D by its function.

To illustrate the effectiveness of this method, I will take two examples from contemporary political science. In their book *The Calculus of Consent*, Buchanan and Tullock[13] ask the reason for the establishment of certain institutional patterns which are commonly observed in modern societies and therefore familiar to us, though the reasons for them are not easy to discern. This is true, for example, of the usual way of determining the collective view of an assembly or college, whereby the view of the majority of members is regarded as the collective view of assembly itself. Why is this rule of the simple majority so often adopted? Why, on constitutional matters, is a larger majority than a mere simple one usually required?

One method could be used to answer this question – historical material could be used to find exactly when and in what circumstances these rules were adopted in a particular society. In other words, use the method of historical research. The other method is the one used by functionalist theories. Assume that an assembly of N people is trying to find the best way of converting their N individual opinions on a particular subject into a collective opinion – for example, that the assembly has to decide collectively whether to adopt measure A or measure B, policy A or policy B. Clearly the ideal situation would be one where everybody chooses the same option – the collective opinion would coincide with each individual opinion. Nobody would have to defer; the unanimity rule is in fact the only one which ensures that none of the collective decisions of the assembly has a negative effect on any member.

Of course this ideal rule involves costs: if the assembly is a large one, reaching unanimity can be difficult and time-consuming. In many cases it would be impossible, so the unanimity rule is likely to result in the complete paralysis of the decision-making machinery. To avoid this, n, the number of votes needed to determine the collective opinion, has to be smaller than N. However if n is smaller than N, $N - n$ people have to accept a measure of which they may disapprove. This snag has to be tolerated in order to avoid paralysis. It seems reasonable, however, to accept that $N - n$, the maximum number of people who in theory have to defer to a collective decision of which they disapprove, cannot be greater than n, the number of those who take the decision.

To put it formally: transforming a collection of individual opinions into a collective decision involves two kinds of costs. The bigger n is i.e. the bigger the number of votes needed to pass a measure, the more difficult is the decision; the smaller this number, the more the collective decision is likely to run counter to a significant number of individual opinions. The first kind of cost (C1) increases with n, while the second (C2) *decreases* with n, as figure 4 shows.

The conclusion to be drawn from this analysis is that the sum of the two costs is likely to be at its lowest point when n is around $N/2$; and since $N - n$ (the highest number of those who have to defer reluctantly to the collective

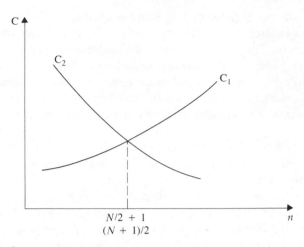

Figure 4   The two types of cost in any collective decisions

decision) cannot be greater than n, the simple majority rule appears to be, in the instant cases, an obvious solution to the problem.

Of course, the C1 curve can have different shapes depending on the kind of decision. For certain matters, it may be more costly to impose a collective decision on a significant minority, in which case a rule will be applied which requires the agreement of a larger number of people.

The conclusion from this analysis is that members of a group who have to choose a method of determining their collective opinion would have, in normal circumstances, *good reasons* for accepting the constitutional rule of the simple majority. Put another way, one would say that the rule is explained in this case by its function – to allow the smooth transformation of divergent individual opinions into a collective opinion.

I would like to refer briefly to a second example which will usefully complete the previous discussion.[14] In many agrarian societies, for example in African or Vietnamese villages at the turn of the century, there were many cases of assemblies of villagers which took collective decisions not by simply majority, nor even by qualified majority, but unanimously. This was something which Western observers for a long time found astonishing. Of course the observers also noted that the unanimity rule almost always involved long discussion. As in the famous American film *Twelve Angry Men*, unanimity is often reached only after protracted discussions. Protracted discussion and unanimity are institutions which usually go together – the one is never there without the other. This is easily *explained* by the previous analysis – the C1 costs of collective decision-making increase with n.

This preference of traditional agrarian societies for the unanimity rule has often been explained in a culturalist way: in these societies, individuals are much less autonomous, more subject to community pressure, seeing themselves as part of a bigger unit. Thus, one part cannot set itself against the whole without risk, which is why, in this kind of society, only unanimous decisions are likely to be regarded as valid and imperative. The unanimist ideal of the group, it is argued, explains why it is attracted to the unanimity rule: its totalitarian nature would not allow an individual to be out of step with the group.

This kind of explanation is commonly accepted, although it arouses one particular suspicion and invites an objection.

The *suspicion* is that not according peasants in traditional societies the same degree of individuality as people in modern societies may amount to what Piaget called sociocentrism. Is this not the 'primitive mentality' dear to the early Lévy-Bruhl?[15] Put more simply, does this kind of explanation not reveal an attitude of condescension on the part of the citizen of industrial societies towards societies which a barely concealed evolutionism calls 'backward'?

The *objection* is that if the unanimity rule stems from the fact that unanimism is the only state acceptable to the group, given the cultural values peculiar to traditional societies, how do we explain that unanimity is reached in most cases only after interminable discussions in which individuals do not hesitate to attack each other strongly and put forward individual points of view? The interminable discussions can of course be interpreted as symbolic and ritual phenomena, but such an interpretation is deceptive – far from being based on facts, it is only an *ad hoc* hypothesis intended to rescue the culturalist interpretation of the unanimity rule.

In fact a much simpler and convincing explanation of why this practice is so widespread in traditional agrarian societies is produced by analysing its function. This kind of society usually has the following characteristics:

1 an economy functioning at a very low rate, approaching what is usually called a 'subsistence economy';
2 a high rate of underemployment;
3 a high level of interdependence between members of the community, where everybody's actions can have significant effects on the well-being of others. Thus, for example, if X decides to improve his or her harvesting methods, Y, who has a right to glean X's field, may be deprived of the means of subsistence.

Now assume people are asked about the rule to be adopted in the village assembly in order to transform the individual opinions of its members into a collective opinion which has the force of law. Assume further that these people do not know whether, in the particular society, they will be richer or poorer, living on the fruits of the harvest like X, or on gleanings from X's field like Y. Obviously, in these circumstances, individuals will demand a right of veto over the decisions of the assembly. If they were Y, and X decided to improve harvesting methods, their living might be put at risk by their neighbour's action. Not surprisingly, therefore, they want a right of veto over this kind of thing; and since we have postulated *typical* individuals, *any* individual, what is true for them is true for others. In this way, it is in the interest of every future member of the society to demand the right of veto. This amounts to saying that future members of the society unanimously desire collective decisions of the assembly to be taken unanimously, rather than by any other rule for transforming individual decisions into a collective decision. In other words, it is the interest of *everybody* in the circumstances to agree to be bound by the collective decisions of the assembly, provided they have a right of veto over these decisions.

What is the cost of collective decision-making? The unanimity rule implies that there will be interminable discussions. However, given the social context, time is much less valuable in these kinds of society than in others – the very high level of underemployment means that people, since they spend only a small part of their available time in productive work, can easily devote much of it to the working of the political system.

In figure 5, two pairs of curves represent our analysis. The unbroken lines are reproduced from figure 4 and show the relationship between the two kinds of costs C1 and C2 as a function of *n* (the number of votes

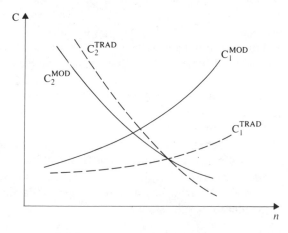

Figure 5   The costs of collective decision-making in a traditional society and a modern society

needed to adopt the collective decision) in 'modern' societies, where time is short and there is a low level of interdependence between members of society. The broken lines represent the same structures for a 'traditional' agrarian society in which time is abundant and there is a high level of independence. In the first case, future members of the society are likely to agree unanimously to accept a decision taken by *simple majority*. In the second case, they will agree to accept only a *unanimous* decision. The majority rule in the first case and the unanimity rule in the second perform the *function* of transforming individual opinions into a collective decision. Conversely, the first rule would be *dysfunctional* in the second case, as the second would be in the first.

These two examples are a good illustration of how functional analysis works, by explaining why a particular institution *comes into existence* in a particular kind of social context, why it *survives*, why it is *accepted and regarded as legitimate* by the members of the society, while disregarding the historical facts about the origin of the institution.

There are of course many other classic examples of functional analysis. Merton used it to explain the existence of the political machine of the Democratic Party in the United States. At a time when social welfare was not well developed in the United States, the Democratic Party assumed this *function*. In return for their vote, it provided poorer voters with social welfare benefits in case of illness or unemployment.[16] In this way, the party machine was in a position to satisfy a quite justifiable demand which was not met by the state. By drawing attention to this *function*, Merton explained the existence of the Democratic Party machine while taking no account of how it sprang up.

In all these examples, there is no mystery in the notion of function – functional analysis shows that a particular institution makes sense for a set of individuals, either because it meets demands and needs which they see as justified, or because it means they can solve a problem facing the group in conditions acceptable to the members.

It is clear that this method is of the utmost importance, not only in cases where historical data is lacking, but even when it is available, because in this case also it can complete historical analysis and explain why a particular institution is regarded as legitimate. This had been well understood by contractualist philosophers, who can be seen as the inventors of functional analysis.

This paradigm, however, also gave rise to all kinds of distortions which gained their legitimacy from its creative capacity and authority. Certain sociologists were led by their enthusiasm for the method to accept uncritically, as a self-evident postulate, that *everything* in a society has a function. Starting from this postulate, societies could be regarded as analoguous to living organisms. In this way the creative capacity of the functional paradigm warranted an organicist view of societies – every institution was regarded as contributing to the efficient functioning of the whole, like organs contribute to the working of the whole body. Here again, a paradigm was being transformed into a *vision of the world*.

Furthermore, in the 1960s, another interesting distortion from the point of view of the history of ideas made its appearance: it was a mixture of functionalism and Marxist teaching. Not only was *everything* in societies regarded as having a function, but this function was defined as maintaining the ruling class in its position of power over the underclass. An example of this kind of functionalism is seen in Foucault's *Surveiller et punir*, which I looked at in the previous chapter – imprisonment is kept because it benefits the ruling class by providing it with the necessary resources to maintain it in power. If it had not been for the authority of the functionalist paradigm, it is difficult to see how such a theory could have retained the attention of the scientific community.

The honours in this field, however, go to Pierre Bourdieu, who asked what purpose is served by culture, education, museums, language, religion, or sport. Answer: the self-perpetuation of the ruling class.[17] How is this done? Answer: by *habitus*. Because of habitus, the ruling class enjoys Beethoven, wants to get into university, and speaks in a refined manner; whereas the lower class goes for tangoes, mass-produced prints, coarse language, and manual jobs. In this way, people stay in their place, and the social order is safe.

Q But what exactly are these habitus?

A They are 'kinds of programmes (in the computer science sense of the word)'.[18]

Q So, Pavlov's ghost would be happier than that of Thomas Aquinas;[19] but how can one tell when these habitus are present?

A I have already told you: when the ruling class is enjoying Beethoven, etc.

Q We are going round in circles. Can one not at least assume that people are aware of their habitus?

A A naive suggestion. Only unconscious habitus can be effective. Can you not see that actors, or rather agents, always find spurious reasons for their own acts and that they 'make a virtue out of necessity'?[20] They think they are free; but they are in chains.

Q So your habitus are as well concealed as the soporific qualities of opium?

A 'The effects of habitus are never as well concealed as when they appear as the effects of structures [. . .] because they are produced by agents who are structure "made human".'[21]

Q I think I understand – the less visible the habitus are, the greater the proof that they exist. You are giving me an idea for the title of our little dialogue: *Bélise flying to the aid of Diafoirus*.[22]

Pierre Bourdieu effectively cancels out what comic effects there might be in his theories by a rhetorical bombardment combining four classic stages:

1 the rhetoric of the 'like' and 'as if', of inverted commas, as in 'structure "made human" ', 'kinds of programmes';
2 the deliberate obscurity of language so that criticism can be fobbed off with the traditional ripost 'that's not what I meant', while giving the impression of profundity;
3 illustrating the theory by specific examples which are sometimes interesting in themselves but which have no probative merit;
4 pseudo-scientific rhetoric:[23] one can always collect lots of data and use fairly learned statistical methods to show that opium is soporific or that social groups have differing tastes without thereby escaping the sophism of soporific virtue or that of the habitus/conditioned reflex.

Without the authority of functionalism (and of popularized Marxism) it would, once more, be difficult to understand how Bourdieu's synthesis of the two paradigms could be taken seriously.

It would be easy to examine other examples of paradigms, and to show that in most cases they start from an idea which is scientifically very productive. However, they can also be powerful generators of false ideas – because of Münchhausen's trilemma they are not usually questioned by the researcher, and they constitute '*a priori* forms' which give direction to the research. The researcher may therefore regard them as incontrovertible representations of reality, a belief which is likely to derive its strength from the fact that the paradigm is a productive one. This, moreover, is not limited to the social sciences. The Cartesian theory of animal-machines was generated by a distortion such as this – the mechanistic paradigm seemed to Descartes so effective in physics that he thought it could be applied to the living world.

In the social sciences, however, these E effects are more readily overlaid by communication effects as well as by position and disposition effects. This is why the utilitarian way of thinking nowadays seems so natural that it has subtly infiltrated social and political philosophy as well as practical political thought. This is also the reason why the exaggerated functionalism of the 1960s and 1970s is still with us, though it is less assertive. These communication effects after all contribute significantly to transforming a paradigm into a view of the world: as soon as it attracts the attention of groups outside the scientific community, it tends to be seen as a view of the world given the seal of scientific approval, and its logical status of hypothesis, or more accurately of *a priori* form, tends to be forgotten.

Up to this point I have been looking at two stages of scientific enquiry – *vocabulary* and *paradigms*, and I have tried to show that at these two stages, false beliefs can develop easily and naturally, without leading us to think that the researcher is blind or dishonest. I will now examine the intermediate stage – that of *models*.

Contrary to what is often thought, there is nothing strange about models in the social sciences. On the contrary, it is a notion which describes a vital stage in scientific analysis, not only in economics or political science but also in sociology or history. In the same way that Molière's Monsieur Jourdain was writing prose without knowing it, all social sciences use models as a method. Of course it is only in certain cases that they assume a mathematical form. The form, however, is of the secondary importance, and it seems to me dangerous to assume that a model has, by definition, to have a mathematical form, otherwise one is likely to miss the vital stage in analysis which is best described by the idea of *model*.

Take the example, as Simmel does,[24] of the historian who wants to explain the result of the battle of Marathon, a theme which, because of its importance for the subsequent fate of the Western world, has long fascinated historians. Why did the Greeks win the battle? Obviously, this can be explained only by reference to one factor – the behaviour of those who took part, i.e. Greek and Persian commanders, officers, and soldiers. Of course we have no real information on the individual behaviour of the participants; but even if each solider had written his memoirs, describing in as objective a way as possible his experience and feelings, this writing would not constitute an explanation of the outcome of the battle. It would reproduce 'reality' (assuming the memoirs were objective), but it would be a compendium difficult to read and digest and which the mind would find hard to penetrate. The conclusion is that although the reasons for the Greek victory could be found only in the behaviour of the people involved, knowing exactly what this behaviour was would not help at all in explaining the victory.

The explanation would be found in building a model – historians decide that a particular Greek or Persian commander played a particularly important part – though of course the *importance* of the role is not discovered directly from reality. Moreover, rather than looking at each individual soldier, historians will probably try to build a credible picture of Greek and Persian soldiers in general. To do this, they will reduce a complex reality to a straightforward image – they will combine all Greek combatants into an *ideal* soldier, whom they will try to bring to life by giving him a 'psychology'. This however will be a basic psychology with a limited number of traits, and probably not very close to what any of the Greek soldiers were really like.

Basically, historians are proceeding here like economists who, in order to explain changes in price of a particular good, start by combining *all* producers and *all* consumers into a single ideal producer and a single ideal consumer, and then give them, as Simmel calls it, an 'abstract' or a 'conventional' psychology. Models are therefore inescapable in history as well as in economics, and it becomes easy to understand why, although they can provide acceptable scientific explanations of phenomena, they can also allow through and legitimate all kinds of belief. This is all the more so in that a model can readily be seen as a copy of reality.

After all, certain models give the appearance of being so abstract and so simplified compared with the complexity of the real world that the people manipulating and using them are unaware of the realist illusion. This is true, to take an extremely well-known example, of Ricardo's 'law of comparative advantages', which Samuelson rightly regards as one of the most spectacular discoveries of social science. This model explains why, in international trade, it may be in the interests of a country – in certain circumstances – to import certain categories of goods, *even when it could produce them more cheaply itself*. Ricardo's 'law' reduces an enigma (why does country A buy goods b which it could produce more cheaply than its trading partner?) to an effect of aggregation of rational behaviour – country A imports goods b because it is in its interest to do so, *even though it would not appear to be so*.

To take Ricardo's example, suppose that in Portugal it takes 80 hours' work to produce x bottles of wine, as against 120 in Britain; and that it takes 90 hours to produce y yards of cloth in Portugal as against 100 in England. Portugal can therefore produce both wine and cloth more cheaply than England. Nevertheless, it is in its interest to import cloth from England, since this is the good where its comparative advantage is smaller. If there were no international trade, a Portuguese who wanted to buy y yards of cloth would have to offer not x bottles of wine, but more – namely, $1.125x$ bottles ($90/80 = 1.125$); and an English person would have to offer 1.2y yards of cloth ($120/100$ = 1.2) to get x bottles of wine. When there is international trade, however, Portugal can offer England x bottles of wine for y yards of cloth; and England will accept this, since at home for this quantity of cloth, only 0.83 bottles of wine could be obtained ($100/120$ = 0.83).

Ricardo's model is presented as an abstract construct, with no claim to be realistic. One is well aware, when one encounters it, that international trade cannot be reduced to a *formula* like this. In other words, the simplifying hypotheses in the model are clear enough for the observer to spot. And, of course, saying that there are simplifying hypotheses means that one accepts that the model corresponds with reality only when reality can be said to be correctly (though roughly) represented by these simplifying hypotheses; that is, the observer will not usually be surprised if, in spite of Ricardo's law, international trade, say between country A and country B, is occasionally unfavourable, for example to B. All that is needed is for a particular hypothesis of the model to be inconsistent with a specific case.

Even in the case of a model which is so obviously idealized, some people may nevertheless believe it to be universal. Also, there are people who claim that Ricardo's law has proved that in reality international trade always benefits those who engage in it. Such an interpretation, however, would assume that the model lacks hypotheses: this is inconsistent with the very notion of model, and in the case which we are looking at, *clearly* untenable, given the immediately visible nature of the simplifying hypotheses.

This example leads people to feel that models are likely to produce a typical E effect. This is shown by the fact that people (for example, the researcher, or one or more of the groups addressed) may tend to forget or overlook the hypotheses without which no model, on any subject, is possible. Of course, I will have to pause when I say 'tend to', since it has very little meaning.

All kinds of facts, however, lend support to the use of 'tend to': let us take an example from the philosophy and the sociology of science. People working in these disciplines subscribe to two or three well-known propositions – the ones associated with Popper, Lakatos, and Kuhn,[25] though for the moment Popper seems to attract only minority support. Without going into too much detail, I want to describe briefly what the debate is about.

For Popper – and I am aware that I am reducing his ideas to their bare bones – science makes progress in the following way: a theory is put forward, which has certain consequences. These consequences may be compared with reality, or rather with data obtained from observation or experimentation. Two situations can then arise: either all the consequences of the theory – at least those which have become clear – are consistent with reality, or else they are not. In the first case the theory is kept; in the second, an attempt is made to amend it or change it until another theory is produced which this time is consistent with the facts: after which, new consequences of the theory will still emerge as well as new data with which they will – or will not – be consistent. And in fact there will always be cases of inconsistency which will crop up.

From this way of looking at it, two ideas emerge: firstly, that a scientific theory is always, to a certain extent, condemned in advance – it may be regarded as true today, then false tomorrow; and secondly, the conclusion from Popper's thought is that scientific progress has to be never-ending. In fact, Popper's thought is a combination of two classical ideas: the *modus tollens* of scholasticism (a universal proposition can be proved to be false, but never proved to be true), and the idea that since a theory is always the product of the mind, it can be evaluated only on the basis of statements made about the real world by its consequences.

By an interesting communication effect, the irony of which can be appreciated, Popper probably owes his present popularity to the fact that his ideas underline certain people's faith in human reason and the progress of science, whereas for others, they confirm the inability of science to establish incontrovertible truths.

For Lakatos as well as for Kuhn, Popper's ideas are questionable. With Kuhn's *Theory of Scientific Revolutions*, with Feyerabend and Feuer, and to a lesser extent, with Lakatos, sociology makes a dramatic entrance: a scientific community representing a discipline goes about its 'normal' work (cf. Kuhn's 'normal science') in the framework of paradigms (Kuhn) or of programmes (Lakatos) which, in the ideal case, produce a consensus and a collective belief in their validity and creative capacity.

Let us assume now that experimental data not really consistent with a theory has been recorded. According to Popper, this event will cause the theory to be questioned. According to Kuhn and Lakatos, the process is much simpler; firstly because the notion of inconsistency between data and theory may be ambiguous. Supposing (says Lakatos) that a physicist of Newton's time discovers that a planet is deviating from the orbit assigned to it by theory T. T could nevertheless be kept thanks to an adventitious hypothesis – the disturbance could be caused by the presence of an unknown planet. Astronomers, however, cannot find the planet in question. Perhaps this is because the planet is too small. A more powerful telescope is built to test the new hypothesis. The hypothetical planet still cannot be traced. Is this sufficient reason to abandon T? No, because cosmic dust may be concealing the planet. A satellite sent to test the new hypothesis cannot find the cosmic dust. Perhaps this is because the presence of a magnetic field has interfered with the satellite's readings, and so on. In other words, decades or even centuries may pass before a 'fact' inconsistent with T leads to its rejection.

There are many other reasons, however, which will prevent the Popperian process of *invalidation*, or, if one prefers, *refutation*, or *falsification* from coming into play automatically. A scientific community can work only within the framework of one or more paradigms. Without a paradigm, it is impossible, for example, to decide which observations and experiments are relevant. For T to be rejected, not only must T's credibility be reduced by the accumulation of data inconsistent with it, and not only must this inconsistency be recognized, but there must also exist – and therefore be put forward – an alternative T' which is more suitable than T. Even if all these conditions are met, it is not inevitable that T' will readily replace T, since many researchers will have a personal interest in keeping T. In other words they are liable for *exit costs* from T, and *entry costs* into T' – costs which are variable, complex, and multidimensional (learning a new language, abandoning a particular view of the world, published work becoming out of date, etc.)[26] It is therefore very likely that many people will try to keep T going by trying to reduce the inconsistencies between T and the facts of the real world by means of adventitious hypotheses which may take a long time to verify or disprove.

The existence of interests linked to social position also lends support to Feuer's theory that scientific progress often comes about through conflict between generations – in fact the exit and entry costs involved in going over from T to T' tend, for structural reasons, to be less for a young researcher than for an experienced researcher. The costs are minimal when the researcher is both young and on the fringe of existing scientific institutions, as in Einstein's case when he was working on the theory of relativity (which is what gave rise to Feuer's theory).

The debate between Popper and the rest is in fact, if one thinks about it, rather strange, by which I mean the very fact that there is a debate about who is right, and that support for each is carefully measured. Both, after all, are putting forward *models*, idealized descriptions of the process by which scientific knowledge is produced. If some models fit certain cases very well, others fit other cases better. In this way, Popper's ideal history (model) is appropriate to the Michelson–Morley experiment, just as Lakatos's model is applicable to other stages in the history of science. All these models introduce hypotheses, which are shown to be more or less true depending on the stage under consideration. There is no point, therefore, in asking who is correct.

The fact that this question is frequently asked, and that hundreds of pages are devoted to discussing it, is the result, in part, of position effects: Kuhn certainly tried to show that he was more successful than Popper, and Feyerabend that he had gone 'further' than Kuhn. Among these position effects, one can also refer to role effects. Sociologists, for example, prefer models with social variables, while philosophers often prefer those without.

Behind the debate, however, there is above all an E effect, namely that very often it is forgotten that a model must contain hypotheses. In this case, faced with two models, the usual tendency would be to decide which one is the *correct* one. However, if it is seen that they are based on different sets of hypotheses, it can easily be accepted – at least in certain cases – that both are *correct*, even if some of their hypotheses are in contradiction. They will be correct in the sense that both give better explanations of a particular type of phenomenon or particular aspect of reality.

Why do people forget what appears to be an epistemological commonplace – that a model is always based on hypotheses? Why is this so often ignored? If it were borne in mind, nobody would argue about whether Popper was better than Kuhn, or Kuhn better than Popper. Similarly, everybody would accept that despite the genius of Ricardo, trade between two countries can sometimes be disadvantageous to one of them. I think that the answer to this question is relatively simple. It is that every model tenders to have visible hypotheses and invisible hypotheses: often, the latter are not only hidden from view, they have to be carefully winkled out. In general, people will only bother with the former. To this E effect, based on the contrast between the two sorts of hypotheses, will be added position and disposition effects by virtue of which both the researcher and the audience will be more or less inclined to perceive the invisible hypotheses.

To illustrate this idea, I will quote again an example which I have used before, since I cannot find a better one to support what I am saying. I like the example for another reason, namely that it took me quite a long time to realize the weaknesses of a model whose effectiveness I had long admired. In other words I experienced for myself in this example the difficulty that sometimes exists in getting a model to reveal unspoken hypotheses.

The example is given in an article[27] which tries to explain why peasants in West Bengal adamantly refused to adopt an innovation which would certainly have improved the productivity of their land. The study therefore started with an enigma – why did these peasants refuse to do what was obviously in their interest? The article is even more interesting in that the author, an Indian Marxist, made sure he did not fall into the trap which snares many people who study this kind of question, whereby they attribute apparently irrational behaviour to the irrationality of the actor. The article in question shows that the peasants rejected the innovation because, *despite appearances to the contrary*, it was rational for them to reject it. It is after all an agrarian economy; productivity and the standard of living are low. However, it is also a money economy, and society is divided into two classes – landlords and tenant farmers. The tenant farmers hire out their labour and sometimes provide their own tools. In return, they receive part of the harvest according to the terms of a contract. This, however, is not enough for them to live on, and therefore they have to borrow. Since they do not have enough security to borrow from banks, they borrow from their landlords. Since their level of income remains the same over the years, they are in a state of chronic indebtedness. Despite having sold their labour willingly, they are bound to their landlord through debt. It is a kind of semi-feudal system.

Why was the innovation which would have meant an increase in productivity rejected? Because it would probably have led to a reduction in landlords' income. The increase in productivity would have increased the amount of rice which went to the landlord, but by increasing the income of the tenant, it would have reduced the latter's level of indebtedness. In this way, the trading profits of the landlord would have risen, but this increase might not have offset the possible loss on the debt.

The proof is presented as a mathematical model leading to a conclusion which goes beyond this thinking, and which is not really arrived at intuitively. The model shows in fact that for a hypothetical increase in productivity, the landlord can, from year to year, suffer a heavy loss, even when the tenant turns to personal use a large proportion of the additional income from the increase in productivity. In technical language, even if the tenant has a high marginal propensity to consume, and, as a result, uses only a small amount of the extra income to reduce his or her debt, the landlord's financial loss can, on balance, exceed the trading gain from the increased productivity.

This is a very powerful model. It suggests in effect that in a production system like that of West Bengal, any innovation is very likely to be rejected. In other words, a semi-feudal production system tends to bring about economic stagnation which continues indefinitely. Is the necessary corollary that the economic modernization of West Bengal depends on the abolition of the prevailing relationships of production? This conclusion would be rather too hasty, because the model has visible parameters and invisible parameters, as well as visible hypotheses and invisible hypotheses. The visible hypotheses deal exclusively with the relationships of production. The visible parameters describe the share of the harvest which goes respectively to landlord and tenant, the tenant's marginal propensity to consume (which is assumed to be constant – that is, independent of income), the rate of interest at which money is borrowed, and the increased production brought about by the innovation.

Within the theoretical framework defined by these hypotheses and these parameters, the clear conclusion is that the innovation involves the landlord in a risk of substantial loss, and therefore the landlord will be led to reject it.

However, the model also contains invisible hypotheses and parameters:

1   The model concentrates on relationships between landlords and tenant farmers and *competition* between landlords is not taken into account. However, landlords who decided to go along with the innovation before the others could reduce the price of their rice, sell more of it, buy more land and emerge better placed. At the same time, other landlords would follow suit.

2   Relationships of power are not taken into consideration either: each landlord is assumed to have the final say in whether the innovation is accepted or rejected. The model assumes, therefore, that the authorities can try to persuade, but cannot urge or pressurize people; and also that tenants cannot exert pressure on the landlord.

3   The suggested innovation involved financial investment, though this was not high. There are however other kinds of innovation which do not need financial input but which could bring about considerable productivity gains (reorganizing the sowing and harvesting teams, changing growing methods, and so on). These are cost-free innovations which play an important role in agrarian societies at an early state of development, and yet the model assumes that innovation is always expensive. By doing this, it introduces a parameter; but it is an invisible parameter, and appears only when one scratches the surface of the model. For an innovation not involving financial input, another invisible hypothesis already referred to has to be regarded as much less likely – that tenants have no means of exerting pressure on the landlord. Although this hypothesis is possible for an innovation involving a financial input, it is much less relevant for one which is cost-free to the landlord and which is bound to have a positive impact on productivity.

4   The model also introduces invisible hypotheses concerning the psychology of the actors, namely that the landlords are scared of taking risks. However, although innovation involves them in risk, it also gives them an opportunity. As the model shows, for certain combinations of two parameters – the amount of increased productivity and the tenant's marginal propensity to consume – innovation is, in the theoretical framework of the model, unfavourable to the landlord; for other combinations however, it is personally beneficial. This can clearly be seen intuitively: if the productivity gains are substantial enough, and if the tenant's marginal propensity to consume is high enough, the commercial advantages to the landlord will exceed the financial loss. Although the expected increase in

productivity can be calculated, if only roughly, the tenant's marginal propensity to consume is not only not known, but can also be assumed to vary between individuals, and with changes in income. The model concludes that the innovation will be rejected only by introducing a hypothesis which, although almost hidden, has to be regarded as too stark, in that it asserts not only that all landlords are strongly averse from taking risks, but even that *none* of them is willing to take the slightest one. If one of them accepted the innovation, he or she would drag the others along, simply by being in a position to steal their clientele by selling rice more cheaply.

In this way, the model offers a brilliant and possibly valid explanation of why the innovation was rejected *in the context and the conditions under consideration* but it does not permit the conclusion either that semi-feudal production relationships lead to inevitable stagnation, or that economic development necessarily depends on their abolition.

The point is that if one is convinced of the validity of the paradigm that productive *relationships* are the main determinant of productive *forces*, one will *give no thought* to uncovering the hypotheses hidden in the model; where one is convinced of the validity of this classical Marxist paradigm, an extremely rigorous effort of methodical criticism is needed to flush out these hypotheses.

This example allows us to understand why models in the social science are usually perceived in a *realist* way, and are regarded as having too wide a scope and too much validation. To explain this, it is not sufficient to refer to a 'tendency' to give these models more generality than they deserve. This word merely identifies a complex problem rather than helping to account for it. The key to the problem, I think, lies in the fact that not only does every model contain, by definition, hypotheses, but that it contains hypotheses of varying degrees of visibility. Whether the frontier between visible and invisible hypotheses is clear depends on the particular case. It is usually clearer in the case of a mathematical form of model. However, the distinction between the two kinds of hypothesis is always there, whatever the nature of the model. After all, a model can exist only when some of its hypotheses are made explicit. At the same time, however, it remains a simplification of reality, and to perceive exactly what the nature of this simplification is, we need to compare the model with the reality which it is supposed to be explaining. Even though it may seem to be a vicious circle, such a comparison is not in principle impossible, as is shown in the previous analysis. However, it can never be regarded as complete, because the invisible hypotheses are situated in the area between the model and reality;

and to prise them all out, we need to be able, like gods, to embrace reality in all its complexity.

To this E effect, which in my view is basic, other effects[28] are often added. A model is normally constructed in the framework of a paradigm. In our previous example, the paradigm is clearly visible and can easily be described – relationships of production determine the totality of economic phenomena. Somebody who believes in this paradigm will have more difficulty in perceiving some of the invisible hypotheses which fall outside this framework.

When a model such as the one I have just been considering is made available to everybody, it will give rise to communication, position and disposition effects. Thus, for example, sociologists who believe in the Marxist paradigm which is the framework for the model, but who have no clear idea of a concept such as the marginal propensity to consume, will inevitably regard the model as a black box. They may however be attracted by its conclusions, and by the brilliant and authentically scientific nature of the analysis.

Similarly, a Marxist politician may see in it the specific confirmation of the idea that economic development depends on the abolition of archaic relationships of production.

Finally, I need to remind the reader of an essential point to which I have referred several times: in contrast to the natural sciences, the social sciences tend to operate in the public gaze, to choose subjects for research according to the requirements of the moment rather than because of intrinsic need, and to arouse the interest of different audiences. This means that E effects are significantly amplified by the communication effects to which I have referred. Although it may be difficult for researchers to perceive the boundaries of the paradigm to which they subscribe or the invisible hypotheses of a particular model, it is even more so for the researcher's audience. Conversely, although natural sciences are also subject to E effects, they are much less open to this phenomenon of amplification through communication effects.

Ideologies therefore may be based not only on sophisticated theories, but also on authentically scientific theories. However, the second case is more important and more interesting than the first. The fragility of a sophisticated theory or one made up of bits and pieces becomes readily apparent. Conversely, it is much more difficult to eliminate the ideological effects of a scientific theory, since determining how valid it is, is a complex operation of which the results, moreover, are not easily made visible. At the same time, if one sees that the ideologies are also based on authentically scientific theories, it is all the more easy to understand why beliefs in false or dubious ideas are so widespread.

As Simmel clearly showed at the end of the nineteenth century,[29] the influence of Marxism is to a large extent explained by the fact that Marx defined paradigms and models which were authentically scientific, and this is why he gained so much credit. However, he also tried to give these models and paradigms a greater validity and scope than they warranted: hence the ideological nature of Marxism.

To end this chapter, I will simply mention a final point which I will not be able to develop further. In this chapter, I have dealt only with the *explanatory* side of the social sciences, and not with their *interpretive* side. There is a problem of explanation when one ponders, for example, on the reasons for the Greek victory at Marathon, or on the causes of economic stagnation in a particular society. However, the questions which social sciences try to answer are not always of this kind. Just like traditional philosophy of history, the social sciences also tackle questions which can be called, very roughly, questions of *meaning*. Thus, for example, some people try to show that there are dividing lines in time and space (the dividing line of 'modernity', or that between modern and traditional societies, or between 'holistic' societies and 'individualistic' societies), or that it is possible to see lines of development in history. Of course, these lines and divisions can only become apparent by emphasizing certain problems and relegating others to the background, by stressing certain traits and disregarding others. The picture of reality produced in this way may be reasonably successful, convincing, and interesting. If it is successful and convincing, it may give rise to ideological effects, as can be seen from the great nineteenth-century evolutionist surveys or the discontinuist philosophers of history of our own day (Karl Polanyi, Michel Foucault, Louis Dumont).[30]

However, the relationship between ideological phenomena and the social sciences is at the same time simpler and more complicated when they are looked at in their interpretative dimension. It is simpler in that ideology is, as it were, inherent in interpretation itself. It is more complicated in that an *interpretation* – rather like a work of art – is influential only if it is in tune with the times, and if, therefore, it expresses ideas which are widespread in any case. This is why it is *divisions* which are now in vogue rather than broad evolutionist visions. The ideological influence of the social sciences is thus much more difficult to isolate, as far as their interpretative dimension is concerned. Presumably, it would need another book to give this problem the detailed treatment it requires; but it was important to raise it.

It must of course also be said that the concept of interpretation and explanation are not indicative of mental activities which are totally separate from each other. This is clear, for example, in the way Dilthey saw the task of the biographer:[31] his view was that the biographer has to look for the final goal (*Endzweck*) for which the subject was aiming. Once the meaning which the hero gives to his or her life has been discovered, the biographer can then *explain* – in theory at least – each one of the subject's acts.

Part III

9

Two case studies

In this chapter, I will elaborate briefly on two case studies of present-day ideologies to which I have already referred: developmentalism and Third Worldism. The first one says that only the West has the ability and the responsibility to lead underdeveloped countries to a developed state. The second, on the other hand, asserts that poor countries should take charge of their own fate and not trust the West, which still practises colonialism. Although these opposing views are easy to summarize and immediately reveal their ideological character, both call upon an imposing scientific armoury. I will try to show that the spread of these two ideologies is clearly based on the three types of effect which I have analysed earlier, without trying to describe them in detail.

The first case study is based more specifically on the examination of a 'theory' which, in the twenty years between 1950 and 1970, came to appear as a kind of collective dogma, and had a considerable political influence. I refer to the theory that it was impossible for poor countries to achieve economic 'development' without help from outside. This 'theory', which was one of the mainstays of the system of ideas prevalent at the time, and which was given the name of 'developmentalism', was the main inspiration behind development policies. The governments of developed nations as well as international organizations and many governments 'on the spot', regarded it over a long period of time as a kind of creed.

How did this collective belief become established? Initially, a group of researchers regarded as specialists in the field of socio-economic development put forward similar theories which concluded scientifically that outside aid was vital. To understand why these theories were influential, we must look at why they were able to convince people. Why were they seen, not only *outside* scientific circles, but *inside* as well, as well-founded and possessing the demonstrative strength characteristic of scientific theories? To understand this persuasive force, we have to look at some of these theories in detail, and I will dwell a little on one of the best known, the theory of the 'vicious circle of poverty'. Originally put forward by Ragnar Nurkse,[1] a Swede, this theory had a long run, since it survived the decline of developmentalism – Galbraith[2] later produced a new revised version more in tune with the 1980s.

Nurkse's theory of the vicious circle of poverty can be summarized in the following propositions:

1 In a poor country, savings capacity is low.
2 When savings capacity is low, investment capacity is low.
3 Productivity gains usually come from capital investment.
4 When investment capacity is low, productivity gains are therefore difficult.
5 Increase in standard of living depends on productivity gains.
6 Since productivity gains are unlikely in a poor country, its standard of living and therefore its savings capacity are bound to stagnate.
7 Since development cannot happen endogenously, it has to be induced by aid from outside or the injection of foreign capital.

The persuasive force of the theory of the vicious circle of poverty comes primarily from the fact that it is offered as a *general* theory of under-development, possessing a significant *explanatory power*. Secondly, from the fact that it is made up of a series of propositions, each of which can be taken as obvious.

In fact, they have the appearance of *analytical* propositions in the Kantian sense of the word. The first proposition, for example, represents a simple statement of the notion of poverty: is it not true that one way of telling whether a nation is rich or poor is to assess its savings capacity? Or the second proposition: is it not obvious that investment capacities depend on savings capacities? Although the third proposition is synthetic rather than *analytical*, can it seriously be questioned? Is it not an obvious fact, even if this time it is *empirical* rather than *analytical*, that productivity gains are brought about particularly by investment in capital goods. Do we not observe every day and in all areas that increase in productivity comes from replacing human work by increasingly efficient machines? And it is of course another commonplace of economic theory that an increase in the standard of living comes from productivity gains.

One is dealing, therefore, with a theory which not only has significant explanatory power, but which also consists of a series of propositions each of which could be taken to be either analytically obvious or empirically commonplace. Moreover, the theory explains at a stroke a host of factual data which the hastiest of observers cannot challenge – one could name dozens of countries which seem to be doomed to indefinite economic stagnation. In other words, this is a theory which conforms to the traditional canons of things scientific, and this is why it was largely accepted by the international scientific community.

However, two further reasons for its favourable reception must be mentioned. The first is that many other theories were put forward at the same time which, by different avenues, led to the same conclusions. Since space does not allow me to go into great detail on this point, I will give one further brief example. One of these theories stresses that communication and transport infrastructures (overhead capital) are an essential condition of development – if the road or railway network is inadequate, markets will remain constricted. The result will be that possible entrepreneurs will have no real motive to replace labour with capital equipment, even assuming they are in a position to do this. Moreover, in developing countries, the authorities usually do not have enough resources to finance large infrastructure projects. Once more, the conclusion from this set of propositions – each of which is readily acceptable – is that foreign aid is necessary for development.

This coincidence of conclusions from a range of developmentalist theories gave rise to what may be called a *convergence effect*, whereby each theory reinforced the credibility of the others. I think this effect is worthy of attention, since it is present in most of the processes by which ideologies are formed. It presents some logical problems, however. Thus, for instance, the starting point of the theory of the vicious circle of poverty is a hypothesis which is incompatible with those of the theory that constricted markets deter investment. In the first case, the assumption is that savings capacity is zero; but in the second case, the assumption is that savings accrue, but are unlikely to be turned into investment. The two theories therefore lead to the same conclusion, but on the basis of different conditions.

The two reasons I have given for the positive reception of developmentalist theories by the scientific community are of an *epistemological* nature: the theories were perceived as sound and powerful, and at the same time as convergent. However, this reception is just as much due to reasons which can be called *sociological*, and which were responsible for powerful communication effects. In fact, at the time that these theories were conceived, the world seemed to be dominated by the West, and particularly by the United States. In any event, the Third World was not yet seen as a proper political actor on the international scene. Theories of development through outside aid, whereby nations in the *Centre* were responsible for those on the *Periphery*, were consistent with this view of the world.

Moreover, although there was in some countries, particularly in Latin

America, home-grown thinking on the problems of development, this was strongly dependent on theories emanating from the developed world. Any original thinking had but minor influence. It is true that some Latin American researchers had put forward themes such as that of the worsening of the terms of trade and tried to show that international trade *benefited* developed nations in particular.[3] However, the time had not yet come when this ideology became in any way prominent.

Developmentalist theories – of which the theory of the vicious circle of poverty is a major example – were therefore able to spread from one stage to another without hindrance. Samuelson gave a mathematical form to Nurkse's theory, thereby increasing its prestige and credibility.[4] Moreover, international organizations as well as governments endorsed and applied the conclusions to which developmentalist theories directly led – for example, foreign aid or injection of foreign capital. This was because they were regarded as being based on scientific theories which not only seemed intrinsically sound and *convergent*, but also occupied a *quasi-monopolistic* position.

Furthermore, there appeared another convergence effect: sociologists proposed, in parallel with economists, 'theories of modernization',[5] many of which tried to show that technical innovation and the development of education and mass communication would inevitably provoke chain reactions in developing countries. In particular, sociologists stressed that these factors would lead to a drag-along effect on economic development.

In fact, developmentalist theories had neither the explanatory power nor the basic soundness which were attributed to them. While it is true that they had a clear enough scientific form to allow them to get past the first stage (the scientific community), the reason why this was easy to do, and why it was not difficult to spread them among civil and political society was that they were in tune with the times. Why were these theories, which have only limited validity, as we will see, regarded as theories having general application, not only by intermediate and final recipients, but also by the international scientific community?

Let us return briefly to the theory of the vicious circle of poverty. All its propositions appear to be analytically or synthetically obvious, which partly explains why it was so authoritative. A moment's thought, however, is enough to show that the incontrovertible nature of the theory is pure illusion. In reality, the theory conceals, behind obvious statements, a significant set of invisible hypotheses and parameters.

A poor country has a low capacity to save. This, however, is true only if its income distribution pattern is very narrow. Income distribution, however, may be characterized at the same time by a very low *average* and by a very large *range*, i.e. by extensive inequality. In such a case, which is not uncommon, there is by definition a minority group which has a capacity to save. The basic proposition of the theory of the vicious circle of poverty is therefore presenting in an analytical form something which in fact comes from observation. In doing this, it is conferring on the theory a persuasive power and a general applicability which it does not deserve. This is all the more true in that, as observation shows, inequalities are often very large in countries which we call developing countries.

Another basic proposition of the theory of the vicious circle of poverty is that productivity gains are usually achieved by substituting capital equipment for manual labour. This proposition is an 'empirical generalization' which is very likely to be accepted – is it not true that *in the societies in which we live*, productivity gains are brought about by the investment of capital goods?

The theory of the vicious circle, however, is intended to be applied not to advanced industrial societies but to developing societies, where the primary sector is generally predominant. Where this is so, productivity gains are very often brought about by other methods besides the injection of capital equipment – changes in farming methods, or a redistribution of tasks. The traditional Japanese method of growing rice, for example, although much more productive than the Indian method, does not require more physical capital – it is only the organization of labour which distinguishes the two methods.

In other words, the third proposition of the theory of the vicious circle of poverty – that productivity gains depend on capital investment – seems to be empirically obvious because it evokes phenomena which are in fact typical, but typical of *industrial societies* rather than of societies which the theory addresses. Belief in the validity of this proposition is therefore based, to use Piaget's term, on a *sociocentric* reference. The proposition is likely to be regarded as true by somebody from a developed society, even though it has minimal relevance to the societies addressed by the theory. Here, there is a perspective effect (an important category, as we have seen, of disposition effects) just like those which I described when discussing magic.

Moreover, it has to be remembered that even in developed societies and even in the industrial sector, productivity depends on many factors besides the accumulation of capital – the decline in US productivity in the 1970s was not only the result of a fall in investment.

A final remark is that the theory of the vicious circle of poverty introduces, but not explicitly, many other hypotheses on which its validity depends. There is the *tacit* assumption, for example, that the ideal society with which it is dealing has no significant links with the outside world. If it did, the society in question could, even if its own productivity were not rising, benefit from productivity gains in other countries. It could even import the same goods over the years at decreasing cost, and this would have the same effect on its standard of living as an increase in its own productivity.

To conclude this rapid critical survey, we can see that the theory is in fact valid only *under extremely specific conditions*. It assumes that the range of income distribution is very narrow, but this is not true of several countries. It assumes that productivity gains are the result mainly of capital investment, though this applies far more to industrial societies than to relatively undeveloped societies. It also assumes a society with no links with the rest of the world, which is rarely the case. Overall, the ideal-typical society (to use Weberian terminology) which is addressed by the theory of the vicious circle of poverty is a kind of patchwork. It cannot serve as a simplified description of what relatively undeveloped societies really are. However, by its recourse to sociocentric representations, by the quasi-analytical nature of its component propositions, the theory gives the impression that it is a faithful description of the 'structural' traits common to all preindustrial societies. In doing this, it diverts the attention of those who use the theory (just as in the case of its authors) away from the invisible parameters and hypotheses concealed by its apparent validity.

It has to be said on this matter that the idea of an idealized description of developed societies as a whole should be treated with some caution and that in any case, it sets up a *paradigm*, in other words an *a priori* concept. What comparison can there possibly be between societies such as Colombia and Congo in the 1950s and 1960s? Both are of course developing societies, but the point is that they are widely divergent. The assumption that they can be subsumed under one idealized heading comes from the *a priori idea* that underdevelopment is a central political problem. It is an idea which of course is not enough in itself to confer on the phenomenon of underdevelopment a unity which it does not have in reality; but it creates in somebody who subscribes to it a mental disposition favourable to theories which purport to offer explanations of underdevelopment taken as a single phenomenon. It also prevents one from perceiving the obvious fact that developing societies are extremely diverse.

From the outset, an *extrinsic* objection could be made to theory of the vicious circle of poverty: if it is as true as it seems, how can we explain that some poor countries, for example eighteenth-century Britain, or nineteenth-century Japan or Prussia, experienced spectacular growth without foreign aid or the injection of foreign capital? The fact that this objection has not cast doubt on the theory is also explained by the strength of certain collective beliefs, particularly the one that developed nations are responsible for the development of what was beginning to be called the Third World.

Of course, some people from the 1950s and 1960s onwards were beginning to question the soundness of developmentalist theories in general and of the theories I have dealt with here in particular. At the time, however, no real attention was paid to such doubts. The collapse of developmentalist theories was less due to criticism of them than to geopolitical changes from the 1960s onwards, when decolonisation gave the Third World an increasingly important role in world affairs. The view on which developmentalist theories were based and which said that the West played a vital part in the development of these countries was discredited, not only because certain groups regarded it as 'neo-colonialist', but also because it was inconsistent with reality and *as a matter of fact* it had become impossible to regard these countries as laboratories.

This is why developmentalism was replaced by new ideologies such as dependency theory: the latter reintroduced Lenin's theory of imperialism and tried to show that the main cause of underdevelopment was the relationship of dependence which the nations of the Centre imposed on those of the Periphery under the guise of interdependence.

This new ideological phase can be analysed in exactly the same way as the developmentalist phase, and I will return to this point later. 'Dependency theory' was originally presented as a set of scientific theories which a significant part of the scientific community was able to take on board. It then spread through a certain number of stages, providing a legitimation of the collective representations summarised in the idea of 'Third Worldism'.

The case study which I have outlined suggests that the way in which the belief system called *developmentalism* was established needed to be analysed as the aggregate effect of acts, each of which can be regarded as easily *meaningful*, in the Weberian sense of the word. When he put forward his theory of the vicious circle of poverty, Nurkse, like many others, was trying to solve a *problem* which is perceived as crucial: what are the causes of underdevelopment (taken as a single phenomenon) and how can it be remedied? Of course, he asked the question in terms which were often used at the time, and he accepted without much discussion that it was possible to speak of underdevelopment as a single phenomenon. This generalist perspective, however, is traditional in the social sciences, and it is certainly characteristic of economic theory in particular. Therefore the idea that there was a problem of underdevelopment coincided with professional ways of looking at things. This is also why Nurkse's theory, like the many theories of the same kind which were produced at that time and which came up with conclusions which accorded with his, was immediately seen as interesting by the international scientific community and particularly by economists.

It is also easy to see why it was regarded not just as interesting but as valid. What Nurkse puts forward in his vicious circle theory is a *model*. This model is a valid construct only under extremely restrictive conditions, so restrictive, as we have seen, that it is not certain that the model can be taken as the idealized image of any real society. However, it is *meaningful* that its author did not really make these restrictive conditions clear. Firstly, because it is self-evident to an economist that all models are idealized constructs; secondly, because a researcher can hardly be expected to dwell at length on the imperfect validity of the theories which he or she is putting forward; and thirdly, because making clear such limitations raises considerations relevant to history rather than economics, and a propounder of theories tends to think that historical facts are outside his or her scope. In other words, we need only introduce simple hypotheses on the division of labour within the scientific community to *understand* that what was merely a model, valid in very restrictive conditions, has been presented as a *general* theory of underdevelopment as a single phenomenon, and widely seen as such by the international community of professional economists.

Of course, as I have said, objections were made very quickly to this interpretation; but they came from researchers who, like P. T. Bauer,[6] were not identified as closely with the body of thought which is summed up in the phrase 'economic theory'. Because he had had long and direct contact with the situation on the ground, P. T. Bauer realized early on that development phenomena could not be analysed effectively using the language of economic theory, and that it was necessary to take account of the diversity of underdeveloped societies. He argued, in other words, that the development economist should also be an historian and, as such, pay particular attention to differences and unforeseen events. Of course, Bauer was not the only person to think like this; but this interdisciplinary perspective involved costs, in that those who adopted it were to some extent marginalized, and their audience was rather limited. It did not help that, very often, the historico-economic perspective not only appeared scientifically tainted, but also seemed to lead to scepticism and ineffectiveness: did it not lead to the conclusion that there is no miracle cure for underdevelopment (as a single phenomenon), or that there is no means of telling that a particular approach will automatically bring about the expected development effect? Conclusions such as this brought no encouragement to politicians or to people who were politically aware or committed.

Arguments attacking developmentalist theories were therefore not very influential, and the theories themselves became dominant, not only because they were firmly situated within economic theory, but also because they led to optimistic conclusions and a well-defined political line: all that was needed was to inject foreign capital into underdeveloped countries or to build up infrastructures through foreign aid, and development would take off.

Having received the seal of approval of the scientific community, developmentalist theories were able to continue through a series of stages. It is easy to understand why they attracted the interest of Third World governments as well as governments in advanced countries, international organizations, political parties, and the Press. Obviously, when a theory appears to offer a simple solution to a major political problem, *mediators* (for example journalists) and decision-makers do not always look at it critically. In the breakdown of roles, this critical examination is the function of the scientific community, which in this case had given its approval to developmentalist theories. Moreover, *criticizing* a theory is a thankless task, involving costs and implying particular cognitive and intellectual resources more likely to be found in the scientific community, especially for relatively technical theories.

The reception given to the theory by the scientific community is also easy to understand. The reason why a theory such as Nurkse's must be regarded as weak is not, I repeat, because it lacks substance or coherence, or is sophistic, but because its validity depends on all kinds of implicit conditions which are unlikely to be found together in the real world – as we have seen, it was unlikely that these conditions would immediately be made explicit and become socially visible.

This is why the developmentalist ideology held sway for a time and was toppled only when it was seen to be in contradiction with new collective images generated when the Third World began to play a role in international affairs.

The Third Worldist ideology which replaced it was based not only on sentiment, as is often thought, but also on a body of scientific theories which usually come under the heading of *dependency theory*. Since this theory has nowadays acquired the status of a kind of paradigm, or of a theoretical framework for wide-ranging research, it is not surprising that it has numerous variants. The version by S. Amin and A. G. Frank is different from that of F. Cardoso,[7] and nuances and distinctions abound. There are so many variants and versions of the theory, and pieces of research on it or inspired by it, that scholarly work could be undertaken on them.

It is more interesting, however, and more relevant to my argument, to concentrate on the main strengths and the primary propositions or intuitions. The major intuition is that certain societies are dependent on others, that some are of the periphery and others of the centre, and that this duality gives rise to numerous consequences which tend to be to the disadvantage of the former and the advantage of the latter. In his theory of international trade, Ricardo, on the strength of a model based on all sorts of simplifications, proved that when two nations begin to trade, they can both benefit from this relationship, even when one of them imports goods which it could produce more cheaply than its partner. I have referred to this model earlier, and do not intend to return to it. Against this optimistic classical view of international trade, the 'dependency theorists' emphasize that dependent countries tend to export raw materials cheaply and to import manufactured goods at a high price. It is argued that, generally speaking, the relationship between dependent societies and independent or central societies entails effects of *exploitation* by the latter of the former, *disarticulation* effects (as when capitalists in the dependent societies ally with those in other countries or when inequalities in dependent societies are alleged to increase merely by the fact of dependence), as well as *immobility* effects (the 'development of underdevelopment', to use G. Franck's well-known phrase).

To deal with the matter briefly, two categories of data can be set against these hypotheses of dependency theorists. Firstly, studies based on series of data: P. T. Bauer,[8] for example, argues that, according to statistics issued by the Economic Commission for Latin America (a UN agency in which some of the ideas later taken up by the dependency theorists were particularly influential), gross national product rose 4.2 per cent a year in Latin American countries between 1935 and 1953, which was considerably better than in the United States. Since, as Bauer stresses, transactions in Latin America are largely monetary ones, statistics on gross national product are more meaningful than in most underdeveloped countries. In South-East Asia, exports of rubber were negligible in 1900, but rose to a value of £400 million by 1963; two-thirds of the rubber was produced on native-owned plantations. In the mid-1950s, income per head of population in Ghana was four times higher than at the beginning of the century, although the total population had itself quadrupled in this period. On the worsening of the terms of trade, A. Lewis reminds us that the terms on which primary products were traded for manufactured goods were better in the 1950s than at any other time during the previous eighty years, because of the rise in demand caused by the Korean War. Between 1955 and 1962 these terms became worse, but improved subsequently, and in 1970, when dependency theory began to make its mark, they were at their best point ever. The point is that it is impossible to speak of a persistent worsening of the terms of trade. Moreover, Lewis's data[9] does not take account of the fall in production costs or the considerable increase in exports of primary products, nor the better quality of imported goods and the effect which this had on welfare. In other words, we can point to a host of statistical data which hardly fits in with the view that 'dependence' inevitably causes immobility effects or the 'development of underdevelopment'

Secondly, the general views of dependence theorists can be attacked using the findings of research into specific cases. An example which has led to considerable research is that of Nigeria[10] – firstly because Nigeria's 'dependence' dates back to the beginning of the sixteenth century, when trade relations with Europe started; and secondly because colonization not only led to a spectacular increase in agricultural production, but also did not prevent (in fact may have encouraged) the rise of a class of Nigerian entrepreneurs in trade and transport at the regional and national level, in the distribution of imported goods and in banking and industry. All this must be understood, of course, in the context of Nigerian history – it is true, for example, that the slave trade prevented certain kinds of development when the income it generated allowed the substitution of local products by imported goods. Conversely, when the slave trade – the inhuman nature of which is obvious – came to an end, there were many traders with skills which were then transferred to the cotton or palm oil trade, allowing the setting up of trading networks and traditions which were passed on from generation to generation. Subsequently, these networks had no problem in marketing cocoa, rubber, and wood, as Nigerian growers adapted to the growth of European demand. Overall, Nigerian agriculture before British colonization was characterized by its ability to produce a large agricultural surplus, and also by a surplus of labour and arable land. Moreover, the organization of Nigerian society was such that very often members of local communities were free to decide how to use communal land and its produce. Factors such as these explain why Nigerian agriculture adapted very easily to foreign demand. Moreover, trade was not just developed, but accepted, and moral standards in commercial matters were well defined and adhered to.

The reaction of British colonialists to this situation was to conclude that Nigerian growers could meet the demands of British firms, in that there was a surplus of labour and arable land, individual freedom of decision hallowed by custom, and a proven ability to produce a sometimes considerable surplus and to adapt to changes in trading patterns. They also saw that it would be very risky to try to reduce growers and farmers to the level of agricultural labourers.

Nigerian growers responded to European demand and brought about an 'economic revolution'. Although their work was a function of the needs of British industry and the British market, and despite the colonial situation, the position was one of interdependence rather than dependence. European needs created opportunities for Nigerian growers and other economic agents, and this interdependence brought about remarkable growth and development. Nevertheless, the 'dependence' of Nigerian agriculture on British demand was limited by the fact that the goods which were exported, apart from cocoa, were consumer goods; and since economic development led to urbanization, domestic demand grew steadily, so that the system was reasonably well protected from the fluctuations of external demand. Moreover, the growing importance of all sectors – primary, secondary, and tertiary – in Nigeria led to an increase in disposable capital. Schatz has clearly shown that although there were not as many Nigerian entrepreneurs as one might have hoped, this was not because of lack of indigenous capital.[11]

The case of Nigeria is particularly interesting, since it is a society which for eighty years, until 1960, was subject to colonial rule. Despite this political dependence, economic 'dependence' undoubtedly accelerated growth and development, though it had negative effects on Nigerian society.

Is this case an exception? Obviously colonial rule was of a particular kind, as history helps to explain; but it would be risky to regard the Nigerian case as an aberration. On the contrary, it suggests that in general, it is better to speak of interdependence rather than dependence and that in any case the consequences of dependence are totally negative for the 'dependent' society only in marginal cases.

The example of colonial Nigeria is of course not the only one which can be cited to show inadequacies in dependency theory. In a very interesting article, Bienefeld[12] refers to recently industrialized countries such as South Korea, Taiwan, Singapore, and Hong Kong to show that their tremendous growth disproves that version of dependency theory which argues that a 'peripheral' society will only sink deeper into underdevelopment unless it makes a total break with capitalism. Bienefeld shows clearly how growth in these countries is the result of unfavourable trends in productivity and therefore falling competitiveness in most industrialized countries since 1970. At the same time, however, economic expansion continued, leading to an increase in demand for raw materials, and profit margins in OECD countries fell. These factors taken together led to the need to reduce production costs, to find new markets for manufacturing industries and to look for investment opportunities giving an adequate return. The result was that producers and traders looked towards these 'newly industrializing countries' which were able to expand because of wider markets in industrialized countries.

What is interesting from our point of view is that Bienefeld refused to see in these examples a refutation of dependency theory, but on the contrary said that he found that they confirmed it. He argued that dependency theory has always stressed the importance of the international context – an importance confirmed by the case of newly industrializing countries. It goes without saying that these countries did not merely wait for opportunities to come their way; they used opportunities to pursue a voluntarist policy made possible, or at least helped along, by the fact that they were cases where the state dominated the economy. According to Bienefeld, therefore, the fact of interdependence underscores the validity of dependency theory, which suggests it is acceptable only if it is deprived of almost all its specific content! After all, there was no need to resort to dependency theory to see that, when country A addresses a demand to country B, this demand creates an opportunity for country B which it can grasp or not, depending on a whole host of factors, and that this demand constitutes a relationship of interdependence between A and B.

Doubtless aware that his analysis, though very interesting, had no need for dependency theory, Bienefeld tries to grab hold of its branches, by saying, for example, that the remarkable growth of newly industrialized countries went hand in hand with a very high level of political repression. This is of course true, but one may ask whether repression can really be regarded (as he suggests) as a condition of growth – did it for example lead to a lower demand for wage rises? The answer is 'no', and this hypothesis can be disproved merely by looking at how wages developed. Since the mid-1970s, according to Bienefeld, skilled workers in South Korea and Taiwan have had considerable wage increases and wage differentials have narrowed. Therefore, the case of Brazil, which has not experienced a narrowing of wage differentials to the same degree, in no way proves that, where a country of the 'periphery' starts experiencing strong growth even when dependency theory says it should not be doing so, differentials are inevitably preserved or increased. Similarly, it is doubtful whether the repressive nature of a regime is a necessary condition or an inevitable consequence of growth in societies of the 'periphery'.

Some dependency theorists assert that for them the important issue is 'reality' and history. Thus, for example, they condemn, because it is too abstract, the classical theory of international trade. However, a corollary of this emphasis on 'reality' is surely a rejection of dependency theory itself. It is axiomatic that societies have developed to different degrees and that their influence in world affairs varies; it is a gratuitous statement to say that dependence is always to the advantage of the dominant society – in so far, that is, as the concept of dependence is amenable to definition, since it could be said that Canada is at least as 'dependent' on the United States as, say, Argentina. There are countless ways in which a society can be interdependent with its environment, and the effects of this interdependence are infinitely variable.

The propositions put forward by dependency theory give rise, in fact, to a basic question of methodology, the full scope of which cannot be examined in the context of the present discussion – namely, is it meaningful to analyse the effects of *dependence*? After all, although in certain cases a proposition such as 'X is the effect of Y' has a clear and distinct meaning ('the fire was caused by a gas leak'), in other cases it lacks this.

Taking for example as fact X that my watch tells the time, of what Y is this the effect? Would any good come out of analysing the effects of the invention of the wheel on modern society? They are both all-pervading and impalpable, like the consequences of the fact that Nigeria was a British colony and Brazil a Portuguese one. In the final analysis, it is perhaps because it claims to have the answer to the question about the *effects* of 'dependence' that dependency theory seems so hard to pin down. On this point, we must once more stress how it differs from the classical theory of international trade which, although it relies on obvious simplifications, has a clear objection – to analyse the effects of a move from self-sufficiency to mutual trade, in certain precisely defined conditions. The difference is that whereas the theory of international trade never claimed to replace history, dependency theory tried to rediscover, in a abstract form, the 'fundamental' workings of history. It is, in its principles, a return to what was called in the nineteenth century the philosophy of history: the only difference is that the 'laws' that it is trying to make salient are not evolutionary but 'structural' laws.

In other words the very questions which dependency theory asks are intelligible only when one sees that they show that there are *a priori* assumptions in the minds of those who ask them. It is not difficult, however, to see that these *a priori* assumptions are fragile, and to identify the disposition effects on which they are based.

How can we explain why dependency theory is so successful and influential? Its influence has been and still is uncontestable: it is still a commonplace view that the industrialized societies are the cause of all the problems of the Third World, and it is not difficult to see how this view became prevalent. It offers an easy explanation for all kinds of phenomena which challenge the basic values of democratic societies and to which citizens of these societies are inevitably sensitive. Moreover, the explanation points to guilty parties who in any case are the object of extremely unfavourable prejudices on the part of certain specific groups.

For this reason, it is more interesting to look at the way dependency theory was received in the scientific community, in that, as I have shown, it achieved the status and the stature of a true paradigm, in Kuhn's meaning of the phrase – it provided the inspiration for a large amount of research in various parts of the world. Although the theory began in Latin America, much North American, Polish, German, and French writing is inspired by it. Why did the theory gain so much influence?

Firstly, it needs to be emphasized that dependency theory is built on the debris of other paradigms to which I have referred earlier: modernization theory and development theory. I have already covered this point and will merely say, in summary, that at the end of the 1960s, doubt began to be cast on these paradigms, which had been central to the social sciences in the preceding period, not only because they had been disproved by the facts, but also – and perhaps especially – because they ran counter to images which became dominant at that time. Both modernization theories and development theories were by implication a view of social change which was based on technical expertise. Moreover, they seemed to contain a sociocentric point of view which was less and less acceptable as soon as the Third World began to assert itself in international affairs.

Secondly, the 'structuralists' of the Economic Commission for Latin America had initiated themes such as the worsening of the terms of trade of primary products against manufactured goods.[13] 'Structuralism' therefore took on board, and made its own, the obvious point that there was conflict between developed and underdeveloped societies. However, it went beyond the way in which terms of trade worsened, and pointed to a new kind of explanation for it as well. Whereas development theorists and modernization theorists looked for the causes of underdevelopment within the underdeveloped societies themselves, structuralists showed that the causes should be sought in the *relationships* between developed and underdeveloped countries. At precisely the time, therefore, when development theories and modernization theories were seen to be in an impasse, 'structuralist' ideas hinted at an alternative paradigm. The theory of the deterioration of terms of trade was probably weak and easily refuted by factual data, but the paradigm behind the theory (the analysis of underdevelopment as a consequence of the *relationships* between developed and underdeveloped countries) not only was not refutable in the same way (a paradigm is by definition not refutable), but it was also clearly different from the paradigms in use for twenty years and apparently at the end of their useful life. All that was needed, therefore, was to give a name to this paradigm, and the notion of dependence made it clear that the causes of underdevelopment lie in the *relationship* between developed and underdeveloped countries, and that these relationships are asymmetrical.

Therefore the paradigm behind 'structuralism', which later became 'dependency theory', not only avoided completely the charge of sociocentrism, but in fact reversed this sociocentrism – developed nations no longer held the key to development, they were responsible for underdevelopment. This paradigm shift not only opened up new avenues of research, or at least was seen as a potential boost to research into development, but furthermore, it created a situation in which the context of research was in tune with representations and dispositions which, during the 1960s, had become dominant in certain specific groups. It must also be emphasized that the new paradigm had become accepted – it carried on the tradition of analysing 'imperialism' as a consequence of capitalism. The high point of this tradition was, of course, Lenin's *Imperialism, the Highest Stage of Capitalism.*[14]

Without going into details, I will simply remind the reader that Adam Smith, in *The Wealth of Nations*,[15] made a vigorous attack on what was later called colonialism. He argued that, because it placed restrictions on the freedom to negotiate, colonialism – a form of the 'mercantilism' excoriated by Smith – meant that goods were imported into European countries at an unnecessarily high price. The reason for this was not only the costs of transport, but above all the fact that the colony did away with competition between suppliers, and constituted an unintentional and unjustified subsidy of the trader by the consumer.

The same point was made at the beginning of the twentieth century by Hobson:[16] the conclusion of his influential book was that colonies benefit only traders and speculators. A further point of his was that inequalities within industrial nations were such that if surplus capital were used to increase productivity, the resulting level of production would be more than could be absorbed by consumption: colonies were therefore needed to mop up surplus capital which could not be used at home because of these inequalities. Hobson's analysis was refined by the famous Austrian economist Hilferding,[17] who stressed that in the case of *financial* capital in particular, which could find no other investment opportunity, colonies could be used to mop it up. Lenin's book is of course merely a juxtaposition of the ideas of Hobson and Hilferding, and he makes explicit reference to these writers.

It is important to refer briefly to these historical points, since they explain why Lenin's theory of imperialism was accepted in circles which were not only not Leninist, but which were resolutely opposed to Marxism-Leninism. They help us to understand, for example, why Hannah Arendt, in her book *The Origins of Totalitarianism*[18] adopts Lenin's arguments uncritically. The reason is that she was well aware that Lenin had added practically nothing to the arguments of Hobson (to which she frequently refers) and Hilferding.

I think that the points I have raised help to explain why Lenin's theory of imperialism, if not in its details, then at least as far as its main argument is concerned (that imperialism is the consequence of capitalism), is regarded as a kind of focus by very broad groups, and is readily accepted by them, including people who are only moderately attracted by Marxism. It is not appropriate in the present discussion to go into criticisms of Lenin's theory;[19] but its weakness is shown by certain facts, such as that the British Empire expanded considerably between 1840 and 1870, well before the time (Lenin puts it at around 1890) when it was difficult for European capital to find investment opportunities in Europe. The fact that these obvious objections to Lenin's theory are ignored by such a learned writer as Hannah Arendt is a good illustration of how far the theory of imperialism had become common ground, because of its ecumenical origin.

We see, therefore, that 'dependency theory' offered an alternative paradigm at a time when existing ones had come to the end of their useful life. Moreover, it had the double attraction of classicism and modernism. It was something new and at the same time reassuring because of its implied reference to a tradition of thought which was well established and widely accepted. On the other hand, it did not claim that it was returning to this tradition. Although it clearly rediscovered this tradition and gained some of its authority from it, it nevertheless claimed to be based on a criticism of previous paradigm.

This criticism of existing paradigms was, moreover, very powerful, in that it pointed up a major weakness in many development theories. When Rostow[20] spoke of 'stages of growth', for example, he omitted the obvious point that (on the assumption that there are in fact stages) for a society which has reached a particular stage, it makes all the difference whether it has reached it *before* or *after* the others. In other words, it was certainly odd to put forward a theory of development which took societies to be independent of their environment. Gerschenkron[21] stressed this point in his examination of the development of Prussia and France, and Gunder Frank quite rightly developed and generalized the argument: it was clear that many modernization and development theories included by implication the dubious premiss that societies can be treated as closed systems.

Once it had begun to gain ground, dependency theory in fact worked like a paradigm, being flexible enough to inspire research in a variety of human sciences: Wallerstein, a historian and sociologist, latched on to the Centre–Periphery dualism,[22] Emmanuel, an economist, endeavoured to use tools of economic analysis to formulate ideas on dependence;[23] sociologists[24] used the armoury of statistical analysis to try to show that dependence, measured for example by Galtung's[25] index of the structure of transactions between a particular society and the rest, affected the growth of GDP. All kinds of research, from historical research, to statistical analysis common in sociology, to economic modelling, could be marshalled to defend and illustrate dependency theory.

Apart from those already adduced, one of the main reasons why the theory of imperialism became dominant to the extent of being common ground is that no *general* theory can be put forward to refute it, except perhaps Schumpeter's attempt[26] to defend the hypothesis that imperialism, far from being necessary for the survival of capitalism, is on the contrary a vestige of the precapitalist era.

One has to admit that, even though it is easy to put forward many historical arguments against Lenin's theory of imperialism, and to show that it runs counter to a host of obvious facts, it is not easy to find a general theory which carries more conviction, no doubt because in this area *any* general theory is unlikely to carry the day.[27] We saw earlier, for example, that it is impossible to understand the form which British colonialism took in Nigeria without taking account of the peculiarities of Nigerian society.

This is why theories based on the concept of dependence cannot explain *at a general level* disparities between nations, or the way these develop over time. In this respect, they are no better and no worse than economic theories which stress the 'vicious circle of poverty' or sociological theories which regard the close interdependence of institutions (political, religious, economic, and family) which characterizes traditional societies as a necessary cause of immobility and stagnation.

Despite this, it is not impossible to understand why the paradigm of dependence achieved dominance for a time. It is not merely based on vague sentiment (a love for the Third World, a dislike of capitalism), but as it spreads, it sets in train complex mechanisms. The main point is that it gains some of its authority, as does any influential paradigm, from the fact that it is scientifically interesting. It must also be recognized, however, that exaggerated belief in it on the part of several groups reveals the presence of various kinds of situation and communication effects, as well as E effects.

I will merely point to some examples of these effects from among those which, by implication, I have referred to in my discussion. For example (E effect), the dependency theorist rarely questions the *a priori* idea that a general theory of underdevelopment (taken as a single phenomenon) is possible, an idea which is a corollary of the very notion of 'economic theory'. Similarly (communication effect), it is obvious that dependency theory readily attracts the interest of many Third World intellectuals who are favourably disposed towards it, even when they are not in a position to treat it as a white box. Again (position effect plus perspective effect), it is easy to understand why Third World elites, like many intellectuals and politicians in developed countries, are often more aware of the inequalities of development than of the positive effects of interdependence. The former are immediately visible, whereas the latter can be highlighted only by fairly complex analyses. The final point (disposition effect) is that many social actors accept uncritically the argument that, to explain why an apparently unjust and morally offensive state of affairs persists, we must look for, as it were, those who benefit from their wrongdoing. As we know, dependency theory has the advantage of pointing the finger at the guilty party.

Epilogue

10

Against scepticism

A book on ideology is, in the nature of things, bound to be irreverent: if one wants to preserve the criterion of truth and falsehood in the definition of ideology, and, at the same time, use examples to back up one's argument, one is obliged to adopt a critical attitude with regard to those theories which are used as illustration and which confer on received ideas the authority of science.

However, rational critique must not be confused with polemics, nor discussion with pamphleteering. I have endeavoured, of course, to avoid the pitfalls of the latter. Above all, I would like to emphasize something which seems to me extremely important at a time when the ideology of 'anything goes' reigns supreme – namely, that rational critique, far from reducing all theories to the same common denominator, allows us to locate them in a hierarchy according to validity. After all, even though the ideological influence of a theory may be completely independent of the question of how far it is valid, we cannot conclude that all theories are equally correct. The confusion between the *validity* of a theory and its *interest* is, moreover, as I have tried to show, one of the main sources of ideology. The sceptical ideology of 'anything goes' merely systematizes this confusion in a way which is at the same time blind and, paradoxically, dogmatic.

The point is that even though any theory, whether scientific or sophistic, can prop up received ideas and ideologies by means of the various effects which I have tried to identify and define, the scientific quality of the theories which I have covered in the course of my analysis is in fact quite varied.

Without wanting to establish a kind of league table, I will go back over some of my examples to show that it is quite easy to establish hierarchies in this field. Thus, for example, I think that the Weberian theory of magic is so sound as to stand any test. On the other hand the theory put forward in

The Protestant Ethic, giving a hypothesis which is attractive, significant, and to a certain extent correct, had its scope restricted and its meaning clarified by subsequent research. The theory of the 'vicious circle of poverty' is an authentically scientific theory, as is the Marxist theory of the influence on economic stagnation of semi-feudal relationships of production. There is however in both a danger affecting the very way in which they are formulated, in that they may be regarded as applicable to the real work – that is, in this case, as more general than they in fact are.

The theory in *The Great Transformation* is a delicate and fragile synthesis: it has an interpretative dimension (the major dividing line of the market economy, the argument that liberal society is impossible) which is mixed in with an explanatory dimension. The data used, however, is both considerable and accurate, and, although the argument is eclectic, it keeps within the bounds of the procedures normally used in historical analysis. In this work, it is particularly the idea of a dividing line which is arbitrary, since it is inspired by the philosophy of history rather than history itself. However, as Simmel has clearly shown,[1] history is bound to contain an admixture of philosophy of history; and the quality of the final mix depends on how much is added.

Habermas's theory of pure and perfect communication is a *model* which is interesting, congenial, and inspired by the sincerest of motives; but it always reminds me of the story of the expert in operational research who, when asked the best way to get an elephant on to a boat, started from the assumption that the weight of the elephant was negligible.

Foucault's theory in his book *Surveiller et punir* uses forms of argument which are perhaps not visible to the naked eye, but which depart from those which metholodogy and sociology consider legitimate. If we want to give this theory an indulgent interpretation and see in it an application of the 'invisible hand' model, then to make it work we must introduce into it very broad hypotheses – so broad that Foucault himself had to wrap them up in the discreet language of the conditional and the 'perhaps'.

We see, therefore, that all theories do not have the same validity, but since their ideological influence is only to a limited degree a function of their validity, the impression sometimes emerges that all of them are correct. However, equality as far as ideology is concerned does not inevitably mean equality as far as rational critique is concerned. On the other hand, the ideological influence of certain scientific theories does not mean either that scientific theories *are* ideological. Some theories put forward in the social sciences are, in themselves, at the same time non-scientific *and* ideological; but many others may have an ideological influence, even though they are authentically scientific. The latter case is infinitely more important than the former for the theory of ideologies, since a received idea is of course much more likely to catch on if it is based on an authentically scientific theory than if it is based on sophisms.

I think I have made the point sufficiently clear, but I had better repeat it – my analysis does not give rise to scepticism, but on the contrary tries to show that the scepticism of 'anything goes' is mainly the result of an ideological confusion between two dimensions essential to any theory – its validity and its interest.

In the present book, I have confined myself to the study of ideologies *in statu nascendi* rather than fully-fledged ideologies, and this for a very simple reason of method, the importance of which was underlined by Weber in his work on the sociology of religion: it is much easier to understand what an idea means (to paraphrase him somewhat) when one looks at it as it is emerging. It is then that is relationship with 'everyday concerns' can be seen clearly – his analysis of magic is a case in point. What frequently happens then, however, is that the idea becomes more complicated, it takes on a gloss or a dogma, the manipulation of which become the responsibility of specialist groups, and it ends up by having a semi-independent existence; and since 'material' processes (as Marx would have said) develop in parallel to the main process, the relationship between the original idea and the state of society may become more and more difficult to grasp.

I have endeavoured here to bring in the idea of method, which I think is very important. Thus, for example, instead of looking at developmentalist ideology or Third Worldist ideology themselves, I have tried to show how and why certain clearly identifiable theories, authentically scientific in nature, were so well received that they were briefly dominant as if they had been dogma, and why these theories contributed towards the endowment of certain received ideas with scientific authority.

After all, this is how a received idea takes shape: at least initially, it has more or less to be regarded as true, as having the warranty of Authority, the best-known form of which nowadays is Science. Then there come complex dissemination processes, of which the principal ingredients, I think, are the various kinds of effects which I have tried to outline: communication effects, situation effects, and E effects. However, when the received idea has reached a certain level of visibility, the task of the sociologists comes to an end and they hand over to the historian – people who are historians of ideas, political historians, or just plain historians.

As I tried to show in another book,[2] for example, nobody can really argue that the particular form of despotism in the Soviet Union after 1917 was a kind of direct consequence of Marxist doctrine. Lenin did not limit himself to putting Marx's *Capital* into practical effect; the reason why he organized Russian social democracy on democratic centralist lines was that he was doing it at a time when the activity of workers' movements, which had previously been very high, had somewhat diminished, whereas the intelligentsia was again in ferment. This new situation led Lenin to substitute the principle of 'guide and mentor of the masses' for that of the 'uprising of the masses' of which he had been strongly in favour during the economic upturn. He came round to the idea, developed in *What Is To Be Done?* that the best way of organizing the dictatorship *of* the proletariat was to ensure the dictatorship of the (social democratic) party *over* the proletariat. The concept of dictatorship of the proletariat was doubtless taken from Marx, but Lenin's interpretation of it is meaningful only in the social and economic context of 1905. The effects of this interpretation – which were felt throughout the whole world – would have been different, of course, if Lenin had not seized power.

Similarly, it seems obvious that the Calvinist doctrine did not imply directly – in itself – a theocratic conception of the state. It implied even less that a despotic theocratic state should be set up, or that there should be in Geneva a group of inspectors to root out any jam – which was a forbidden delicacy – from people's cupboards.

In other words, we must be careful to differentiate between the social diffusion of received ideas and ideologies, and the political use to which they are put. The first is a matter for sociology, the second for history. If the two aspects are confused, there are two dangers: that more power will be conferred on received ideas than they in fact have; and that they will be regarded as being exclusively political in origin, whereas, nowadays especially, they are often of scientific origin. If received ideas and ideologies are regarded as being purely political in origin, it becomes difficult to explain their credibility, in other words to answer the question which I think is central to any theory of ideologies.

Another distinction must be brought in, however. Some ideologies are grafted on to *partial* theories which are scientific (like developmentalism), or pseudo-scientific (like the functionalist neo-Marxism of the 1960s). It is these partial theories which I have particularly had in mind in this book. In this case, there is often a convergence effect in that many of these partial theories give, downstream, convergent conclusions; or else, upstream, tend to reinforce a common paradigm. The case of developmentalism is significant in this respect, and in Chapter 9 I referred to the upsteam and downstream convergence of the totality of theories which are usually grouped under this heading. Similar remarks could easily be made about the second example – Third Worldism.

Ideologies can also however be grafted on to *syntheses which claim to be all-encompassing*. Generally, these syntheses contain scientific nuclei quite skilfully linked by reasoning taken from other language registers.

The case of Marx belongs, of course, to this category, as does that of Spencer, which I would prefer to dwell on, for reasons which will become apparent.

The all-encompassing nature of the works of these two writers helps to explain their huge readership: at the height of his fame, Spencer's books sold more copies than those of all but a few philosophers have ever done, and in this he may be in a unique position.[3] Spencer's synthesis, like that of Marx, has an unexceptionable scientific nucleus. In his *Social Statics*,[4] for example, Spencer very clearly identified and demonstrated the importance of mechanisms which later constituted the basic framework of Darwin's *On the Origin of Species*. At the same time, he saw clearly that processes which are apparently leading towards an end (such as the processes of evolution) could be interpreted in a way which is not teleological but teleonomic – that is, not as the effect of a will or plan or design, but as the unintended result of mechanisms which can be analysed in a purely casual manner. This idea, of course, was not entirely new, and Adam Smith had applied it, for example, in his analysis of the division of labour. It is this idea which is summed up in the concept of the 'invisible hand'. However, Spencer was certainly the first to see its crucial importance and to have applied it systematically – so systematically in fact that he thought he was in a position to put forward the hypothesis that there were common mechanisms (which he subsumes in a single expression, the 'law of evolution') behind all kingdoms – the social kingdom as well as the living, and even inanimate, kingdoms. He was of course aware of the complexity of social phenomena and of the fact that, in this area, the 'law of evolution' came up against what he called 'circumstances'. He was for example convinced that evolution was taking us in the direction of a withering away of the State, and of a move from 'military' societies to 'industrial' societies. However, he recognized at the same time that, realistically, history could go backwards and lead to a strengthening of the state and thereby of the 'military' (that is, constraining) nature of societies. Despite this, he saw the 'law of evolution' as lying behind everything, and as revelatory of the divine presence. Of course, Spencer's God could hardly appear directly on this earth,[5] since evolution had to be seen in a teleonomic and not a teleological way – that is, as the result of causal links and not an overall plan. Yet at the same time, the universal nature of the 'law of evolution' conferred a unity on the Universe, which could be interpreted as the manifestation of the presence of God.

The example of Spencer is particularly interesting in that it illustrates a case in point of which Marx and Comte, as well as Saint-Simon or Fourier, are manifestations, but in a much clearer way than that of Marx and Comte. In all these examples, we see that a desire to encompass everything is grafted on to scientific nuclei. In Spencer's case, however, the indisputable scientific nucleus is particularly easy to identify. Moreover, the Spencerian synthesis is simpler and more open than that of his two main rivals, who were also his near contemporaries.[6] It is quite easy to understand, on reading the *Treatise*, why it was regarded as so remarkable when it first appeared.

Spencer's ideas, however, unlike those of Marx and Comte, were not concretized in institutions; nor, unlike those of Marx, did they form the basis of a state. Spencer's synthesis was gradually discarded, disappearing more or less completely from the scene when the turmoil of the 1920s led to increased intervention by states in the workings of the economy. By increasing the role of the state, not only was history moving from an 'industrial' society to a 'military' society, but such a development, which Spencer would have seen as a backwards step, was regarded as progress, particularly in the United States at the time of the New Deal. Only the scientific nucleus of Spencer's work survived, though he was not credited with having created it.

It would seem that nowadays, apart from Marxism, only traditional religions can inspire all-encompassing syntheses, which perhaps amounts to saying that there has been a revival of religious feeling; it seems that, although modern ideologies have scientific bases, the development of science has killed scientism, which is why it can no longer easily generate all-encompassing syntheses.

Moreover, all-embracing syntheses arising from science are characterized by a high degree of inflexibility and by the fact that they cannot easily, by their very nature, avoid being refuted by reality, as is seen very clearly in the case of Spencer. This is why none has survived, apart from Marxism. Developing Robert Bellah's ideas,[7] we can argue *a contrario* that syntheses based on religion, because of the language registers they use, and particularly because these introduce supernatural elements, possess greater capacities of transformation and adaptation.

However, the most fundamental reason why scientistic syntheses are weak is that science, despite the hopes it raised at one stage, is unable to answer the main question of metaphysics and religion – what is the meaning of life? To this must be added the point that scientism, by claiming to be all-encompassing, contradicts the very nature of science.

The Marxist exception is explained to a great extent by the fact that, alone of its kind, it finds form in ideocratic states. Since the death of scientism, ideologies inspired by science can be no more than *partial*, like Third Worldism, though this is not to say that their social and political influence is negligible.

I think I have fulfilled another of my promises, and have shown that, to explain the diffusion of received ideas, one could keep to the classical version of methodological individualism, that is, the one propounded by Max Weber, consisting of two principles – firstly, considering every collective phenomenon as the product of individual actions; and secondly, trying to interpret individual action as rational, even if it means accepting the existence of an irrational residue. Although fanaticism, blindness, and perversion certainly have a role to play in spreading ideologies, I think I have shown that one could go a long way to explaining how false ideas take hold without assuming that social actors are subject to irrational forces outside their control. It is not because they are irrational that bankers apply economic theories without always examining what lies behind them.

Following on from this, I also tried to suggest that the influence of the dominant theory of ideologies – the irrationalist theory – could be explained, at least in part, by the authority and widespread influence of the classical philosophical theory of falsehood. Although modern-day sociologists are not really trained in philosophy, they are imbued with Durkheim and Marx, whose training was full of philosophical tradition.

It is clear that I do not believe at all in the argument about 'the end of ideology': ideologies are the effect of social mechanisms which are simple, ordinary, and, as Durkheim would have said, 'normal'. Like mushrooms in the undergrowth, ideologies which appear to be buried once and for all are always prone to reappear with the slightest shower of rain. In any case, we must beware of asserting the existence of a simple causal relationship between the overarching variables which can be used to describe and differentiate societies, and their liability to be taken over by ideology. Neither the modernity nor the democratic institutions of the Weimar Republic prevented Hitler giving them an ideological battering, helped by the economic and political turmoil of the times. More recently eugenic myths have made headway in the most solidly based democracies.

In an important respect, ideologies are unlike mushrooms in that the former always reappear in new *forms*. Pareto was well aware of this – for an old, discredited idea to become prevalent again, it first has to undergo a *metamorphosis*, since it has to be capable of being readily seen as a new idea. This is why, for example, the Marxism of the 1960s and 1970s is different from the Marxism of the turn of the century, and can appear unrecognizable to somebody who fails to look at it closely.

Of course, when I say that I do not believe in 'the end of ideology', I am merely stressing, firstly, that a society without an ideology, in the meaning in which I have taken the word, is almost inconceivable; and secondly, that any society is *capable* of being open to total ideologies. After all, neo-Marxism, despite its primitive nature, was only recently very widespread in Western democracies; and, although it is unlikely that it will return in force in the near future (in a form which would inevitably be new), it would be dangerous to assert that the ideological moderation which has only just begun to characterize Western societies is here to stay: in the matter of ideologies perhaps even more than other kinds of social phenomena, determinist patterns should be studiously avoided.

This does not mean that ideological cycles lack causes, nor that causes far removed from the realm of *ideas* cannot have ideological effects. The Marxism of the 1960s, for example, gained ground because of the high growth rates of the time, and it survived for a time after these fell; at the time, the growth of production was regarded as natural and permanent, and a traditional target was there to be attacked – distributive injustices. More precisely, the high growth rates of the 1960s certainly promoted the return of egalitarian fervour, which raised the level of *interest* in theories (even absurd ones) which attacked social inequalities.

The ideological episodes of the 1960s, therefore, illustrate the fact that a variable as apparently innocent as a rate of growth can have ideological effects. If it is high, it can direct people's attention towards problems of *distribution* and inequality, and call forth egalitarian demons. If it is low, the danger is that it directs attention towards *production* and induces torpor in the demons. This is the stage we have reached now, it would seem.

Although determinist perspectives are dangerous when applied to ideologies (and all social phenomena), this does not mean that ideological changes are inexplicable, or lack causes, or that these causes are inaccessible, but merely that these causes are multiple and all bound up in each other. This is why *explanation* is in this field much easier than *prediction*: these two concepts, which appear to be linked or even coextensive, in the natural sciences, have to be kept completely apart in the area of the social sciences. After all, although it is easy (to return to our discussion) to see what effects rates of growth have on ideological phenomena, it is also patently obvious that no factor – neither this one nor any other – can ever claim to be the only or even the main determinant of ideology.

A return to high growth rates might rekindle egalitarian fervour, or make Marxism flare up again, since Marxism is, for the reasons I have outlined, the only all-encompassing synthesis of a scientistic kind which remains. This is why it represents a self-appointed authority for any theorist who wants to pander to egalitarian fervour. However, this scenario is by no means certain, since the spread of values derived from egalitarianism in the three decades after the war also made more visible certain consequences of these values, particularly the oppressive and debilitating nature of egalitarian policies, as well as the contradiction between equity and equality, that is, between justice and equality.

It is therefore better in the social sciences, as well as in other areas, not to try to make sweeping predictions, except about the short and, perhaps, the medium term. One can perhaps thank God for the ideological moderation which seems to have temporarily established itself in France and other Western democracies; but we must accept that this situation is a result of all sorts of factors whose future development cannot accurately be predicted.

I have said that this is not a sceptical book: ideologies are often based on scientific theories (that is, they use procedures regarded as normal by all sciences) which can be judged in the court of 'rational critique'. However, ideologies must not be confused with the scientific nucleus around which they sometimes weave their cocoon. Although ideologies have hard kernels which are vital to their credibility, it is nevertheless true that they are built from bits and pieces. My view is that Foucault's bits and pieces, because they have no hard centre, do not have an inspiring future. Those of Marx's *Capital*, since they have hard centres, will no doubt go on inspiring exegetical, scientific, and rhetorical language. They are doing this at this very moment – despite the 'conservative revolution', Marx has for the first time acquired the stature of a popular classic in some sections of the American intelligentsia;[8] and I have already noted that dependency theory inspires a considerable amount of research, and that it is a paradigm which encompasses a great host of historians, economists, sociologists, and political scientists.

However, although the hard kernels of ideologies (provided they are scientific) derive from rational critique and therefore from the criterion of truth and falsehood, ideologies themselves do not. This distinction is no doubt what Raymond Aron was thinking of when he said that ideologies did not derive 'directly' from the criterion of truth and falsehood.

I do not think that we can therefore say that all ideologies are equally correct, but, since ideologies are not derived 'directly' from truth and falsehood, it cannot be proved by recourse to procedures for determining the validity of a scientific theory. Critique of ideologies as ideologies, in other words, can only be based on the direct affirmation of certain fundamental values.

From this point of view, it is not difficult to perceive certain differences between ideologies, and even to outline a typology of ideologies. Some endeavour to change humankind and make people good despite themselves: they try to put the individual, who may be reluctant, at the service of the community, perhaps relying on his or her assent which will be given later, after the big change. Some ideologies are characterized by a dislike of other people, directly or indirectly depending on how far their sociocentrism (Piaget) is disguised. On this point, there are of course different sorts of sociocentrism – positive ones, which reject the out-group, and negative ones, which reject the in-group by idealizing the merits of the out-group, at the same time despising it as much as they idealize it. Here one thinks of the musings on society-communities or, as they are sometimes called, 'holistic' societies which might have existed in some far-off place or time.[9]

Other ideologies take people as they are, in that they decline to cast judgement on them, rejecting all concepts (alienation, false consciousness, and so on) which assume that the observer can stand over the observed and adopt a transcendent point of view in order to judge and possibly reorder the latter's preferences. As a consequence, they make individual preferences the ultimate criterion for assessing social and political institutions. At the same time they are aware of the complexity of social systems. They refuse to take analogies seriously – organicist analogies, for example – which would reduce them to systems of a kind which is too simple. Moreover, they are aware of the fact that, though the preferences of individuals are an ultimate criterion, the objective of revealing and combining these preferences cannot be achieved in a completely satisfactory way; or (which they are also aware of) in a direct way. The objective assumes the intervention of complex institutions which, though always capable of improvement (i.e. in the way they perform this function of revealing and combining preferences), cannot ever hope to be perfect.

I think the superiority of the liberal ideology lies above all in these differences, since liberalism is also a composite corpus, combining beliefs based on philosophical, ethical, anthropological, historical, economic, sociological, and political theories. Between Locke, Montesquieu, Adam Smith, or Toqueville – to name but the main figures of liberalism – there is not much more in common than the few principles to which I have referred. There is likely to be agreement, however, that these principles are crucial.

To summarize, though the scientific nuclei of ideologies certainly derive from the criterion of truth and falsehood, I think ideologies themselves derive rather from the criterion of *soundness*.[10] Though it is impossible to prove – since here we have, to use the famous distinction in *The Nicomachean Ethics*, a discussion on principles and not a discussion from principles – I would say that theories within the framework of the liberal tradition are based on sounder principles than, for example, those which claim to judge social actors from a transcendent point of view, to tell them what to think, believe, or prefer, or even explain to them what they *really* think, believe, or prefer.

I will add that it is only at this point that one can evoke the idea of an interchange – some people might prefer collusion – between methodological individualism and the liberal ideology. The assumption that people are rational not only introduces a premiss which I think has been sufficiently proved to be scientifically creative, but also respects the social actor. *A contrario*, when an individual is said to behave irrationally, it is often because the measure being used reveals the prejudices and the dislikes of the observer for the observed. 'Irrational' is, in fact, often only a polite and apparently neutral synonym for adjectives which are not polite and neutral.

In any event, *irrationalist* individualism (which, to turn Weber's view on its head, sees people above all as irrational, that is, subject to forces which at the same time go beyond them and escape them) can hardly avoid, because of the logic of its premisses, reducing the social actor to the state of marionette. Holistic[11] methods, when they are raised to the status of ideals, tend quite simply to reduce people to nothing, or, as the phrase goes, to 'propping up structures'. A further point is that it is often difficult to differentiate between irrationalist individualism and holism in that the forces which in the former case are supposed to pull the strings of the marionette are often seen as rooted in *society*, as people in the nineteenth century said, or in *social structures*, as we prefer to say in the twentieth century.

On this point, we must remember that social actors, as seen by methodological individualism, far from being suspended in a kind of social vacuum, are socially situated.[12] They have been through education, and been members of different groups; they have a social position, and dispositions against which they develop patterns of conduct including, in those cases in which the sociologist is interested, a rational dimension. These dispositions however have to be seen either as facts (either I know something about physics, or I do not), which actors must take into account when deciding where they are situated, or as guides for action (for example, a disposition towards temperance) which are always rather fluid and in any event subject to monitoring by consciousness.

Finally, by emphasizing the role of science in the origin of ideologies, I may have given the impression of being mainly interest in elites. Pareto noted that the *derivations* which elites find so attractive are usually different from those which attract other social strata. He was certainly right, for example, in arguing that derivations from seventeenth- and eighteenth-century contractualist philosophy, which for him were merely rationalizations intended to confirm feelings, were by their very nature confined to an educated group. His analysis is wrong, however, in that it does not adequately deal with the first point. It completely ignores the crucial fact that contractualist philosophy contains an incontrovertible and extremely important scientific innovation, which was later widely used in the social sciences – it propounded a method by which the reasons for the existence of institutions could be analysed even when there was no information about how they began, which means that we can *explain* a particular institution in the absence of knowledge of how it started. The basic idea of the contractualist method is that if we can show that a group in a particular position would unanimously choose to adopt a given institution, then we can understand the meaning, for the group, of that institution. In this way, contractualist philosophy contains the essence of what was later called the paradigm of functional analysis.[13] It was therefore the scientific importance of contractualism which ensured its salience and its reputation.

It is however true, on the one hand that contractualist philosophy was ideologically influential, and on the other hand that this influence was directly exerted only on a small section of the public. Because of its scientific nucleus, it was probably aimed, as Perelman[14] would say, at a universal audience (the Chinese of Max Weber), but, given the subtlety of its analyses, it encountered only specific groups. Nevertheless, by being passed from one stage to another – as we saw when we looked at the influence of Rousseau and the analyses of Cochin in this respect – some principles of contractualist philosophy eventually came to the attention of a much wide variety of groups.

In this way, by means of a succession of communication effects, an intellectual good which has the status of a *scientific theory* for the original proponent will often become a *myth* when it reaches the end recipient. The truths in the original theory will be divested of their conditional character. Only the main thrust of the analysis will be preserved, and exegetical and rhetorical modes of reasoning will tend to replace scientific reasoning. The convictional strength of these variants, however, will still be based on the scientific authority of the theory.

The fact that effective ideologies usually have sound scientific nuclei which can be treated as white boxes only by a tiny elite does not mean that they are incapable of having a wide audience. It is simply that, as they pass from stage to stage, their message changes. The spread of ideologies is not a mechanical process, but depends on actors and mediators who interpret the message for their own audience as they perceive it. This is why, generally speaking, even the most homespun ideologies have a scientific origin. Surely the assimilation of social processes to the processes of natural selection – which one might possibly suggest helping in a small way – is squarely based on one of the major scientific discoveries of all time?[15]

In contrast to a received idea – which writers as eminent as Talcott Parsons and Karl Popper have endorsed – ideologies cannot be reduced to arguments which are improper from a scientific point of view.[16] In any event, in order to understand modern myths and those of our own day in particular, we may be obliged to reject the easy solution whereby the symbolic and imaginary dimension of social life is artificially isolated.

Just as in the case of magic, we must see how these myths tie in with the 'concerns of everyday life', and also recognize the effects of the division of labour and of social differentiation on their production and diffusion. Only by looking at these links as a whole can we understand why fairy tales can be based on 'normal science': if it had not been for dependency theory, the myth of the Revolution would not have had the credibility it did in the Third World.

A final point: this book might be seen as pessimistic, since it shows that social actors often believe in false or dubious ideas for the best reasons. However, the whole thrust of my argument also rests on a premiss which, at least in my eyes, has the status not of a working hypothesis, but of an obvious fact, and which means that an optimistic interpretation of the book is the correct one. This premiss is that, despite the crisis of values which we hear so much about nowadays, one value in particular remains unchanging and certain, so much so that we might say that it is independent of all historical and social conditioning, and that in this sense it can be regarded as transcendent. This value finds expression in the fact that most people unconditionally prefer the truth to its opposite.

Notes

Preface

1 *Revue des sciences morales et politiques*, 2 (1983) p. 314.
2 I would like to thank Jacqueline Lécuyer and Béatric Marin for their efficient help in the preparation and writing of this book.

Chapter 1   A question (among others) on ideology

1 It is taken from P. Berger, *Pyramids of sacrifice – political ethics and social change* (Basic Books, New York, 1974).
2 In fact, possible contradictions between individual rationality and collective rationality were identified and described analytically, for example by Rousseau (*The Social Contract*) in the field of political philosophy, by theorists of collective goods in economics, by ecologists (G. Hardin, K. Boulding), or by game theorists. Obviously the best historians (Thucydides, for example) and sociologists (Marx, Spencer) were also conscious of the complexity of the relationships between individual rationality and collective rationality. However, in contrast with the student of economics who cannot get away from the theory of collective goods, or the student of philosophy who will have to look carefully at the aporia thrown up by classical political philosophy, the student of anthropology or sociology has hardly any opportunity of looking at this question.
3 *L'Inégalité des chances* (Colin, Paris, 1978 (1973); Hachette, Paris, 1985).
4 K. Popper, *The Poverty of Historicism* (Routledge & Kegan Paul, London, 1944).
5 J. Watkins, 'Ideal types and historical explanation', in Readings in the Philosophy of Science, ed. H. Feigl and M. Brodbeck (Appoleton, New York, 1953), pp. 723–43.
6 *Theories of Social Change – a critical appraisal* (Polity Press, Oxford, 1986); originally published as *La place du désordre* (Presses Universitaires de France, Paris, 1984).
7 *The Unintended Consequences of Social Action* (St Martin, London, 1982);

originally published as *Effets pervers et ordre social* (Presses Universitaires de France, Paris, 1979 (1977)).

8 A point made by W. Dilthey. See Chapter 8, note 31.

9 T. Kuhn, *The Structure of Scientific Revolutions* (Chicago University Press, Chicago, 1962).

10 Pages 84–93.

11 K. Mannheim, 'Die Bedeutung der Konkurrentz im Gebiete des Geistigen', *Schriften der deutschen Gesellschaft für Soziologie* (Tübingen), 6 (1929).

12 K. Mannheim, *Man and Society in an Age of Reconstruction* (Harcourt, New York, 1940 (1935)).

13 Among recent books which can be regarded as remarkable examples of their kind are: J. Baechler, *Démocraties* (Clamann-Lévy Paris, 1985); A. Jardin, *Histoire du libéralisme politique* (Hachette, Paris, 1985); H. Lepage. *Pourquoi la propriété* (Hachette (Pluriel), Paris, 1985); S. C. Kolm, *Le Contrat Social Libéral* (Presses Universitaires de France, Paris, 1985).

14 I gave an account of the conception of rationality which I am propounding here in a paper called 'L'acteur social est-il si irrationnel (ou si conformiste) qu'on le dit?', at a conference on 'The Individual', proceedings published by Royaumont and Le Seuil, October 1985. The premiss that explaining the behaviour of an actor amounts to finding the *good reasons* for it covers, as specific variants, Weber's teleological rationality (*Zweckrationalität*) and axiological rationality (*Wertrationalität*), but it covers many other cases as well. Thus, for example, the knowledge which I have on a particular question may influence my interpretation of it. Here we can speak of *rationality relating to dispositions*. Similarly, my position may influence the way I perceive and apprehend a particular phenomenon, so that we may also speak of a *rationality of position*. Numerous examples of these two points are given throughout the book. We can show the various conceptions of rationality as concentric circles as illustrated in the accompanying diagram.

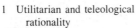

1 Utilitarian and teleological
     rationality
2 'Weberian' rationality
3 Situated rationality:
     the 'good reasons'
4 Acts which are affective,
     impulsive and so on
5 Irrational acts

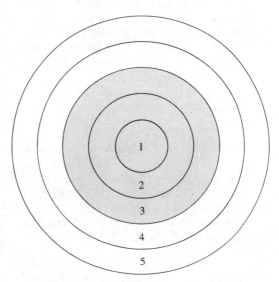

The smallest circle represents utilitarian or teleological rationality, though these are not the same thing – one may wish to please other people without wishing thereby, as one's primary purpose, to please oneself; and one may try to achieve an aim in as satisfactory a way as possible without being motivated primarily by the material or symbolic rewards to be expected. The next circle, subsuming the first, is Weberian rationality, which adds axiological rationality to teleological rationality. The next circle is coextensive with the 'good reasons' of any kind which actors may have for doing what they do or believing what they believe. A non-physicist, for example, has good reasons to believe in the truth of the theory of relativity. This however is neither a teleological rationality nor an axiological rationality. The third circle thus encompasses the last two kinds of rationality which I mentioned before (rationality of position, and rationality relating to dispositions). The next one contains acts of an impulsive and affective kind or reflex actions: both Weber and Pareto stress that, though they are of crucial importance *for the actor*, they play only a small part in sociological explanation. Finally there are actions which are evoked in actors by forces which are beyond the control of their consciousness, and which give rise to a theory of the psyche inspired by the early Freud or the Marx of the *camera obscura* (see Chapter 2). This largest circle therefore represents the irrational model of action, the usefulness of which I doubt, even in explaining belief in false ideas.

Circle 4 corresponds to what may be called the *classical* conception of irrationality, and circle 5 to the *modern* one. In the classical conception, an irrational act (for example, an impulsive act provoked by anger) is both more or less conscious and more or less transparent – I know that my reaction was one of anger, and other people can see this as well. In this case the irrational motivation is readily confirmed both by internal experience and external observation. However, the opposite is true of irrational acts in the modern sense – here the irrational motivation is a *construct* inaccessible both to internal experience and external observation. In this way, the 'instinct of imitation' (Tarde), the 'mimetic desire' (R. Girard), the 'resistance to change' (various writers), the 'blindness through interest' (Marx), the 'unconscious impulses' of the early Freud, the 'false consciousness' (F. Mehring, F. Engels) can be neither experienced nor observed, only inferred. Notions such as these raise serious methodological, psychological, and sociological problems, as I point out in the paper mentioned at the beginning of this note, as well as in various parts of this book.

Chapter 2   What is ideology?

1   The two volumes of *L'Analyse de l'idéolgie* (Galilée, Paris, 1980, 1983), edited by Gérard Duprat, are extremely valuable. In giving an overview of the debate on ideology in the various social sciences and the different traditons of thought, they show clearly how confused it is.

2   K. Marx and F. Engels, *Die deutsche Ideologie* (Dietz, Berlin, 1932), p. 22.

3   Cf. Chapter 5.

4 'Marxian' refers to Marx himself; 'Marxist' means pertaining to the doctrine founded by Marx and developed by those who came after him.

5 On this subject, see G. Labica and G. Bensussan (eds), *Dictionnaire critique du marxisme* (Presses Universitaires de France, Paris, 1982).

6 For example: 'As soon as it is no longer a question of an independent ideology, formulated by the mass of workers themselves in the course of their movement, the problem is posed *exclusively in the following way*: bourgeois ideology or socialist ideology. [. . .] *Any* weakening of socialist ideology implies a strengthening of bourgeois ideology. [. . .] Bourgeois ideology is older than socialist ideology'. *What Is To Be Done?* (Lawrence & Wishart, London, 1944), II, b. 'The cult of the spontaneous'.

7 L. Althusser, *For Marx* (Allen Lane The Penguin Press, London, 1969), pp. 231–2 (original emphasis).

8 Durkheim, however, uses it in passing in *The rules of Sociological Method* (The Free Press, London, 1982) and gives it a meaning which as it happens is very close to Engels's meaning (see Chapter 3, note 4): for Durkheim, sociological analysis is ideological, for example, when it equates the history of ethics with the development of ethical ideas.

9 R. Aron, *The Opium of the Intellectuals* (Greenwood, London, 1977).

10 It is necessary to distinguish between those courses of reasoning which are based on principles (οἱ ἀπὸ τῶν ἀρχῶν λόγοι) and those which try to establish principles (οἱ ἐπὶ τὰς ἀρχάς), *The Nicomanchean Ethics*, I, 4.

11 Contemporary philosophy of science sometimes tends to give to the notion of rightness (Richtigkeit, justesse) an intrusive role, thus failing to achieve rightness – see for example Richard Rorty, *Philosophy and the Mirror of Nature* (Blackwell, Oxford, 1980), or Nelson Goodman, *Ways of World-making* (Harvard University Press, Cambridge, 1984). This new philosophy, by limiting the notion of truth to its congruent part, abolishes to a large extent the distinction between interpretation and explanation and between hermeneutics and science, but also between science and ideology. My reaction is to suggest, in the conclusion to the present book, that although the scientific core of ideologies stems from truth and falsehood, ideologies themselves in fact stem from rightness. However, I believe that nothing is to be gained from putting the confusion into shape. This new philosophy seems to me to be inspired by the praiseworthy desire to break free from the aporia engendered by the epistemology of 'anything goes'. By regarding rightness as sacred, it is no longer necessary to accept that 'anything goes', and at the same time the difficulties of positivism and neo-positivism are avoided; but this synthesis which is in keeping with the times is achieved at the price of the abolition of costly classical distinctions.

12 E. Shils, 'The concept and function of ideology', *International Encyclopaedia of the Social Sciences*, vol. 7, pp. 66–76.

13 Ibid., p. 73.

14 Ibid., p. 74.

15 R. Nisbet, *The Sociological Tradition* (Heinemann, London, 1967).

16 Cf. Chapter 9.

17 T. Parsons, 'An approach to the sociology of knowledge', in *Transactions of the Fourth Congress of Sociology* (Milan, 1959), pp. 25–49.

18 C. Geertz, 'Ideology as a cultural system', in *Ideology and Discontent*, ed. D. Apter (The Free Press, Glencoe, 1964), pp. 25–49

19 F. Sutton, S. Harris, C Kaysen, J. Tobin, *The American Business Creed* (Harvard University Press, Cambridge, 1956). The authors give many applications of their hypothesis that a function of ideology is to reduce the tensions encountered by individuals in performing their role. For example, business people will reconcile their ethic of responsibility with any failure of their business operations by readily adhering to propositions such as 'profit levels are not what they were', 'workers today care more about job security than doing a good day's work', and so on.

20 Ibid., pp. 4–5.

21 In his *Philosophy of History*, Hegel – who had never previously used the term – contrasts *ideologues* (*people of principles*) and statesmen in his survey of the 1830 Revolution. See Z. Pelczynski, 'The roots of ideology in Hegel's political philosophy', in *Ideology and Politics*, ed. M. Cranston and P. Mair (The Hague, Sijthoff and Noordhoff, 1981), pp. 65–74.

22 J. Locke, *Some Thoughts Concerning Education, Works*, 1823, p. 186.

23 Montesquieu, *The Spirit of Laws*, Book I Chapter 1.

24 K. Marx, *The Poverty of Philosophy*, II, p. 2; J. M. Keynes, *A Treatise on Money* (Macmillan, London, 1953 (1930)).

25 A. Smith, *An Inquiry into the Nature and Causes of the Wealth of Nations* (London, 1776), Book IV, Chapters 7 and 8.

26 The theory of surplus value is in fact based on a model of the capitalist firm which could just stand as a simplification acceptable in the early period of capitalism; but its hypotheses make this impossible in a capitalist economy of moderate complexity. On the assumption of two classes of actor (capitalists and workers), the model attributes to the firm a single function, that of production, and ignores that of the co-ordination of tasks within the firm, that of developing new products, and on a more general level, the adjustment of supply to demand and the marketing of the product, as well as the costs and levels of remuneration relating to these functions. It is only in the context of these hypotheses that profit can be interpreted as confiscation. Marx moreover saw that his theory begged a major question: why is this confiscation accepted? He suggested an answer which is interesting (cf. Chapter 5) but which assumes the theory of surplus value to be true.

There is no need to stress that the theory of surplus value is the cornerstone of Marxian sociology, and particularly of the Marxian theory of class. This is why later Marxists tried to replace it as soon as the increasing complexity of the capitalist firm made it gradually apparent that it was faulty. The modification took the form either of a change of *scale* (cf. in Lenin and modern dependency theorists, the hypothesis of world-wide confiscation by international trade), or of a change of variable (domination as confiscation of Power and Culture). This is an illustration of one of the most interesting aspects of Pareto's theory of derivation: a discredited idea has to assume a different form in order to have a chance of playing a part again in the market of ideas.

27 R. Nisbet, *The Sociological Tradition*.

28 R. Hofstadter, *Social Darwinism in American Thought* (Braziler, New York, 1959 (1944)) gives a good analysis of the development of social Darwinism in the United States and the way in which it spread by a complex system of intellectual and political relays. The case of Sumner is particularly interesting: as a keen supporter of Spencer, and on the basis of his reputation from his book *Folkways*, he strongly attacked protectionists and socialists and called with increasing vigour for a social order based on the survival of the fittest. G. Lemaine and B. Matalon, in *Hommes supérieurs, hommes inférieurs* (Colin, Paris, 1985), show clearly that Darwin himself seems, towards the end of his life, to have given support to social Darwinism.

29 Cf. Chapter 9.

30 See, for example, the classic work by R. M. Hare, *The Language of Morals* (Clarendon, Oxford, 1952), I, p. 2.

31 I am now aware that my article 'Le phénomène idéologique; en marge d'une lecture de Pareto', *L' année sociologique*, XXXIV (1984), pp. 87-126, may give the impression that I adhere strongly to Pareto's theory of ideologies. This article is based on a lecture I gave in Pareto's native city of Turin, in which I tried to show how Pareto's theory of ideologies was interesting and relevant to the present day, and to rescue it from the oblivion to which it had been consigned, partly no doubt because of the vehemence of language which characterizes the *Treatise*. This is why I emphasized the positive aspects and minimized the negative aspects of the theory.

Chapter 3   Is *Homo Sociologicus* (always) irrational?

1 K. Mannheim, *Ideology and Utopia* (Routledge & Kegan Paul, London, 1954 (1929)) p. 55.

2 F. Bacon, *Novum Organum*, 'Section ' symbol 38.

3 I think that J. Elster established this point in *Making Sense of Marx* (Cambridge University Press, Cambridge, 1985). In contrast with G. Cohen (*Karl Marx's Theory of History,* Clarendon Press, London, 1978), which tried to axiomatize the Marxian theory of history, I think that the book which will finally show us the *true* Marx, or at least give us the least dubious view of him, is one which shows him as a profoundly eclectic writer. It is this which will allow us to explain more readily why Marx is influential and why there are so many ways of adhering to Marxism. Although there are orthodox Marxists who are faithful to a particular aspect of the dogma, there are also at the other extreme fideistic Marxists. For my part, I tried to show in *Theories of Social Change - a critical appraisal* (Polity Press, Cambridge, 1986) p. 126 ff. the absolute incompatability between the analysis of the crisis of feudalism in *The Poverty of Philosophy* and that in the *Manifesto*, which were written within a year of each other, and suggested that this was because they were addressed to different audiences. I further suggested in *The Unintended Consequences of Social Action* (St Martin, London, 1982) Chapter 7, that although Marx often applied an individualist method, this was not the case with, for example, his theory of surplus value. The claim of eclecticism is plausible when one

remembers that Marx was an avid reader with detailed knowledge of the works of Hegel, Adam Smith, and the complete corpus of economic history available at the time, as well as Cervantes and Camoens. Since Marxist exegesis, however, is generally the work of Marxists or anti-Marxists, it tends to postulate the *unity* of *the* thought of Marx, or, at any rate, that of the 'early' or 'later' Marx. Elster's book seems to me to be the only one which is a step in the right direction.

4 Marx-Engels, *Werke* (Dietz, Berlin, 1968), vol. 39, p. 97. It should be pointed out that the ideologues referred to in this letter are, as the subsequent paragraphs indicate, those who think that political questions can be settled by discussions internal to a particular intellectual discipline – law, theology, political philosophy. In this respect, Engels mentions Luther and Calvin, who claimed to have refuted Catholicism just as Hegel claimed to have refuted Kant, or like the physiocrats claimed to have refuted the mercantilists.

5 Ibid.

6 It is interesting to note that the close relationship evident here, in the case of the Marxian theory of ideology, between classical philosophy and the social sciences, is not unique: indeed, it appears very frequently. For example, when Durkheim undertakes in *The Elementary Forms of the Religious Life* to explain the origin of certain notions and certain procedures frequently used in science (for example, the notion of cause, the notion of force, classification procedures), he reproduces almost word for word the classic idea of Kant – these notions and procedures do not derive from experience; on the contrary they make experience possible. However, whereas Kant saw in human nature or the human mind the location and the origin of his famous *a priori forms*, Durkheim saw them as the product of social experience. When we do something in botany, physics, chemistry, or astronomy, we are using naturally, as it were, notions such as force or cause, or classification procedures. These notions and procedures, however, are not inspired by our experience of chemical, astronomical, or botanical phenomena. On the contrary, it is they which allow us to understand these phenomena and make sense of them. Up to this point, therefore, Durkheim is happy to follow Kant, but he diverges at precisely the point where Marx diverges from Bacon, and goes down the same road as Marx did – the notion of force is inspired by the feeling of constraint which social life evokes in us: classification procedures are suggested to us by social classifications which can take very different forms from one society to another, but which are characteristic of all societies.

There is a corollary to these remarks, which is that the widely held belief that the social sciences arose from a break – which is now total – with philosophical tradition is an innocent one. In contrast with a received idea which is largely due to the extraordinary influence of Auguste Comte, sociology no more 'broke with' Bacon, Spinoza, or Kant than economics 'broke with' Locke.

7 Analogy is sometimes defined, over four terms, by the formula '*a* is to *b* what *c* is to *d*'. I do not think this definition covers all uses of the notion of analogy.

8 P. Ansart, *Idéologies, conflits et pouvoir* (Presses Universitaires de France, Paris, 1977), pp. 56–7.

9   Unless we accede to a proposition usually accepted by neo-Marxists, which can in fact be derived from Marx's writing, like the one to which I refer here, and which is any case is certainly a part of the Marxist creed – that intellectuals are 'the undergroup of the ruling class'. Either this proposition has no meaning, or else it has a meaning. Personally, I do not think it is meaningful, since it underestimates in an absurd way both the diversity of intellectuals and the fact that intellectual production is independent of social conditioning. If one assumes that it has a meaning, it is self-destructive, since if intellectuals were at the service of the ruling class, they could not produce Marxist theories, at least not this one.

10   K. Marx and F. Engels, *Die deutsche Ideologie* (Dietz, Berlin, 1953 (1932)) p. 44.

11   Elster, *Making Sense of Marx* pp. 489–90. On commodity fetishism, see also Ansart, *Idéologies*, p. 56.

12   R. Aron, *The Opium of the Intellectuals* (Greenwood, London, 1977).

13   The analogy of the *camera obscura* introduces the hypothesis of an unconscious to which a causal effectiveness is ascribed. This hypothesis is of course totally unscientific and remains a simple *flatus vocis* as long as the existence of such an unconscious is proved only by its presumed effects.

14   Why does Weber introduce this hierarchy between rationality and irrationality? The reason is simple, I think – as soon as the sociologist declares that a person or a group has acted in a particular way through inertia, passion, fanaticism, blindness, or perversion (which of course *may* be true), not only is the discussion brought to an abrupt halt, but the suggested explanation is likely, if it stops there, to be circular. In this regard, we need only refer to all the research which explains the rejection of a particular innovation by social actors' 'resistance to change', by their incurable traditionalism or by saying that there are programmes (in the computing sense) in their brains which direct their behaviour. Since these programmes are obviously not observable, only the behaviour which they are supposed to explain can be evoked to show that they exist.

Of course, I am not making a plea for a model which assumes the absolute sovereignty of consciousness, and it must be recognized that the classic notion of *disposition* is indispensable for sociological analysis. What is unacceptable is to reduce the social actor to a system of *dispositions* which function in an autonomous way, independently of the intentions of the actors. It is for this reason, I think, that Weber suggested that at first one should postulate rationality, but be ready to identify later the part played by the irrational.

15   K. Mannheim, *Ideology and Utopia* p. 2.

16   Ibid., p. 3.

17   Ibid., p. 71.

18   Ibid., p. 76.

19   Ibid., pp. 70–1.

20   Ibid., p. 85.

21   K. Mannheim presents the two cases which I have just quoted (the taboo against charging interest on loans during the early capitalist era, and the

patriarchalism of the Junkers) as examples of 'false consciousness', a notion which is attributable not to Marx but to F. Mehring, and which Engels uses in his famous letter to Mehring quoted at the beginning of this chapter. Like the notion of 'the unconscious', the notion of 'false consciousness' can give rise (and indeed has given rise) to all kinds of conceptually unacceptable uses (on the unconscious, see Chapter 6, note 10). However, it can also give rise to a totally acceptable interpretation, as is the case in Mannheim.

22   The quotations in this paragraph are from C. Geertz, 'Ideology as a cultural system', in *Ideology and Discontent*, ed. D. Apter (The Free Press, Glencoe, 1964), Chapter 2, p. 63.

23   Ibid., p. 63. My diagnosis that Geertz's theory does not add much to Mannheim's raises, if one accepts it, an interesting point, which is that writers and researchers as a general rule accept without much debate an idea which often amounts to an ideology, that of scientific *progress* – any important theory ought to contradict, at least in part, and go further than those which precede it. This is certainly how the theory of Geertz was seen – as an 'important stage' in the theory of ideologies. However, though Geertz's article is important, it did not for me represent a turning-point, but rather reminded us in its own way of old and forgotten ideas. Of course, though the *a priori* idea of *progress* which can be summed up in the equation 'important = new' might be ideological in some cases (as here), it is in no way irrational: on the contrary, it is hard to see how one can indulge in scientific research without believing in it. However, it is based on a strong hypothesis – that the present preserves all interesting things which have been said in the past. It sometimes leads us to think that something is new whereas it is merely a rehash, or to emphasize recent matters and forget the importance of work done in the past. This is why the idea of progress can sometimes hinder the progress of knowledge.

24   J. Baechler, *Qu'est-ce que l'idéologie?* (Gallimard, Paris, 1976).

25   J.-P. Sartre, *Being and Nothingness* (Methuen, London, 1957 (1943)) p. 48, 'Bad faith is a lie to oneself [. . .] the person to whom one lies and the person who is lying are one and the same person, which means that it follows that I know, as the person deceiving, the truth which is hidden from me as the person deceived. It further follows that I know this truth very precisely *in order* to hide it from myself more carefully – and this not at two different moments in time.'

26   A. C. MacIntyre, *The Unconscious, a Conceptual Analysis* (Routledge & Kegan Paul, London, 1973 (1958)). In speaking of 'the early Freud', I am referring to MacIntyre's hypothesis that Freud moved from an *explanatory* to a *descriptive* conception of the unconscious.

27   D. Colas, *Le Léninisme* (Presses Universitaires de France, Paris, 1982).

Chapter 4   Journey around a table

1   E. Durkheim, *The Elementary Forms of the Religious Life* (Allen & Unwin, London, 1915 (1912)).

2   It is with good reason that C. Lévi-Strauss said of Sartre that he was a 'false mind' (Raymond Aron, *Histoire et politique – textes et témoignages*, Julliard, Paris, 1985, p. 122). There are in fact several gems in his philosophy: people decide to be sad (*Being and Nothingness*, Methuen, London, 1957 (1943)) p. 61; Jews exist only in the mind of antisemites (*Réflexions sur la question juive*, Gallimard, Paris, 1954); one can believe at the same time and equally strongly in two contradictory propositions (*Being and Nothingness*, p. 84 *ff.*), and so on. His absolutist conception of the sovereignty of the consciousness (one decides to be sad, and perhaps also to be hungry) takes to excess that of eighteenth-century sensualists and twentieth-century behaviourists. At the same time, he does not hesitate to attribute to this sovereign consciousness experiences which no human being seems ever to have had.

3   V. Pareto, *A Treatise on General Sociology* (Dover, New York, 1935 (1916)).

4   Ibid., Chapter II, § 180 *ff.*

5   Aristotle, *The Nicomachean Ethics*, Book VII, Chapter 2.

6   M. Weber, *Economy and Society*, II, (Bedminster Press, New York, 1968 (1922)) p. 416.

7   Ibid., p. 476.

8   Ibid., p. 410.

9   Durkheim, *The Elementary Forms of the Religious Life*, p. 415.

10   L. Lévy-Bruhl, *La Mentalité Primitive* (Alcan, Paris, 1922). Lévy-Bruhl of course later considerably modified his earlier views in *Les Carnets de L. Lévy-Bruhl* (Presses Universitaires de France, Paris, 1949).

11   K. Mannheim takes his inspiration – but in a qualified, exact, and careful way – from the classic arguments of German historism (history is a succession of singularities whose meaning, for the observer, varies according to the historical position of the latter). *Historism* is not to be confused with its opposite, *historicism* (in Popper's sense – establishing the laws of history). According to historism, God could never be a historian, since history can taken on meaning only for actors who are situated. According to historicism, the task of history is to find evidence of the hand of God in the turmoil of history.

12   According to the methodology, outlined by P. Lazarsfeld, of the construction of 'attribute space': cf. R. Boudon and P. Lazarsfeld, *Le Vocabulaire des sciences sociales* (Mouton, Paris, 1965), pp. 147–70.

13   Pareto, *A Treatise of General Sociology*, Chapters 4 and 5.

Chapter 5   Outline of a restricted theory of ideology

1   M. Merleau-Ponty, *Phénoménologie de la perception* (Gallimard, Paris, 1945); *La Structure du comportement* (Presses Universitaires de France, Paris, 1963).

2   A. Schütz, *Der sinnliche Aufbau der sozialen Welt* (Springer, Vienna, 1932).

3   P. Berger and T. Luckmann, *The Social Construction of Reality* (Doubleday, London, 1966).

4   R. Linton, 'Cultural and personality factors affecting economic growth', in
    The Progress of Underdeveloped Areas, ed. B. Hoselitz (Chicago Univer-
    sity Press, Chicago, 1952), pp. 73–88.

5   For a critique of this contemplative theory, see T. Kuhn, Scientific Develop-
    ment and Lexical Change, Thalheimer Lectures, (Johns Hopkins University,
    1984, duplicated).

6   On historism, see Chapter 4, note 11.

7   As a general rule, I use the word 'disposition' in the sense in which it is used,
    for example, in G. Ryle, The Concept of Mind, or L. Wittgenstein,
    Philosophische Untersuchungen § 149 'When one says that knowing the
    alphabet is a state of the mind, one is thinking of a state of a mental apparatus
    (Seelenapparat) (perhaps of the brain) by means of which we explain the
    manifestations (Aüsserungen) of that knowledge. Such a state is called a
    disposition (Disposition).' Dispositions are therefore cognitive resources,
    skills which we have acquired and which we can call upon. The word 'disposi-
    tion' can also of course have a meaning which is not cognitive, but affective
    or ethical, as in Aristotle (for example, the disposition [ἕξις] to
    temperance).

8   And also in other texts of the Gesammelte Aufsätze zur Religionssoziologie
    (1922–3). I am simply trying to emphasize the importance of the theory of
    magic outlined by Weber and not show – or state – that others are thereby
    discredited, which would involve a long discussion completely outside my
    argument. What needs to be stressed, however, is that theories of magic are
    connected with a typology similar to the one I developed in Chapter 4 con-
    cerning ideology. This will be evident by reference to a few classic examples.
    For Frazer (in The Golden Bough), magic is a false science. Magic ritual is the
    vehicle of false beliefs which depend on feelings (for example, fear of
    superior powers). Wittgenstein argues (in 'Bemerkungen über Frazers The
    golden bough', Synthese, 17 (1967), pp. 233–53) that magic should not be
    approached by reference to science: it is not a representation of the world, but
    the expression of a wish ('die Magie aber bringt einen Wunsch zur
    Darstellung; sie aüssert einen Wunsch'). Wittgenstein bases his interpretation
    on an important statement, namely that the rainmaker is not seen as having
    the power to bring rain, because the only time he is asked to beg the assistance
    of the skies is during the rainy season. Evans-Pritchard thinks (Witchcraft,
    Oracles and Magic Among the Azande) that magic is an interpretative system
    which has logical coherence but which runs counter to the scientific mode of
    thought characteristic of our society. Adding Weber's theory to these exam-
    ples gives us the typology outlined in Chapter 4.

9   H. Von Wright, Explanation and Understanding (Routledge & Kegan Paul,
    London, 1971).

10 D. Kahneman and A. Tversky, 'Subjective probability: a judgement of repre-
    sentativeness', Cognitive Psychology, 3 (1972) pp. 430–54; A. Tversky and
    D. Kahneman, 'Availability: a heuristic for judging frequency and prob-
    ability', Cognitive Psychology, 5 (1973), pp. 207–32.

11 The question which I put here is in fact of my own making, I have tried to
    synthesize into it the spirit and the results of the large number of experiments

referred to in R. Nisbett and L. Ross, *Human Inference*, (Prentice Hall, Englewood Cliffs, 1980).

12   As J. R. Tréanton notes in 'Faut-il exhumer Le Play? ou les héritiers abusifs', *Revue française de Sociologie*, XXV (1984) p. 465, even experienced scientific researchers can fall in this trap: H. Le Bras and E. Todd in their book *Invention de la France* (Librairie générale française, Paris, 1981, 38–9) note that there are between thirty and forty French *départements* where the Left does well in elections and where there is a significant proportion of community families (families of the same generation living in the same household). Despite the resemblance in kind between assumed cause and effect (the community family values solidarity more highly, therefore it is not difficult to imagine its members voting more readily for parties which espouse solidarity), these cases of consistency, numerous though they are, do not prove Humean causation (correlation). Any causation is further discounted in that since the unit of observation is a collective one (the *département*), even if a correlation was objectively shown to exist, it would not prove that voting for the Left is more frequent among community families. Here we see how implausible it would be to impute to 'primitive thought' a statistical pre-knowledge so rigorous that it would prevent primitive person from falling into traps from which even the best research scientists are not always protected.

13   J. Habermas, *Knowledge and Human Interests* (Heinemann, London, 1972), originally published as *Erkenntnis und Interesse*, (Suhrkamp, Frankfurt, 1968); 'Wahrheitstheorien' in *Wirklichkeit und Reflexion, ed.* H. Fahrenbach (Pfullingen, 1973).

14   Instead of contrasting contemplative and active theories (of knowledge), I could have used the distinction between realist and idealist theory, if I had not feared that confusion would arise over the word 'idealist'. As J. Freund is right to emphasize (in *Philosophie et sociologie*, Cabay, Louvain-la-Neuve, 1984), it is Marx who is largely responsible for this confusion, by not keeping separate the two classical distinctions of materialism and spiritualism, and realism and idealism. The classical philosophy of falsehood – which still inspires the theory of ideologies, as I say frequently in my argument – is of course foursquare with the contemplative theory of knowledge, in other words very close to the pre-Kantian philosophy of knowledge. However, it is important also to note that modern philosophy has to a great extent revised the classical model of knowledge from which this classical theory of falsehood derives: firstly, as we have seen, by stressing the active nature of knowledge; secondly, by insisting on the importance of language in knowledge, and on the wide variety of different meanings in language, as well as on the pitfalls of language (for example, the *realist* interpretation of ideal-typical concepts; the belief that the existence of the word implies the existence of the thing itself); and finally by not presenting the subject acquiring knowledge as solipsist.

15   K. Popper, *The Logic of Scientific Discovery* (Hutchinson, London, 1972).

16   T. Kuhn, *The Structure of Scientific Revolutions* (Chicago University Press, Chicago, 1962).

17   T. Kuhn, *Scientific development and lexical change*.

18 In *The Elementary Forms of the Religious Life* (Allen & Unwin, London, 1915 (1912)).

19 In the same way, Jean Baechler intended to make clear his opposition to the paradigm deployed by Durkheim in his analysis of *suicide* by entitling his book *Les Suicides* (Calmann Lévy, Paris, 1975).

Chapter 6   Ideology, social position, and dispositions

1 The novel cannot do without teleology. It is hardly likely that novelists will explain the behaviour of their heroes – prosaically – using a register which scientific discourse would consider legitimate. After all, if a *social actor* cannot have a destiny, the hero of a novel cannot not have one, or the reader's attention would not be engaged. For instance, it is more or less unimaginable that the novelist can account for an accident – the one which Sartoris has, for example – in the same way that a sociologist would, or a police inspector in charge on an enquiry. Each of these observers will normally use a register which is different from the one used by the others.

Let me make it clear that, contrary to certain absurd interpretations of 'register', it is one thing to accept the obvious fact that there is a whole range of registers, and quite another to see in them the sign of a breakdown in human thought. After all everybody, except perhaps J. F. Lyotard (in *La Condition Post-Moderne*), is capable of distinguishing between a novel and a scientific proof, and therefore of mastering this distinction.

However, because of the seductive force of the language normally used in novels – as in tragedy or drama – the social sciences are open to the literary temptation and occasionally succumb to it. Here, however, we must respect the message of Wittgenstein's second period – the one of *Philosophical Investigations*: the human brain is complex enough to allow multiple linguistic registers. It is important to see, however, that often, one of them is not reducible to another, and to know in which register one is, since in this matter there is no value in mixtures. This is why sociology which claims to be literary easily becomes sub-literature.

2 J. Elster, *Making Sense of Marx* (Cambridge University Press, Cambridge, 1985), p. 182 and the quotation from *Capital I*, on co-operation.

3 In any event, it is based on a hypothesis on which there is no unanimous agreement – the labour theory of value. Cf. Chapter 2, note 26.

4 L. Coser, *The Functions of Social Conflict* (Routledge & Kegan Paul, London, 1956).

5 Coser bases his argument on E. Hobsbawn, 'The machine breakers', *Past and Present*, I (1952) pp. 57–67 and on E. Thompson, *The Making of the British Working Class* (Vintage, New York, 1966).

6 A. Sauvy, *General Theory of Population* (Weidenfeld and Nicolson, London, 1969 (1952)), I, Chapter XIV; *L'Economie du diable* (Calmann-Lévy, Paris, 1976), pp. 33–4; *La Machine et le chômage*, (Dunod, Paris, 1980).

7 *Theories of Social Change – a critical appraisal* (Polity Press, Cambridge, 1986).

The book is S. Epstein, *Economic Development and Social Change in South India* (Manchester University Press, Manchester, 1962).

8 W. Sombart, *Why Is There No Socialism in the United States?* (Macmillan, London, 1976 (1906)).

9 E. Chinoy, 'The tradition of opportunity and the aspiration of automobile workers', *American Journal of Sociology*, 57 (5) (1952) pp. 453–9.

10 The notion of *the unconscious* can be used to designate all kinds of observed phenomena. For instance, we perform all kinds of acts (for example, walking) without realizing it, unless at the level of our consciousness. Phenomenology has of course studied these phenomena (see, for example, A. Schütz, *Das Problem der Relevanz*, Suhrkamp, Frankfurt, 1971). We can also say that *habits* are (more or less) unconscious, even though they can be the object of an abrupt realization when the slightest incident appears in the development of the behaviour for which they are responsible. We can also speak of the unconscious in the context of what we call *dispositions*: I know that two and two are four, even when this knowledge is not present in my consciousness. We can equally speak of the unconscious, though in a completely different sense, in the context of what theologians have called *implicit faith* (a notion which reproduces on the theological level a well-known analysis in Plato's *Menon*), and of similar phenomena: I know theory *T* in detail, but I have not taken cognisance of its consequence *C*, even though it is clear; alternatively: I know *T*, but I have not seen that *T* is based on principle *P*; or again: I believe in *T* and *T'* even though *T* and *T'* are contradictory, but I have not realized the contradiction (for example, the case of the egalitarian who rejects the utilitarian paradigm). We can also speak of the unconscious when we observe fragments of behaviour (on the part of somebody else, or even of ourselves) which we clearly feel have a common meaning, without immediately being able to say what this meaning is. This is true of dreams, which Freud regards as a rebus, without in this case giving the unconscious any causal virtue. We can also speak of the unconscious when we proceed by trial and error, feeling ourselves merely shunted about until the solution to a problem (the plan for an article, the meaning of a sentence, and so on) appears to us in a flash of inspiration. We can speak of the unconscious when we project on to persons observed, without realizing it, data which apply to our situation but not to theirs (cf. Weber's analysis of magic). Or when we trip over our words (a slip of the tongue) during the dangerous process of trying to make others think that we believe the opposite of what we in fact believe. In other words, all kinds of psychic phenomena can be called unconscious, without raising any problems over the word.

Conversely, it seems dangerous to make of the unconscious a Pandora's box and a logical mainspring which allows us to draw any conclusion from any premises. When we accept, without going into further detail, that people can fail to see what they see and see what they do not see, and fail to believe what they believe and believe what they do not believe, the relationship between the behaviour of actors and its interpretation of necessity takes on an arbitrary form. Everything then becomes a matter of rhetoric; and the door is wide open to the egocentrism and sociocentrism of the observer.

Partly because they think they have distanced themselves from philosophy, the social sciences often do not realize that they give rise to and make generally available a *theory of the unconscious*, which may be more or less acceptable. For example, individualist sociology adopts as a whole or in parts the theory of the unconscious which was developed particularly in German philosophy and sociology (Simmel, Weber, Husserl), but also in British philosophy (Ryle, MacIntyre). It accepts the existence of an unconscious, but gives itself the right neither to transform it into a Pandora's box, nor to attribute causal power to it. This tradition of thought accepts, for example, the existence of habits, but refrains from concluding that they can transform social actors into sleep-walkers. It agrees that there are lies and bad faith in the ordinary sense, but not bad faith in the Sartrean sense (the subject's ability to believe simultaneously and with the same force in two contradictory statements). It accepts that people may fail to see what is in front of their eyes, but not that they can see what they cannot see. Certain sociological theories, of psychoanalytical origin, Marxist as well as Durkheimian ('rationalization', 'false consciousness', 'collective consciousness') give rise on the other hand to a theory of consciousness which is unacceptable to the extent that it postulates the existence of states of consciousness which no human being has ever experienced. It is difficult to see why personal experience should not be brought in here: we are well aware that we *can* hesitate between two contradictory statements; this is a state of consciousness which is easily experienced and communicated. Similarly, we are well aware that we cannot believe simultaneously two statements which are both unambiguous and contradictory: this type of state of consciousness can be neither experienced nor communicated. As I indicated earlier, Mannheim clearly saw the difficulties of the notion of 'false consciousness'; he therefore gave it a meaning which was very restricted (cf. Chapter 3, note 21) and perfectly acceptable.

There is in fact a very interesting book waiting to be written on implied theories of consciouness in the social sciences. After all, concerning the theory of consciousness, the break which the social sciences are alleged to have made with the philosophical tradition has had particularly undesirable consequences. If this philosophical tradition had not been lost sight of, a certain number of models of the social actor – particularly those which consider the social actor to be a mechanistic product of the environment – could not have established themselves so easily.

11 H. Spencer, *The Study of Sociology* (The International Scientific Series, 1873).

12 J. Hintikka, *Knowledge and Belief* (Cornell University Press, Ithaca and London, 1962), 5.3, p. 106 *ff.*

13 E. May, *Lessons of the Past* (Oxford University Press, New York, 1973).

14 V. Ferkiss, *Futurology* (Sage, London, 1977) gives a list of these forecasting errors, of which two are particularly diverting: in 1880, Brockhaus (the major German encyclopaedia) said in its article on *automobile*: 'name sometimes given to a strange vehicle powered by a combustion engine . . . This invention which has now been forgotten experienced only failure and the disapproval of scientific authorities.' And Firkiss shows that demographic forecasting in

Britain between 1924 and 1932 never mentioned the subject of over-population, but was almost entirely concerned with the low level of fertility of elites and the effects of this on the genetic heritage of the human race.

15 This case in point is the central plank in the theory of ideology of A. Downs, in *An Economic Theory of Democracy* (harper, New York, 1957).

16 Perhaps wrongly, in my opinion, since measures meant to eradicate them often involve social costs such that, if they knew about them, the members of the society would unanimously vote against the measures in question. This is clearly seen in the case of egalitarian education policies which have ended up by displeasing everybody. A measure which provokes or would provoke unanimous hostility cannot be regarded as democratic. Egalitarianism is therefore in no way a necessary corollary of democratic values.

17 In an interesting report, Antoine Prost ('La Politique de démocratisation de l'enseignement – essai d'évaluation, 1950-80', duplicated) showed that streaming, which he reminds us was meant, at least in part, to promote the educational staying-on rate of groups which up to then had benefited least from education, did not reduce the differences in staying-on between social classes. However, his report does not show that streaming did not improve the staying-on rate of the less well-off. See, on these matters, the article by O. Ekert-Jaffé, 'La scolarisation entre 17 et 20 ans – démocratisation ou poursuite des inégalités?', *Population*, 3 (1985), pp. 491–504, which confirms the trend towards democratization in France during the period 1960 to 1970, while at the same time revealing that it varied with age (it was more marked at seventeen than later) and that it depended on family size.

18 A. Tversky and D. Kahneman, 'Judgment under uncertainty: heuristics and biases', *Science*, 185 (1974), pp. 1124–31.

19 R. Boudon, *L'Inégalité des chances* (Colin, Paris, 1978 (1973); Hachette, 1985).

20 On questions of method for measuring lack of equal opportunities in education, see J. P. Grémy, 'Les différences entre pourcentages et leur interprétation', *Revue française de sociologie*, XXV, (3) (1984), pp. 396–420. See also Ekert-Jaffé. 'La scolarisation entre 17 et 20 ans'.

Chapter 7   Ideology and communication

1 M. Foucault, *Discipline and Punish* (Allen Lane, London, 1977).

2 H. R. Trevor-Roper, *Religion, the Reformation and Social Change, and other Essays* (Macmillan, London, 1972).

3 B. Groethuysen, *Origines de l'esprit bourgeois en France* (Gallimard, Paris, 1977 (1927)).

4 E. Voegelin, *The New Science of Politics* (University of Chicago Press, Chicago, 1983 (1952)).

5 L. Coser, *Refugee Scholars in America* (Yale University Press, New Haven, 1984).

6 K. Polanyi, *The Great Transformation* (Beacon Press, Boston, Mass., 1957 (1944)).

7   On this point, see Louis Dumont's preface to the French translation of *The Great Transformation - La grande transformation* (Gallimard, Paris, 1983).

8   Polanyi, *The Great Transformation*, p. 61.

9   M. Hechter, 'Karl Polanyi's social theory: a critique', in *The Microfoundations of Macrosociology* ed. M. Hechter (Temple, Philadelphia, 1983), pp. 159-89.

10   See A. Jardin, *Histoire du libéralisme politique* (Hachette, Paris, 1985).

11   A. Cochin, 'La campagne électorale de 1789 en Bourgogne', in *L'Esprit du jacobinisme* (Presses Universitaires de France, Paris, 1979 (1904)) pp. 49-78.

12   I base my remarks in this section on ideas which I presented in 'Anomie, contradictions et philosophie publique dans les sociétés industrielles', *Contrepoint*, 22-23 (1976), pp. 39-69; *The Unintended Consequences of Social Action* (St Martin, London, 1982), pp. 66-74; *The Logic of Social Action* (Routledge, Chapman and Hall, London, 1981), pp. 134-5; 'The FMS movement in France: variations on a theme by Sherry Turckle', *Revue Toqueville*, 2 (1980) pp. 5-24. See also F. Bourricaud, *Le Bricolage Idéologique* (Presses Universitaires de France, Paris, 1980), pp. 141-8, who rightly stresses the role of mediators in the spread of ideologies.

     It must be emphasized that these mediators do not always belong to those who *because of their role* (journalists, and so on) have a mediatory function. Artists and writers may perform this mediatory function by giving artistic or literary expression to ideas which arise in other areas. The obvious example is the 'committed' singer or actor. This is, however, merely one example of a more general case in point. For instance the literary vibratos on the nineteenth-century journal *Progrès* would no doubt have been less inspired, and would have been seen as less convincing if they had not been able to base their work, more or less consciously and more or less discreetly, on Comte, Marx, Spencer, or Darwin.

13   J. Medvedev, *Grandeur et chute de Lyssenko* (Gallimard, Paris, 1977).

14   M. Weber, *The Protestant Ethic and the Spirit of Capitalism* (Allen and Unwin, London, 1976 (1904-5)).

15   G. Marshall, *In Search of the Spirit of Capitalism* (Hutchinson, London, 1982).

16   J. Schumpeter, *Business Cycles* (McGraw-Hill, New York and London, 1939).

17   S. Eisenstadt, 'The Protestant ethic thesis in analytical and comparative context', *Diogenes* 59 (1967), pp. 25-46.

18   Trevor-Roper, *Religion*, Chapters 1 and 2.

19   Foucault, *Discipline and Punish*.

20   G. Tullock, 'Does punishment deter crime?', *The Public Interest*, 136 (Summer 1974), pp. 103-11. G. Becker, 'Crime and punishment - an economic approach', *Journal of Political Economy*, 76 March-April 1968, pp. 169-217. F. Jenny, 'La théorie économique du crime: une revue de la littérature', *Vie et sciences économiques*, 73 (1977), pp. 7-20.

21   Foucault, *Discipline and Punish*, p. 265.

22   Ibid., p. 271.

23 Ibid., p. 272. Note the reference to 'serving a purpose'.
24 Ibid., p. 276. Note the word 'secretly'. What becomes abundantly clear here
    is a structure of reasoning typical of exaggerated functionalism. An institu-
    tion gives rise to unintended consequences, but it is nevertheless maintained.
    This must be because it is useful to somebody, and this somebody has the
    power to impose it. But who can this somebody be other than (by definition)
    the ruling class whose existence is thereby, if not proved, at least confirmed,
    even though in a totally circular manner? To which must be added that this
    power, to be effective, must remain invisible and be exercised *secretly*. See
    R. Boudon, 'The three basic paradigms of macrosociology: functionalism,
    neo-Marxism and action analysis', *Theory and Decision*, 6 (1976), pp. 381–
    406. On the influence of this mode of thinking on contemporary thought on
    the state, see M. V. Cabral, 'L'Etat-providence et le citoyen', *Encyclopaedia
    Universalis, les Enjeux*, pp. 788–95.
25 Foucault, *Discipline and Punish*, p. 285.
26 Pushing this audacious logic further than Foucault, P. Bourdieu accepts
    without turning a hair that an unintended consequence can be regarded as the
    cause of behaviour, even when this consequence is harmful to the actor. For
    instance, the fact that the lower classes have modest educational ambitions
    means that overall, as statistics show, their educational achievement is low.
    This consequence is then interpreted by the inventor of reproduction theory
    as the cause of the modest ambitions observed among the lower classes, who
    would see in the statistics the proof that their fate is sealed. Transposed to
    another example, this reasoning would explain why the middle of Paris is
    choked with traffic at six o'clock in the evening in the following way: car
    drivers note that they cause traffic jams (an unpleasant and unintended con-
    sequence); they therefore acquire a *habitus* which encourages them to think
    that they cannot escape traffic jams; and it is because they are – unconsciously
    of course – impelled by this *habitus* that they make for the centre of Paris
    each evening. It would of course be 'sociologically naïve' to consider that the
    traffic jams are caused by the fact that people want to get home from work.
    Similarly, it would be 'sociologically naïve' to suppose that educational
    inequalities are due to the fact that a working-class family and a professional
    family do not have the same resource levels, the same view of the risks
    entailed by investment in education, the same references (in the sense of the
    theory of reference groups) or the same dispositions (in the Aristotelian
    sense). This naïve interpretation will be found in my book *L'inégalité des
    chances*, (Colin, Paris, 1984 (1973)), and the learned interpretation appears
    in P. Bourdieu and J.-C. Passeron, *Reproduction in Education, Society and
    Culture* (Sage, London, 1977). It would be superfluous to say that the clas-
    sical notion of 'causality of the probable' is not enough to make this learned
    interpretation scientific.
27 Foucault, *Discipline and Punish*, p. 277.
28 See, however, J. Merquior, *Foucault* (Presses Universitaires de France,
    Paris, 1986).
29 S. Sieber, *Fatal Remedies, the Ironies of Social Intervention*, (Plenum, New
    York and London, 1981) p. 70, suggests another classic example, also in the

field of penal policy, of these perspective effects: the effect of the use of hard drugs on the crime rate is so visible that those responsible for deciding penal policy often tend to underestimate the negative effects of banning them. Such a move leads to the appearance of illegal dealing and offers another opportunity for organized crime. Since prices on this illegal market rise to astronomical levels, the drug-taker is led into crime against persons and property. Just as in the case of the effects of prison, the *net* effects of banning hard drugs are difficult to determine. By a perspective effect similar to the one to which Foucault and his followers fall victim, there is a tendency to confuse these net effects (complex, abstract, and not easily measured) with the most obvious gross effects.

30 M. MacLuhan, *Understanding Media – the Extensions of Man* (Routledge & Kegan Paul, London, 1964).

31 Several examples of this will be found in the well-documented and well-argued book by L. Ferry and A. Renaut, *La Pensée 1968* (Gallimard, Paris, 1985), which I received just as this book was going to press. It will be interesting to see how reviewers react to Ferry and Renaut's book, which is iconoclastic in its findings but critical (in the sense in which one speaks of a critical mind) and analytical in its method. Perhaps people will try to *discredit* it: it will be more difficult to *refute* it.

Chapter 8   Science and ideology

1 T. Kuhn, *The Structure of Scientific Revolutions* (University of Chicago Press, Chicago, 1971). It is not without hesitation that I use the word *paradigm* here. Perhaps the obscurity of the concept of paradigm would be to a large extent removed if one used instead an older concept, that of *principle* ($\dot{\alpha}\rho\chi\dot{\eta}$). The idea which Kuhn is trying to get across by his notion of paradigm is of course that every scientific initiative is based of necessity on things which it does not question. This is of course the idea contained in the notion of principle, which has, as a bonus, the advantage of summarizing it in its etymology. The development economist, for example, starts from the *principle* that the word 'development' has a meaning, that it can properly be used in the singular, and so on. I myself, in this book, start from the *principle* that I refuse to use the notion of the *unconscious* in the way that it is used in the earlier works of Freud. In other words, I would argue, *cum grano salis*, that, *logically and epistemologically*, the concept of 'paradigm' does not add much to 'principle', and that in most of Kuhn's work the latter could replace the former. *Sociologically*, however, if Kuhn had done this, he would certainly have lost the benefit of the exegetical writing on what the notion of paradigm *really* means, and his analyses would have been less easily perceived (I am not saying that Kuhn wanted this to happen, merely that it did). His work would have been just as interesting, and perhaps clearer, but it would have been less visible.

2 H. Albert, *Traktat über kritische Vernunft* (Mohr, Tübingen, 1975 (1968)). Albert got the Münchhausen reference from a passage from Schopenhauer,

Ueber die vierfache Wurzel des Satzes vom zureichenden Grunde (Hamburg, 1957 (1813)), p. 25, where he compares Spinoza's notion of self-cause (*causa sui*) with a famous Münchhausen adventure – having fallen into a pond while riding his horse, the Baron gripped the horse's flanks and got out of the water by pulling his own pigtail.

3 G. Lukács, *Der junge Hegel* (Europa, Zurich, 1948).

4 F. Tönnies, *Community and Society* (Harper and Row, New York and London, 1957).

5 C. Camic, 'The utilitarians revisited', *American Journal of Sociology*, 85 (3) (November 1979), pp. 516–50, shows clearly that the major utilitarians mostly regarded the utilitarian paradigm as having limited application. Camic takes the concept of utilitarianism, as I myself do here, in the sense in which it is generally used nowadays, and which is summed up in the premiss that individual behaviour springs from a comparison between the costs and advantages of alternative lines of action. However, the notion of utilitarianism also denotes, classically, the social philosophy that the best policies and political institutions are those which maximize the total good which is made available to members of society.

6 In *The Unintended Consequences of Social Action* (St Martin, London, 1982), I tried to show that the utilitarian paradigm could usefully replace others in analysing certain sociological phenomena. I also tried to show that, though this paradigm could in no way claim universality, and it is more suited to economics than to other social sciences, it can also be effective in these other areas, as is evident from numerous classic and modern works in sociology, political science, criminology, or anthropology. However, to assert that the utilitarian paradigm *can*, depending on the phenomenon being studied, be applied for example in sociology and history, and saying that the model of *Homo œconomicus* is of universal and exclusive application in these disciplines, are two distinct statements. I have always limited myself to the first, but I recognize that I was thereby opposing the *received idea* developed by Parsons, as well as by Durkheim and others, that sociology sprang from an alleged break with utilitarianism. This break – it surely goes without saying? – has in fact never been consummated. Although it is obvious that social actors are guided by values and myths (such as the ideological myths with which this book is concerned), it is difficult to see how their 'material interests' (Simmel) can be disregarded. The effectiveness of sociology such as Weber's stems largely from the fact that it rejects and avoids this break. Even where religious myths or magical practices are concerned, Weber always insists, as we have seen, that both must be understood as a response to the most down-to-earth 'cares of everyday life'.

7 F. Engels, *The Origins of the Family, Private Property and the State* (Progress, Moscow, 1948 (1884)).

8 R. Cloward and L. Ohlin, *Delinquency and Opportunity* (Free Press, New York, 1960).

9 A. Downs, *An Economic Theory of Democracy* (Harper, New York, 1957); B. Barry, *Sociologists, Economists and Democracy*, (Chicago University Press, Chicago, 1970).

10 J.-J. Rousseau, *The Social Contract*, Book III, Chapter 2.

11 G. Simmel, *The Problems of the Philosophy of History – an epistemological essay* (Free Press, New York, 1977 (1892)).

12 I will mention only, for the record, the case of those sociologists who, in a totally contradictory manner, claim to be inspired by egalitarianism (therefore postulating that human beings are motivated by appetite and envy) and, at the same time, rage against the utilitarian paradigm. The explanation for this contradiction is mainly that it is not seen as such. Furthermore, it reveals a corporatist type reaction to the perceived enemy and rival – economics. It is a myth which is highly dubious but often propounded that sociology 'discovered' (in contrast with economics) that human beings were not motivated by their interests alone. Sociology did not of course discover this self-evident truth which all utilitarians, from Adam Smith onwards, took for granted. On this matter, see Smith's theory of moral sentiments.

13 J. Buchanan and G. Tullock, *The Calculus of Consent* (University of Michigan Press, Ann Arbor, 1967 (1962)). To understand the difference between *functional* analysis and *historical* analysis, the approach of Buchanan and Tullock can be contrasted with the writings of Léo Moulin which show that the electoral and deliberative techniques normally used nowadays were refined by medieval religious orders: 'Sanior et major pars – étude sur l'évolution des techniques électorales et délibératives dans les ordres religieux du VIe au XIIIe siècies', *Revue historique du droit français et étranger*, 3 and 4 (1958); 'Les origines religieuses des techniques électorales et délibératives modernes' *Revue internationale d'histoire politique et constitutionnelle*, April-June 1953, pp. 106–48.

14 S. Popkin, *The Rational Peasant* (Berkeley University Press, Berkeley, 1979).

15 L. Lévy-Bruhl, *La mentalité primitive* (Alcan, Paris, 1922).

16 R. K. Merton, *Social Theory and Social Structure*, 9th edn (The Free Press, Glencoe, 1964).

17 P. Bourdieu and J.-C. Passeron, *Reproduction in Education, Society and Culture* (Sage, London, 1977 (1970)); P. Bourdieu, *Ce que parler veut dire* (Fayard, Paris, 1982); *La Distinction* (Minuit, Paris, 1979). The description 'neo-Marxist' can be applied to a research and intellectual movement which developed world-wide but more particularly in France in the 1960s and 1970s, and which was characterized by an attempt to explain any institution by its presumed macro-social effects. For this intellectual movement, *explanation* amounted to answering the question 'what purpose is served by . . .?': prison (Foucault), education (Althusser, Bourdieu), culture (Bourdieu), cities (Castells), the state (Miliband). The answer to the question '*whose* purpose is served by . . .?' is of course known in advance: that of the ruling class. We are justified in speaking of neo-*Marxism* in this context, since this type of functionalism is present in certain analyses of Marx (see, for example, his theory of the state, of law, of religion, and his general theory of ideologies). It needs to be made clear however, in deference to Marx's memory, that we are speaking about a *neo*-Marxism, in that there are in his work, as I have stressed several times, analyses which in no way derive from this stark functionalism.

There are, of course other neo-Marxisms besides the one to which I am referring here.

18   *Entretiens avec 'Le Monde': La société* (La Découverte and Le Monde, Paris, 1985), p. 110.

19   The *hexis* of Aristotle, like the *habitus* of Thomas Aquinas, is neither unconscious, nor unamenable to the will, nor mechanical, nor fixed in content, nor determined in a totally social way, nor *a fortiori* determined only by position in the social stratification system. In Aristotle (*The Nicomachean Ethics*, II, p. 3, for example) the *hexis* is an orientation which subjects give *to themselves*. For instance, people who have chosen temperance will derive pleasure from stopping after two glasses; people who have opted for intemperance (the opposite *hexis*) will derive pleasure only from managing to sate their desires. In Thomas Aquinas, *habitus* are, in the same way, placed under the control of consciousness (*voluntas*); cf. *Summa theologica*, Q 49, art. 3 'Commentator (i.e. Averroes) dicit, in 3 *de Anima*, quod habitus est quo quis agit cum voluerit'; Q 50, art. 1 'Objectio illa procedit de habitu secundum quod est dispositio ad operationem, et de actibus corporis qui sunt a natura: non autem de his quis sunt ab anima, quorum principium est voluntas'; Q 52, art. 3 'Usus habitum in voluntate hominis consistit'. The classical notion of disposition, as defined by eminent authors from Aristotle and Aquinas to Wittgenstein and modern psychologists such as Nisbett, has absolutely nothing to do with programmes (in the computer science meaning of the word). See also J. Stoetzel and P. Lazarsfeld, 'Définition d'intention et espace d'attributs' in *Le Vocabulaire des sciences sociales*, R. Boudon and P. Lazarsfeld (Mouton, Paris, 1965), pp. 189–93, which shows that the notion of *disposition* or *attitude* is used in social psychology in a way which is very close to the classical philosophical meaning.

20   A formula which appears repeatedly in Bourdieu, *La Distinction*.

21   P. Bourdieu, 'La causalité du probable', *Revue française de sociologie*, XV (1974), pp. 16–17. For an application of his theory of *habitus*, see Chapter 7, note 26.

22   In *Le Style du Général* (Julliard, Paris, 1959), pp. 69–72, J.-F. Revel rightly stressed the importance of rhetorical behaviour, which he calls 'a Bélise-type argument', after a character in Molière's *Les femmes savantes* ('Ils m'ont su révérer si fort jusqu'à ce jour / qu'ils ne m'ont jamais dit un mot de leur amour.') It is a concept which became widely accepted.

23   This adjective is borrowed from Marc Beigbeder's *Une bouteille à la mer*.

24   Simmel, *The Problems of the Philosophy of History*, p. 148 *ff*.

25   K. Popper, *The Logic of Scientific Discovery*, (Hutchinson, London, 1972); I. Lakatos and A. Musgrave, *Criticism and the Growth of Knowledge* (Cambridge University Press, Cambridge, 1970); L. Feuer, *Einstein and the Generation of Science* (Basic Books, New York, 1974); T. Kuhn, *The Structure of Scientific Revolutions*.

26   R. Wicklund and J. Brehm (eds.), *Perspective on Cognitive Dissonance* (Lawrence Erlbaum, Hillsdale, 1976), pp. 298–300, suggest an interesting interpretation of the reactions of chemists to Lavoisier's discovery. Many of them tried over several years to reconcile Lavoisier's discovery with the

theory of phlogiston. The slowness of their conversion to Lavoisier's theory was due to their having adhered so long to the phlogiston theory. This could be explained by the theory of cognitive dissonance, but it is perhaps simpler to interpret it using the concept of 'exit costs'.

27 A. Bhaduri, 'A study of agricultural backwardness under semi-feudalism', *Economic Journal*, LXXXIII (329) (1976), pp. 120–37.

28 I am disregarding an E effect of the division of labour in the social sciences: sociologists often think that phenomena are explained by 'sociological' variables, economists by 'economic' variables.

29 Simmel, *The Problems of the Philosophy of History*.

30 M. Foucault, *Les Mots et les choses* (Gallimard, Paris, 1966); L. Dumont, *Essai sur l'individualisme* (Le Seuil, Paris, 1983).

31 W. Dilthey, *Der Aufbau der geschichtlichen Welt in den Geisteswissenschaften* (Suhrkamp, Frankfurt, 1981 (1910)), *Plan der Fortsetzung zur Aufbau . . .*, 3 (der Zusammenahng des Lebens) and 4 (die Selbstbiographie), cf., for example, p. 248: 'Wir deuten das Leben als die Realisierung eines obersten Zweckes' (we interpret life as the realization of a supreme goal). The '*a priori* form' to which Dilthey subjects the work of the biographer is likely to be satisfactory if the biography being written is that of an Olympic champion. It may well, however, be much less satisfactory in the case of many writers or even politicians. This example shows clearly the ambiguous nature of what I am here calling, without distinguishing between them, paradigms or *a priori* forms. Depending on how they are used, they are capable of the best and the worst: they can either help to reveal reality and make it more intelligible, or help to distort it and make it less visible.

Chapter 9   Two case studies

1 R. Nurkse, *Problems of Capital Formation in Underdeveloped Countries* (Blackwell, Oxford, 1953).

2 J. K. Galbraith, *The Theory of Mass Poverty* (Harvard University Press, Cambridge, Mass. and London, 1979).

3 Economic Commission for Latin America, *The Economic Development of Latin America* (United Nations, New York, 1950).

4 Quoted by P. T. Bauer, *Dissent on Development* (Fakenham and Reading, London, 1971).

5 S. N. Eisenstadt (ed.), *Readings in Social Evolution and Development* (Pergamon Press, New York, London, and Oxford, 1970).

6 Bauer, *Dissent on Development*.

7 A. G. Frank, *Capitalism and Underdevelopment in Latin America* (Monthly Review Press, New York, 1969); G. Franck, *Dependent Accumulation and Underdevelopment* (Monthly Review Press, New York, 1979, 1980); S. Amin, *Unequal Development – an essay on the social formations of peripheral capitalism* (Harvester Press, Hassocks, 1976 (1973)); F. Cardoso, *Dependence and Development in Latin America* (University of California Press, Berkeley and London, 1979 (1978)).

8 Bauer, *Dissent on Development*.
9 A. Lewis, 'A review of economic development', *American Economic Review, Proceedings and Supplement*, 55 (2) (May 1965), pp. 1–16.
10 J. Milewski, 'Capitalism in Nigeria and problems of dependence: some historical comments', in *Dependency Theory – a critical reassessement*, D. Seers (ed.) (Frances Pinter, London, 1981), pp. 109–18.
11 S. Schatz, *Nigerian Capitalism* (University of California Press, Berkeley, 1977).
12 M. Bienefeld, 'Dependency and the newly industrializing countries', in *Dependency Theory*, ed. D. Seers, pp. 79–96.
13 Economic Commission for Latin America, *The Economic Development of Latin America*.
14 V. Lenin, *Imperialism, the Highest Stage of Capitalism* (Lawrence and Wishart, London, 1944).
15 A. Smith, *An Enquiry into the Nature and Causes of the Wealth of Nations* (London, 1776), Book IV, Chapters 7 and 8.
16 J. Hobson, *Imperialism, a Study* (Allen & Unwin, London, 1938 (1902)).
17 R. Hilferding, *Das Finanzkapital – eine Studie über die jüngste Entwicklung des Kapitalismus* (Wiener Voksbuchhandlung, Vienna, 1920 (1910)).
18 H. Arendt, *The Origins of Totalitarianism*, 2nd edn (Harcourt, New York, 1958).
19 J. Gallagher and R. Robinson, 'The Imperialism of free trade', *Economic History Review*, VI (1) (1953), pp. 1–15.
20 W. W. Rostow, *The Stages of Economic Growth* (Cambridge University Press, Cambridge, 1960).
21 A. Gerschenkron, *Economic Backwardness in Historical Perspective* (Harvard University Press, Cambridge, 1962).
22 I. Wallerstein, *Modern World System. I. Capitalist agriculture and the origins of the European world economy in the sixteenth century* (Academic Press, New York, London, and Toronto, 1974).
23 A. Emmanuel, *L'Echange Inégal* (Maspero, Paris, 1968). See the swingeing attack on Emmanuel's theory by P. Samuelson, 'Illogisme de la théorie de l'échange inégal', *Commentaire*, V (17) 1982, pp. 52–62.
24 D. Dan Walleri, 'Trade development and underdevelopment', *Comparative Political Studies*, XI (1) (1978), pp. 94–127.
25 J. Galtung, 'A structural theory of imperialism', *Journal of Peace Research*, 2 (1971), pp. 81–117.
26 J. Schumpeter, *Imperialism and Social Classes* (Blackwell, Oxford, 1951).
27 R. Boudon, 'Individual action and social change – a non-theory of social change', 46th Hobhouse memorial lecture, London School of Economics, *British Journal of Sociology*, 34 (1) (March 1983), pp. 1–18.

Chapter 10   Against scepticism

1 G. Simmel, The Problems of the Philosophy of History (Free Press, New York, 1977 (1892)).

2   R. Boudon, *Theories of Social Change – a critical appraisal* (Polity Press, Cambridge, 1986).
3   Sartre's case is obviously different. Here the philosopher is sitting on the shoulders of the writer. Nobody, or very few people, had read *L'Etre et le néant*, which is a hasty recasting of Husserl and Heidegger. However, the success of the writer carried the philosopher. And the most serious reservations which Heidegger expressed publicly (Sartre: a writer perhaps; a philosopher, certainly not) passed unnoticed. What happened afterwards proved Heidegger right, since Sartre seems already to have disappeared from the history of philosophy. The case of Gustave Le Bon, the once famous author of *Psychologie des foules* (Retz, Paris, 1975 (1895)) is different again: this was popular philosophy, in the same way that one speaks of popular literature.
4   H. Spencer, *Social Statics* (Williams and Norgate, London, 1851).
5   H. Spencer, *First Principles* (Williams and Norgate, London, 1882).
6   Auguste Comte 1798–1857, Karl Marx 1818–83, Herbert Spencer 1820–1903.
7   R. Bellah, 'Religious evolution', *American Sociological Review*, 29 (1964), pp. 358–74.
8   As was proved by F. Chazel in the case of Sociology, 'Karl Marx et la sociologie américaine contemporaine', *L'année sociologique* 36 (1986), pp. 320–42.
9   R. Horton, 'Lévy-Bruhl, Durkheim and the scientific revolution', in *Modes of Thought*, R. Horton and R. Finnegan (Faber, London, 1973), pp. 249–304, showed clearly the existence of this double sociocentrism: ethnologists of the Victorian era tended to idealize Western societies as compared with primitive societies, and thereby always to propound the themes of discontinuity between the two types of society and the break between primitive mentality and modern mentality. After the Second World War, when what people have called the West's 'bad conscience' made its appearance, many researchers idealized primitive societies as compared with Western societies and again propounded, but this time inverting values, the double theme of the discontinuity between the two types of society and the break between the two kinds of thought, as well as between the two presumed types of relationship between individual and society. However, Horton also stresses that these ideological distortions were avoided by the best sociologists. Durkheim, for instance, (like Weber, though Horton does not mention him), stressed the continuity between scientific and magical thought. It could be added that his distinction between societies which had an organic solidarity and those which had a mechanical solidarity is a prudent one, which gives due weight to the development of the division of labour in modern societies and the social consequences of this, but does not suggest that a type of society in which the individual is, as it were, dissolved (in society) should be set against a type of society in which society is dissolved (in the individual). In any event, Durkheim never remotely suggested that 'holistic' societies could be set against 'individualistic' societies.
    This example allows us to stress an important point – that causality in the processes of production and diffusion of ideologies is complex. Although anthropology has helped, as we see here, to legitimate certain discontinuist

views, the interpretation which it has given of the discontinuities which it was quite sure it could prove, itself seems to have depended on the fashion of the moment.

10   This notion of correctness is illustrated by some of the points I made previously, particularly in the parts dealing with the notion of paradigm. After all, like an ideology, a paradigm can be said to be correct or 'false' (in the sense that a novel rings false), but not true or false. For instance, the utilitarian paradigm rings false if we try to apply it to the reaction to crime. Other paradigms are 'false' not only when they are applied in an irrelevant way to a particular object, but also in themselves. This is the case of the paradigm which claims to reduce behaviour to the mechanical play of dispositions over which consciousness holds no sway, or the paradigm which says that everything in a society has a function. The notion of correctness is, generally speaking, vital for the evaluation of *principles*, as it is for the evaluation, for the sake of knowledge or action, of the application of principles; both these evaluations are subject to Münchhausen's trilemma. What is true of principles implemented in paradigms is also true of principles implemented in ideologies, as in the case of the principle of popular Marxism that individuals could not believe what they believe and not prefer what they prefer, because of the blindness which their 'false consciousness' causes in them. Similarly, one goes beyond the limits of correctness when one starts from the principle that ideal-typical concepts can be interpreted in an essentialist way, or from the principle that one can interpret a particular model as a copy of the real world, by ignoring the hypotheses from which it sprang. These remarks of course do not claim to be a substitute for a proper discussion of the concept of correctness, which is a very important one.

11   We must distinguish between two very different meanings of the adjective *holistic* (or its equivalent, derived from Latin, *totalistic*). The term *holistic* society is sometimes used to describe societies which, in the mind of the person using the word, have the ability to dissolve the individual in the social order, like water can absorb sugar by dissolution. Here, therefore, the word 'holistic' conveys a metaphor which is not very relevant or interesting. *Holistic methods* are different from individualistic methods in that they analyse a particular social phenomenon without taking account of the fact that it is the imprint, at the collective level, of individual beliefs, attitudes, or behaviour. These methods are often legitimate. It may for instance be interesting to note that suicide or birth-rates vary from one country to another or that they vary in a particular way or other over time, even though one has not the slightest idea of the reasons which, at the level of individual actors, explain these overall differences. One will usually try, however, to investigate further, and explain for example how differences of context give rise to different individual attitudes and behaviour. Holistic methods therefore often amount to the initial phase of research: they have a heuristic value, rather than explicative virtue. However, there is also a methodological holism which can be called dogmatic (individuals are no more than elements of a whole, and so on) and which denies on principle that explaining a collective phenomenon can be done by building it up from individual causes. In its most

obscure forms, it tries to exclude psychology from the social sciences, regarding what it invariably calls 'psychologism' as a sin against the spirit (of sociology).

To summarize the whole of my remarks about methodological individualism, I will say that in this matter one can distinguish in social science practice four types of paradigm (1) *methodological individualism* (M1) of the *rational and utilitarian type*: social phenomena stem from individual acts and attitudes inspired in social actors by their interests; (2) MI of the *rational but non-utilitarian type*: it is broader than the first kind, and, like it, insists that social phenomena be (in principle) analysed as the result of individual acts and attitudes. Here, however, explaining a particular individual act amounts to showing that it *makes sense for the actors in question*. However, an act or an attitude can make sense for actors because they serve their interests, but also for all kinds of other reasons: for example, because they are in accordance with a particular value in which they believe (cf. indignation at a crime which does not involve the actor), a particular disposition (cf. the attitude of Western observers to magic), the demands of their role, and so on. This paradigm has an important consequence – as soon as the act is required to be explained because of the presumed *reasons* of the actors, one is excluding *ipso facto* the possibility that the actors can be manipulated by forces outside their consciousness; (3) the MI of the *irrational type* also makes the individual the focus of the analysis, but it reserves the right to postulate in actors the existence of an unconscious which has causal force. This unconscious (a) determines the behaviour of actors like their adrenalin rate determines their mood – without their being aware of it, (b) is itself determined by social forces. The conclusion from this paradigm is that actors could only provide wrong *reasons* for their own behaviour and that the task of the sociologist is to discover the *causes of* rather than the *reasons for* the actors' behaviour; (4) the *methodological holism* which rejects the idea that the individual is the focus of the analysis and which tries to limit itself to the analysis of variables defined at a supra-individual level, as well as to their relationships and the configurations and structures which give shape to these relationships. Paradigm 4 seems to me the one which above all has, as I have said, heuristic value. This is clearly seen in the case of Durkheim: having established the existence of correlations between global data concerning suicide cycles and economic cycles, he went further and, against his own principles, formulated *psychological* hypotheses about why people should commit suicide at a particular point in the economic cycle. Paradigm 1 is of limited validity, as all the major utilitarians saw clearly. Paradigm 3 leads to logical aporia (circular explanations), psychological aporia (it propounds an unacceptable theory of consciousness), or sociological aporia (immaterial social forces work on actors' unconscious). Why is paradigm 4 often seen as having an absolute rather than an heuristic validity? Why does one attribute to paradigm 1 a wider validity than it warrants? Why does one bother at all about paradigm 3? It seems to me that the theory of ideologies which I am putting forward in this book means that we can take account of these phenomena. Since I am not able to develop this statement, I will merely emphasize one point: that behind these phenomena there are black-box effects. Paradigm 3 is based on the authority of Marx and Freud, the most dubious ideas of whom it reproduces (Marx's *camera obscura*, the early Freud's view of the unconscious as a psychic apparatus); paradigm 4 is based on the authority of Durkheim, but ignores his subtleties and hesitations; paradigm 1 is based on the success of economic theory, though these can easily make us forget the decisive role which its main propounder attributed to moral sentiments.

My remarks about paradigm 4 allow me, finally, to clarify one point: *causal analysis*, which Durkheim used in *Suicide*, and which was subsequently formalized, is enormously helpful in sociological analysis. However, its function is, once again, *heuristic* rather than *explicative* since a statistical structure is not explained when the influence of the different variables on each other has been determined, but only when one can deduce the structure from microscopic hypotheses about the behaviour of actors, a process which is obviously rather delicate in practice. The importance of causal analysis lies in its ability to suggest such hypotheses, as is seen in Durkheim himself, whose causal analyses are often, in contrast to his principles, interpreted in the light of microscopic hypotheses. However, I readily admit that, because one is normally more easily convinced by reasons which one has found oneself, it was only after writing *L'Inégalité des chances* that I saw that causal analysis was heuristic rather than explicative in nature.

12   It is therefore only by turning meaning completely on its head that the reproach was levelled at methodological individualism of atomizing society or reducing it to a juxtaposition of 'calculating solitudes'. It was on the basis of this accusation of atomism that G. Gurvitch was silly enough to exclude Max Weber from the pantheon of sociology, in his *Vocation actuelle de la sociologie* (Presses Universitaires de France, Paris, 1950).

13   R. Boudon, 'Remarques sur la notion de fonction', *Revue française de sociologie*, VIII (2) (1967), pp. 198–206.

14   C. Perelman, *L'Empire Rhétorique* (Vrin, Paris, 1977).

15   G. Lemaine and B. Matalon, *Hommes supérieurs, hommes inférieurs* (Colin, Paris, 1985), give an illuminating analysis of the intellectual movement leading from Darwinism to the eugenism of the first third of the twentieth century. At the time, the concerns and theories of eugenics were the same in the United States and in Germany, and they had the same degree of success. This point confirms the idea that, in the *sociological* theory of ideology, there is an advantage in disregarding political factors.

16   It is appropriate to note that the theory of knowledge which I have put forward in this book is quite different from the one outlined by Karl Popper in his *The Poverty of Historicism* (Routledge & Kegan Paul, London, 1944). For Popper, ideology is based on modes of reasoning, the very form of which is not scientifically legitimate. I have tried to show here that this case in point was very special and that it was not the most interesting one. What is more important is the case where ideological beliefs are grafted on to 'normal science'.

Index

Index by Hazel Bell